BEHOLD MY SOUL

(A TRUE STORY ABOUT FORGIVENESS AND THE POWER OF LOVE)

TAJ SIMRIT

TAJSIMRIT.COM

BEHOLD MY SOUL

Taj Simrit
Behold My Soul

Published by Spines

ISBN: 979-8-89569-352-0

BLURB:

"Patience is bitter but its fruit is sweet."

— ARISTOTLE.

His son sarcastically questioned whether all twenty-year-olds should read this book. He responded with a resounding *"yes"* because age isn't a prerequisite for consciousness or lack thereof.

Taj Simrit is the epitome of Friedrich Nietzsche's quote: *"Become who you are."*

His story is as raw and authentic as it gets.

Without sugarcoating, he speaks the truth, not only for others but also for himself.

For transparency, it is necessary to pay the price.

In his belief that suffering and mistakes were essential for growth, he always chose the most challenging path.

If you recognized yourself in this tale of redemption, this was all intended.

Embarking on an exotic and enchanting journey of self-discovery, he will guide you from the snowy peaks of the Himalayas to the

Amazon jungle and beyond by way of the French Riviera and Corporate America.

With his writings, he intricately weaves a fine tapestry that stretches across the time and space continuum.

He combines the major threads of yoga, medicinal plants, energy healing, and the philosophy of Ho'oponopono within the framework of Buddhism, Hinduism, Sikhism, and Christianity.

By following his story, you'll embark on a journey that takes you from modern psychology to shamanism, passing through different stages of unconsciousness, agony, and distress, ultimately culminating in elevated emotions and new-found wisdom.

Bon voyage...

Tajsimrit.com

CONTENTS

—THE 13 MAXIMS FOR A HAPPY AND PEACEFUL LIFE—

#1 Responsibility

Once you understand that you're consistently creating and shaping your own reality, you'll stop blaming others for the misfortunes of your day-to-day existence.

You won't hold anyone else accountable and will take full responsibility for everything that happens in your life from now on. It's a liberating and empowering process that frees you from the syndrome of blame and entitlement that's so prevalent in our societies.

#2 Gratitude

Gratitude is a state of grace that's bestowed on you – straight from the ether. It carries no price, doesn't discriminate, and has its own self-perpetuating cycle. There's nothing more powerful than experiencing and reveling in an overwhelming sense of gratitude.

#3 Empathy & Compassion

"Never judge a person until you walk a mile in his moccasins."

— MARY T. LATHRAP.

You've probably heard this saying countless times, or something similar like

"You shouldn't judge a man until you walk a mile in his shoes."

Our habit of forming opinions about individuals results in their assessment of us without comprehension or empathy. But when you show empathy to others and open your heart with a little compassion, your perspective shifts, and actual communication begins.

#4 Forgiveness

You can't expect to live freely if you don't forgive those who hurt you, including yourself, for any harm you've caused. You'll be replaying the suffering and the pain in your mind on an endless loop, and it will hinder you for as long as you allow it.

Find a way to forgive before you can open your heart to love.

#5 Love

"All you need is love."

— JOHN LENNON, 1967.

John Lennon sensed that love encompassed everything and had the ultimate power to heal. Remove all hindering emotions, such as anger, blame, and resentment, for keys to the gates of love.

#6 Transcend Ego & Spiritual Ego

Yet another pursuit in this lifetime: transcending the imposter, the false identity causing havoc in your heart, in the name of separation. As you 'awaken,' the ugly tail of the spiritual ego emerges.

Learn to eradicate them both if you're searching for a true sense of peace.

#7 Good Deeds

Donating to charity, giving away 10% of your income, or doing volunteer work for a special cause will make you feel great and might also influence the karma wheel – if you take a Buddhist perspective.

When you give with no expectations of returns, you open up a world of infinite possibilities. Trust that good things will come back to you as you put more good out into the world.

#8 Addiction to Sex

Everything consists of energy.

Through sex, we receive the energy and the imprint of all our former lovers. Your partners take on this energy. Hence, it's time to reconsider casual and promiscuous sex and to choose a partner carefully.

#9 Other Addictions

Illicit drugs are at the top of this list, with legal pharmaceutical drugs a close second. Think alcohol, nicotine, caffeine, junk food, sugar, stress, gambling, pornography, guns, and social media – to name a few. Addictions are the enslavers.

#10 Believe in a Higher Power

*"There are only two ways to live your life. One is as though
nothing is a miracle. The other is as though everything is a
miracle."*

— ALBERT EINSTEIN.

Surrendering to a higher intelligence or power means letting go of ego
limitations for a fresh start with limitless potential.

#11 Manifest Your Reality

You are the co-creator of your destiny.

From a blank canvas, your masterpiece awaits the strokes of your
paint brush.

You are the artist. Believe and act on it.

#12 Live in the Moment

The present moment is fleeting, but we can be so stuck in our
stories that we let it pass us by. Don't let life move onward without
enjoying the present, the only moment you have. Dwelling on the past
or obsessing over the future only harms your well-being and that of
those around you.

#13 Non-Attachment

The best way to attract a butterfly is to stop chasing it and wait
until it lands on your shoulder.

Non-attachment is the final and vital step of the manifestation
process.

This book is dedicated to my son.
I can only hope that my perception of the truth will set us free.

"May the wind always be at your back and the sun
upon your face. And may the wings of destiny carry you
aloft to dance with the stars."

— CARL JUNG.

CHAPTER
ONE

"Not until we are lost do we begin to find ourselves."

— HENRY DAVID THOREAU.

4th August, 2023

Marco was sitting on a carriage train on the outskirts of Paris. He was a little spaced out, listening to the '*Mool Mantra*' through his earphones.

It presents the compass to finding your true self, which sits within the opening of your heart. Some say that the most difficult journey in life is moving from the energy of the navel center to the heart center.

Somewhat unconscious of it, he clapped rhythmically to the music.

Until one clap too many saw a middle-aged lady rush over to his seat. Visibly agitated, she yelled at the top of her voice, compelling him to drop his hands in his lap and stop.

Her sheer aggression caught him off guard, grounding him in stark reality.

In just four days back in France, the French wasted no time in showcasing their renowned hospitality.

He had just traveled from Peru, where he stayed with a Shipibo-Konibo family, an Indigenous group. Days earlier, he'd been in a *tambo* (hut) outside of the Peruvian city of Pucallpa, lying in a hammock and finishing the last chapters of his book.

He felt out of tune with the Paris suburbs.

He was heading to a Kundalini Yoga Festival at Château of Jambville in Yvelines. It had been seven years since his last yoga festival in the mountains of New Mexico.

With great eagerness, he wanted to end that seven-year cycle of consciousness and start anew. He was completing a loop in time and suspected the main character would resemble very little of his former self.

Marco was looking forward to grounding himself for the next eight days in the oak forest surrounding the château. The music and the mantras were his umbilical cord to the universe. He was intent on immersing himself into the 'sound current' that would radiate all over the festival grounds.

Unbeknown to him, his first night in a tent on the wet grass would become the perfect setting for a blues song about loss, fatality, and betrayal.

After a fifty-minute train ride from Paris, he arrived at the station of Hardricourt. It smelled like the countryside, with no one on the platform except four yogis seeking a taxi to the château.

He ambled over to the nearest *bar-tabac (a typical French bar that has a license to sell tobacco)* to call a taxi. After a coffee, he returned to the station, feeling proud about solving their transportation problems. One of the German women had called Uber in the meantime and showed little interest in his oncoming taxi.

Adding insult to injury, the taxi never turned up. After a long wait, a different car arrived, and his small backpack was nowhere to be found when he searched for his belongings.

"*Welcome to the New France, how do you like it?*" his nephew later joked.

"*Never leave a small backpack unattended at a train station in France,*" his sister wisely added.

The irony was that he had traveled globally for nearly six years without any thefts. Many countries he visited had extensive danger lists on the U.S. embassy website. It was no wonder a large percentage of Americans didn't even have a passport, he thought.

Now Marco didn't have one either. His French and American passports, credit cards, cash, and jewelry were all missing.

Marco wasn't accustomed to putting all his valuable possessions in a tiny rucksack.

Instead of focusing on the socio-economic ills of France that he'd left over forty years ago, he was guilty of paying more attention to the constellation of stars and galaxies.

It was a shock to the system. Worst of all, his iPad, the most cherished possession that had accompanied him on all his adventures, was gone forever.

All the events of his life were recorded on it, akin to the mosaics adorning a Mediterranean coffee table. Now, a dance of swirling atoms caught his gaze, splitting into infinity.

His iCloud backup was full, and he hadn't bothered to subscribe for more data.

He was deeply disturbed. Someone had invaded his physical and emotional space. He felt as if he'd been stabbed in the belly and gutted.

His intuition had signaled that this might happen. A fear of his iPad crashing meant he transferred his writing to email every couple of days during the first month of writing, but he hadn't kept up with it.

While walking along '*La Seine*' the day before the festival, Marco felt a knot in his stomach. With determination, he'd resolved to send himself the contents of his manuscript that same evening.

Later, he decided to go to the movies and watch Tom Cruise's '*Mission Impossible.*' Upon returning to his hotel late at night, he briefly glanced at his iPad on the table but failed to fulfill his promise. He told himself he'd have plenty of time at the festival.

Ignoring all the signs about his iPad's functionality and data security in the past months, he failed to save crucial content such as photos, videos, and, above all, his writings.

He had allowed this episode to happen, just like a Freudian slip.

The universe had him in a trance while his destiny was being corrected in mid-air like a revised flight path.

He woke during the night, quivering in a damp tent. His only desire was to escape from this doomed place. The unedited book's final 40,000 words appeared as mere atmospheric fluctuations, akin to the raindrops that fell on his tent.

Marco felt drained, disgusted with his lack of insight and, above all, with the totality of himself.

Writing about his life in the early hours of the morning after shamanic ceremonies in Peru was a raw process. To lose the contents left him feeling completely lost and full of remorse.

"When was this moron going to learn anything at all?" he thought to himself.

Conversations with others at the festival centered around the notion that being deprived of his writings was a sign from the universe. Without a shadow of a doubt, there was an underlying reason for this to happen.

Still, Marco wondered why he fought all of the signs he'd received. He intuited that he came from the school of hard knocks.

"What else could I do besides trust in the process, learn from my mistakes, and grow as a better person?" he asked himself.

Then something magical happened. The next day, he attended a singing workshop with a teacher and recording artist from London. Siri Sadhana Kaur has nine records to her credit, and she's a bundle of fun and energy.

Clouds lifted, and the sun appeared for the first time since the theft. Siri Sadhana Kaur had single-handedly – but for the grace of God – turned his disgust into elation.

After ninety minutes of singing, while walking across the vast expanse of grass, he experienced a sense of euphoria – like a butterfly ready to feast on sweet nectar in a flower garden.

The universe conveyed a message through these events, but he couldn't yet grasp the implications. Everything seemed synchronized at this moment.

He realized his task was to play the cards he'd been dealt and enjoy the game. He thought about responsibility, a concept the Indian mystic Sadhguru eulogizes.

According to Sadhguru, it's a pillar of freedom and internal peace that he frames as *'response-ability.'*

"Responsibility simply means your ability to respond. If you decide, "I am responsible," you will have the ability to respond. If you decide, "I am not responsible," you will not have the ability to respond. It is as simple as that. All it requires is for you to realize that you are responsible for all that you are and all that you are not, all that may happen to you, and all that may not happen to you. This."

As opposed to action, which is limited, responsibility is limitless.

The key is to do what you're capable of – instead of picking and choosing what you want to be involved with and therefore being restricted to a life *'half-lived.'*

It starts internally and extends to people around you in all directions.

"Now is the time to show responsibility and commitment to all life, including your own," he mused, paraphrasing Sadhguru.

With a heart full of delightful melodies, Marco decided to take advantage of the favorable winds and change the course of his sailboat.

The destination for his next adventure will be the island of Corsica, a place he always dreamed of visiting. Growing up in Toulon, he often spotted the blue-and-yellow ferries docked in the harbor. He imagined escaping to the '*Isle of Beauty,*' a former French territory that he exoticized.

Marco had no idea it would take him so long to discover the island where Napoleon Bonaparte was born, even after years of roaming the world.

His intentions were manifold. Marco had set his sights on completing the GR 20, dubbed the hardest trek in Europe. It spans 192 kilometers and includes sixteen stages of challenging rock climbing and scrambling.

He planned to rent a small house near the sea for a few months and revise his book after completing the trek. However, he wondered whether this book was worth writing a second time.

What if the message was simple: put it in the junk files and delete it forever?

Being objective with your own writing is difficult, especially when you've not shared the content with anybody. Maybe they were poorly written pieces after all, and the theft would save him from embarrassment.

"Besides, who would want to read about my story?" he thought. The therapeutic effect of writing shouldn't be underestimated, and he wondered whether that alone should suffice.

"Scrap the project," repeated the little voice in his head.

This time, he decided to challenge the nagging doubts that had been bugging him all his life. Twice in the past two years, he flew to Peru to open his heart. He couldn't let this opportunity go to waste.

So he made a decision. In order to benefit his readers, his heart will ultimately triumph over his mind as he tells a better story.

In a week's time, he was supposed to send a copy of his passport to Kathmandu to secure a visa for Tibet. He had booked a two-week-long tour with a three-day *kora* (religious pilgrimage) around Mt. Kailash.

Mt. Kailash is Asia's holiest mountain. It's the axis of the Earth, the abode of Shiva. According to Buddhists, one circuit around this mountain shaped like a perfect pyramid (fifty-two kilometers) will absolve the sins of a lifetime.

He sensed that his book, which was all about redemption but no longer existed in this realm, didn't provide him with the opportunity to vindicate his sins. He was determined to do so in the future.

Once he made that 180-degree turn into his destiny, he never looked back in the rear-view mirror. He was engineered to be this way.

In fact, Marco's uncanny ability to project into the future amazed one of his friends. She once told him that she preferred living in the present and in the past rather than inventing future events.

In response, he stressed that visualizing and feeling as if you already possessed something was essential to the implementation of the Law of Attraction.

Back in 2006, Marco watched the movie *'The Secret'*.

It soon became a cultural phenomenon. Doesn't everyone want to manifest their every desire?

You would be a fool to claim otherwise.

Everybody in Marco's professional sphere tried to jump on the bandwagon. Most of them failed for one simple reason: They could see the silver lining enveloping the clouds above, but they missed the single ingredient that would set the entire sky ablaze.

Do you want to know what this ingredient is?

Marco didn't have a single clue, and he missed the entire forest for the trees. His whole way of thinking, his limited psyche inside his bubbled head, made sure of that.

It would take him years before he started grasping the essence of that voluptuous wildflower called attraction.

When your heart feels empty, what actions can be taken? Wallowing in your misery only attracts more misery.

Therein lies the secret, folks.

Let the winds of destiny untame the young beast inside of you and send it roaring across the stratosphere of imagination.

Paint a fine picture for the Gods to see and feel the strokes of the paintbrush caress the virgin canvas, like a lover's devotion to their muse.

There she lays, ladies and gentlemen, a rose so finely tuned to the grace of God that an army of the prickliest thorns would stand forever against its conquest.

Her sweet fragrance lingering in the hearts of men akin to morning dew on a blanket of wildflowers. The world's sorrows drown in deep blue skies, like lost musical notes in a symphony.

Seize a moment with her and detach yourself. Maybe she will oblige you and be at your command.

Just don't be in a hurry.

After many trials and errors, this universal law shaped Marco's present-day life.

As far as living a life encumbered by the traumatic events of the past, he shouldn't think so. But let's go back to the beginning, shall we?

CHAPTER

TWO

"Throw your dreams into space like a kite, and you do not know what it will bring back, a new life, a new friend, a new love, a new country."

— ANAÏS NIN.

September 2021

L ast night was the Harvest Moon. The moon rises and sets with the sun.

Agriculture workers named it the Harvest Moon because the extended amount of sunlight enabled them to work in the fields longer.

Tonight, Marco's ghostwriter started writing this book to coincide with his first stage on the '*Camino de Santiago*' or '*Way of St James*,' a series of ancient pilgrimage paths across Europe.

He had opted to walk on the '*Camino del Littoral*' or '*Camino del Norte*,' a less popular, more scenic, and harder route than others. It was 820 kilometers long, from Irun on the French-Spanish border to Santiago de Compostela in Galicia.

Adding to the challenge, he planned to continue to Porto, another 280 kilometers. He was in no hurry. Walking an average of twenty-two kilometers a day and resting once a week, he calculated the journey would take a couple of months and involve about 2 million steps.

His taste buds were already savoring the flavor of a tawny Porto, a fortified wine named after the city. It was full of decadent flavors, like caramel, peanut brittle, apricot, plum, raisins, and walnut, making it the perfect way to celebrate his odyssey.

Marco had always admired the pomposity of wine critics.

He often pondered the niche market for a book about his life's ramblings. Procrastinate guilt-free, what a great idea!

It was during an Ayahuasca ceremony in the Peruvian Amazon a couple of months previously that he had a vision with a wider scope. He could hopefully save the readers from making the same mistakes that he did.

You could then empathize with his situation and draw your own conclusions.

If that process happened to make a small difference in your lives, that would be beyond all Marco's expectations.

He intends to take you on a magic carpet ride over five continents. As far as Africa goes, he spent four weeks traveling on a '*magic bus*' tour of Morocco when he was sixteen, which shaped his lust for travel.

But hang on, it might be a rough ride.

The Persian philosopher Rumi once said: "*You have to go through the dark to find the light.*"

You'll find plenty of darkness here – and, hopefully, an exponentially larger amount of light to lead your way along a more memorable life.

Your host could only hope and aspire to be a worthwhile guide.

Knowing Einstein's '*Parallel Universe Theory,*' you'd see our world as an illusion. The past, present, and future don't exist in a linear manner. Everything is happening all at once.

The main character in this book treats these entities in a closed loop and sometimes acts as an imposter. The reason is that lines drawn in the sand are bound to be reclaimed by the sea.

He was on the Camino de Santiago, on a mission from God like the Belushi brothers in the movie '*The Blues Brothers.*'

Marco, an imperfect human, was at the mercy of his emotional immaturity.

If you recognize yourselves in Marco, it's intentional. Let's hope you'll learn something valuable from his follies.

CHAPTER
THREE

"Don't worry about the world coming to an end today. It is already tomorrow in Australia."

— CHARLES M. SHULZ.

Marco's ex-girlfriend Kat, a somewhat tortured soul with a good heart from a little town in New South Wales, Australia, died two weeks ago from cancer. Too young to die; she was about to turn sixty-four.

They met in a post office in Barcelona in 1981, down from the famous _Las Ramblas_, near the _El Monumento a Colón_ (the Columbus Monument).

Marco's decision to visit the post office at 9 a.m. following a night of partying with loved ones remains inexplicable.

They were young and naïve, became infatuated with one another straight away, and traveled to the Canary Islands to celebrate the New Year.

14

Months later, Marco made it to Australia to rejoin Kat. In truth, he used his longing to travel and Kat as a reason to go Down Under.

Marco had already traveled and worked on three continents. There was nothing that excited him more than the unpredictability of overseas travel. Kat picked him up at Sydney's airport, and they drove south for two-and-a-half hours to her hometown.

The first stop was her mom's house. Over coffee and scones, the hostess shot a number of dirty looks and disparaging remarks in his direction.

When they arrived at the horse ranch Kat had passionately spoken about, guess who was waiting in front of her cottage? The ex or current beau? It was difficult to know which.

When Marco glanced at him in the falling evening light, he couldn't believe his eyes. He was a preschool teacher with curly blond hair, tanned skin, and a white, toothy smile. His sweet disposition complemented his good looks.

What was this girl thinking?

Marco, insecure and not terribly attractive, wore his neuroses as a badge of honor.

Comparing him to this demi-God would've been an insult to decency. Maybe she smoked an excessive amount of weed?

In fact, one straightforward truth could summarize Marco's appeal to her. When they were stoned together, they connected really well, whereas her former Apollo didn't smoke at all.

Kat never mentioned that she was still in a complicated relationship with him. Worse yet, her family and friends adored him.

A black sheep had just arrived from outer space with only a backpack and no prospects.

For the record, there were roughly 170 million sheep in Australia in the 80's.

Kat had been squatting on her dad's property.

The father-daughter bond was cold and distant, and the horses appeared to be untamed. That didn't quite fit Marco's glorified image of a horse farm Down Under.

When Kat finally let him ride a horse, it abruptly galloped back to the stall after fifteen minutes, narrowly avoiding crashing into the gate at the last second. Marco miraculously avoided breaking bones, defying all laws of physics.

Two weeks later, Kat dropped Marco at the edge of town to go hitchhiking to Queensland, by way of South Australia and the Northern Territories.

That suited him fine. Another story that concluded in a cul-de-sac was nothing surprising to Marco.

At least Jack Kerouac would be there to keep him company on the deserted road.

"Nothing behind me, everything ahead of me, as is ever so on the road."

Kat's death made Marco wish he'd been more conscious, tolerant, and loving. In that respect, he'd always felt a little backward.

Be careful what you wish for, though.

A wish has to be anchored in something tangible like a past or fantasized experience, or a painful memory that you can transmute to growth.

Otherwise, it's bound to remain just a wish, empty and ill-defined. Now, try to infuse a little gratitude in all the events and precursors of your wishes. In this way, you'll acquire the power to shape your own destiny.

Kat would eventually visit Marco in Queensland, and he paid her a return visit in her hometown eight months later. From the start, it was clear this relationship would fail.

George Bernard Shaw famously said: *"Youth is wasted on the young."*

Marco struck up a friendship with Kat's brother, Jimmy. They went trekking in the Snowy Mountains together. Upon their return, they decided to go to the Hunter Valley.

The father of one of Jimmy's university friends was a doctor who owned a winery near the Blue Mountains, west of Sydney.

This is where Marco met his future wife, who hailed from Boston, Massachusetts.

However, this is a whole different story.

CHAPTER
FOUR

"Follow your dreams. They know the way."

— KOJI YAMADA.

ast forward to 2022. Marco was at an Ayahuasca retreat south of Pucallpa, on the outskirts of the Peruvian Amazon.

Everything suddenly became clear.

Amid doubt and confusion, a steadfast certainty emerged: Life was a journey of challenges and mistakes meant to awaken and elevate our consciousness.

Marco was sitting in a *maloca* (a community house used by the Amerindian tribes of the Amazon for meetings and shamanic rituals). An extensive structure made from wood that's often octagonal or decagonal, it has a high-sloping thatched roof that reaches its highest point in the center.

In the presence of two shamans from the Shipibo-Konibo tribe, he experienced the effects of Ayahuasca. The word *'vine of the soul'* comes from the Quechua language. It is the ultimate medicinal plant that cures whatever ails you.

Once adrift like a jellyfish in the sea, he'd finally found a sense of direction. It was akin to equipping your boat with a new rudder.

The oblivious Marco envisioned becoming a sage and guru, ready to make amends for the shortcomings and the transgressions of his past.

He'll write a book about his life. By describing this transformative process, he'll hopefully inspire the reader to seek a more meaningful life.

They say that one ceremony of Ayahuasca is worth ten years of psychotherapy.

Are you going to revere your local psychologist or venture to *la selva* (the jungle) for a psychedelic experience that promises to cure your disorders?

He didn't know it yet, but he would write an eBook as a precursor to his book, introducing the *'Thirteen Maxims for a Happy and Peaceful Life.'*

The catalyst for this turn of events came in the form of a book that his friend Montserrat gave him on his arrival in Peru.

'Zero Limits' was co-written by Dr. Joe Vitale and Dr. Hew Len.

This book altered Marco's outlook on life and addressed his long-standing uncertainties.

"Ho'oponopono is a profound gift that allows one to develop a working relationship with the Divinity within and learn to ask that in each

moment, our errors in thought, word, deed, or action be cleansed. The process is essentially about freedom, complete freedom from the past"

— MORRNAH NALAMAKU SIMEONA,
CREATOR OF SELF I-DENTITY THROUGH
HO'OPONOPONO (SITH).

This was a traditional Hawaiian practice of reconciliation and forgiveness until Dr. Vitale and Dr. Len brought it into the mainstream.

It comprised four powerful concepts expressed in four simple phrases:

> I am sorry,
> Please forgive me,
> I thank you,
> I love you.

"I am sorry" wasn't something that Marco had a habit of saying. Everyone he'd ever hurt would agree.

Yet today, he acknowledges that we're responsible for our realities. There's nothing on the outside. It's all happening inside of us. Understanding may be challenging initially, but it becomes simple once you grasp the concept.

Taking responsibility is the first step. We live in a society where people feel entitled, especially the younger generations who've already been given everything.

But when we take responsibility for our actions – instead of blaming others for them – it brings the ball (so to speak) back to our court. It frees us to accept our situation and gives us the impetus to make changes.

If somebody did you harm, for example, you'd be the one responsible for creating this situation out of programs or memories that you carried inside of you.

As a matter of fact, you were born pre-programmed, like a computer with software already installed.

However, to fix others, fix yourself first.

Taking responsibility is always the first step, followed by asking for forgiveness.

Don't beat yourself up or feel too guilty about asking for forgiveness. You're not the one to blame. You were unconsciously replaying these memories.

Marco's life took a turn when he understood that gratitude for the necessities, clean air, shelter, and food was the key to liberation.

Complaining was the antithesis of gratitude.

Marco grew up in France. Have you noticed that the French like to complain?

It must be part of their *patrimoine* (patrimony), and they cling to the right to express themselves in that manner.

Complaining attracts the opposite of good things.

It also wastes a significant amount of energy that could be used for more benevolent purposes.

Let gratitude fill your heart as you awaken each morning.

Daily, the global death toll exceeds 150,000 (166,859 in 2024, according to the World Population Review). Many lack fundamental resources like housing and access to clean water. Each day, 25,000 people, including 10,000 children, die of hunger and related causes, according to the United Nations.

Inhale deeply and be grateful for being alive.

Your actions today are a privilege. Embrace them, and your day will unfold smoothly.

Thank you for this blessing of life.

I am free to choose my destiny just by electing the right internal dialogue.

Thank you for clearing these programs and these memories. Clarity opens the door for light to enter.

You ask God, the Creator, the Supreme Intelligence – whatever resonates with you – to clean and purify these memories so that inspiration can come in. It's that simple.

The last step is to say I love you to your friends and family. Don't forget your enemies if you have any.

Try this simple meditation every time you're in doubt: stare at yourself in a mirror and repeat: *"I love you"* until you fall in love with yourself again.

Unconditional love is like a dog's love for his master. This was an epiphany for Marco.

Eight centuries ago, the poet and mystic Rumi wrote: *"Your task is not to seek love, but merely to find all the barriers within yourself that you have built against it, and embrace them."*

Fourteen years ago, Marco's martial arts teacher, who hailed from Hawaii, introduced him to Ho'oponopono. Together, they practiced Qigong with a hint of Ho'oponopono.

Often in life, the messages that are presented to us don't register until years or decades later and then, it all makes perfect sense.

This was one of these magic moments that re-defined an entire existence.

Will Marco be able to make amends for his programming and learn how to love unconditionally?

This is the premise of the book. We're all in search of redemption, aren't we?

I am sorry, please forgive me, thank you, I love you.

Does this hold the power to unlock it all?

Will freedom and peace await beyond the gates?

Marco discovered that dwelling on past mistakes is pointless, as they fuel personal growth and prevent a dull life.

Unfortunately, a sizable percentage of human beings on this planet have no choice but to counteract the stress inflicted by the expectations laid upon them by using stimulants.

Our culture has glamorized alcohol, which is the obvious stimulant that comes to mind. Pharmaceutical drugs and illegal drugs make the top of that list.

Marco played an awesome song called '*Love*' by a Barcelona singer named Manu Om on a loop throughout the night.
That would become both his credo and newfound muse.

"Clear, clear, clear," often said Dr. Len, that's all you have to do.

Joe Vitale wrote his entire book using these magical sentences: I am sorry, please forgive me, I thank you, and I love you.

Marco wasn't ashamed to emulate him and write this book in the same spirit, often listening to '*Love*' by Manu Om on Spotify. He even manifested to be invited to his podcast someday.

Another reason for you, the reader, to keep reading and to share this book with your loved ones and business associates.

They say that the success of a book is 30% percent writing and 70% marketing. I may have a stronger knack for marketing than writing.

If you could bottle up '*Unconditional Love*' and sell it online for the price of a cheap bottle of wine, would this be a hard sell?

You will be the judges.

Marco always longed for a purpose in life. Since he retired, he's been traveling full-time.

It was a blessing, yet always incomplete. It felt a little selfish to travel through those poor countries and indulge in activities like scuba diving, paragliding, and sky diving. Not to mention eating in pleasant restaurants and flying around the world.

In all fairness, his carbon footprint wasn't the greatest.

He saw himself as capable of serving people yet felt somewhat alienated from mankind.

Would unconditional love restore the balance to this conundrum?

After all, Marco was a complex individual. Debbie Ford, in her outstanding book: '*The Dark Side of the Light Chasers*,' had an interesting spin on the polarities inherent in our beings.

Rather than repulsing our dark side, our faults, and defaults, we should instead embrace them because there can't be light without darkness, beauty without ugliness, or right without wrong.

By embracing our most wicked tendencies, we allow the opposite qualities to grow and flourish.

So, instead of fighting against them, all we have to do is recognize, accept, and transform them into something positive and inspiring.

It differs from the concept of paradise and hell from our Judeo-Christian ideology. It's no longer a simple matter of good or evil, and it gives us the freedom to love and accept ourselves.

Many of us have been told since infancy that we were no good or inadequate in many facets of our personalities, and, of course, we ended up believing it.

If we didn't make the effort to change these realities, we would never reach our potential.

By accepting the fact that we're wicked, we can transcend that wickedness and turn it into something virtuous, something godlike.

FIVE

"Close your eyes. Fall in love. Stay there."

— RUMI.

While working door-to-door for a security company in Denver, Colorado, Marco joined a yoga studio and attended morning classes several times a week. He had done yoga regularly after separating from his wife.

One of his teachers often said that you could practice yoga while walking your dog or doing many other activities. You didn't necessarily need a yoga mat or compression pants in order to be *'enlightened.'*

It only takes focus on the moment and consciousness of the breath.

This awareness of breathing makes yoga so powerful.
Combined with energizing, flexible, and stamina-requiring exercises, it has a calming effect on the mind.

Other aerobic activities, like jogging or sports that involve running, can have similar effects. However, certain schools of yoga, when combined with spirituality, have the added benefit of enhancing consciousness.

Marco's life changed when he tried Kundalini yoga in his new Denver studio one morning.

The class differed from his previous experiences.

When the teacher played mantra music from an iPad and the students joined in singing, he had a eureka moment.

Singing mantras is the quickest way to converse with God, his teacher often said. Guru Nanak, the founder of Sikhism, wrote the mantras in Gurmukhi, from which originated the language in Punjab, India.

International artists recorded these mantras in unique styles that Marco found appealing during his years of studying Kundalini yoga.

Fast forward a couple of weeks in that Denver studio, and a different teacher was teaching a class on mantras and meditation. She encouraged the students to sing along.

After decades, Marco finally sang in public.

He had resigned himself to be quiet, even in the shower, since childhood. His older brother Fabrice deemed his voice terrible and called him a worthless singer.

Trying to emulate his idol, Neil Young, with his high-pitched voice didn't help.
But on this day, the teacher complimented his pleasant voice after class.

Marco stood there, mouth agape, unable to utter a single word.

That teacher had an enchanting voice. Maybe she had confused him with another student?

But it turned out that she meant what she said.

That was the beginning of a new credence for Marco, which outlined the fact that it's never too late to change one's beliefs. Marco was one year short of turning sixty.

In fact, singing became one of his new passions and a tremendous source of Divine inspiration.

If you come across something that resonates with you, continue digging for more echoes, in the same way as miners, who bore through carbon to find diamonds.

Marco always had an undying optimism that transcended the harshest situations.

He couldn't stay depressed for long despite experiencing a roller coaster of emotions throughout his life.

When you can't control your emotions, life can be a rocky ride, and the surrounding people suffer.

Calmness brings forth an unfolding life and contagious peace of mind to those nearby.

Then again, to become wise, you must go through various stages of foolishness, mustn't you?

It seemed to work that way, rationalizing Marco to make himself feel less guilty.

Take responsibility, feel empathy, and life becomes a dance under starry skies.

Emotional struggle puts you at the mercy of others, leaving no option but reactive mode.

CHAPTER
SIX

*"You have two ways to live your life. The first one is to believe
that nothing is a miracle, and the other is to believe that
everything is a miracle."*

— ALBERT EINSTEIN.

Marco was in awe of nature from an early age.

He must've known there was a supreme intelligence
– despite his Catholic upbringing, which was the tradition since his
parents didn't have faith in anything and had a pretty low conscience
level.

All that Judeo-Christian dogma made him an atheist, just like
most of his relatives.

At twelve, he celebrated a rite of first communion and tore his
white gown while sliding down a ramp in front of the church like a
chimpanzee. His father's beating led to the end of his relationship
with Jesus and the Holy Ghost.

It took him decades to become an agnostic. He felt a divine power guiding life's play but remained clueless.

Socrates wrote: *"All that I know is that I know nothing."*

At least Marco understood that beyond his ego, which was parading like a rooster in a henhouse, he was insensitive to everybody around him.

That perception made him arrogant.

He was sectarian in his mind. His perspective was the only one to consider.

This wasn't the best way to gain tolerance towards others.

The question bears: How do you make amends for the mistakes of your youth?

Marco, never a choirboy, would often behave like a crazy kid to let off some steam.

He had a great relationship with his brother Bernard. It wasn't very cerebral, but punches came fast and hard.

Taking enough beatings from his father, he had no desire to fight with other kids.

So, he relied on more harmful pastimes, such as breaking windows with rocks or similar acts of vandalism. He engaged in various misbehavior, such as stealing fruit from neighbor's properties, trespassing in vacation homes, and reckless driving on his moped after spending the afternoon in bars with friends, to name just a few.

Marco realized, during the third week of the Camino de Santiago, that the biological age of forty-seven he had conceived no longer applied to him.

After the first few days following the start of the trek, a synovial effusion on his right knee and a sciatic nerve acting up reminded him of his youth gone astray.

Although he'd trekked in many countries in the past, this particular Camino offered a unique set of challenges.

Imagine walking twenty to twenty-five kilometers a day for months, with one day of rest each week. It soon becomes more mental than physical, and you realize that this makes this particular trek special.

They call it a pilgrimage, and, as such, it gives you the opportunity to explore unknown parts of your psyche – hence the challenge and its just reward.

Marco was still a young man by '*World Health Organization*' standards. They state that you don't become elderly until you reach your sixty-sixth birthday.

He figured that with good health, he could go on exploring the world until his eighties, and an interesting insight dawned on him during these solitary walks.

Slow down time by having meaningful experiences. Embrace the past with pride and joy rather than lamenting the passage of time and aging.

It changes your perspective and enables you to carry on without regrets.

Marco believed that losing the ability to dream and witnessing one's increasing bitterness and incapacitation as the years went by would be the harshest reality.

He also sensed that a lack of belief about life after death made the entire process of getting older an unexciting proposal. No wonder such a large number of people required medication.

You have to keep matters in balance. The entire argument of burning life's candle through abuse of food, alcohol, or drugs is a pretty shallow proposition, according to him.

"Your body is your temple," as they say. If you don't take care of it, it's unlikely you could achieve all that Marco has accomplished.

These include getting a paragliding license, learning scuba diving and skydiving, trekking to Everest and Annapurna base camps, and covering over 600 kilometers in the Himalayas. Not counting riding around India on a Royal Enfield for a whole year.

So, as his sister said: *"It takes a toll on the body."*

If you took a glimpse at Marco's bucket list, you'd conclude that he must be mad or, at worst, delusional.

He had never been lacking in imagination.

He realized that dreams, travel plans, and plenty of activities would sustain the fire throughout the night.

Life could change in an instant. You're close to fading into nothingness.

So cherish every breath while manifesting an infinite number to come. Keep looking ahead; don't dwell on the past.

We spend our whole lives chasing the rainbow over the horizon when there's no alternative but the present moment to savor.

It's society's irony.

Besides, there's nothing on the exterior. It's all happening inside of us.

We create our own reality. Let's write a good script since we'll be the principal actors in the play.

Walking the Camino, Marco soon realized that the willpower of men was infinite.

What about the Austrian woman who departed her home country with a Belgian Shepherd five months ago? It was a significant feat, especially since she had to sleep in a tent because of a no-dogs policy in the hostels. On top of that, she was hiking thirty kilometers a day.

Marco faced a test of endurance as he continued hiking, dealing with his own aches and pains. He wouldn't have it any other way, hence the proportional amount of satisfaction.

On the Camino, rain had come and gone for five straight days.

Always dress in layers to avoid getting soaked.

Marco had lived his first twenty years on the French Riviera. He wasn't a big fan of the wet, the wind, and the cold.

Sunshine had been a rare sight, but it was bound to change like it always does.

Marco's recent state of mind was positive, and he thrived on challenges.

Live life fully to embrace the reminder of mortality.

You don't get any younger by acting half your age, but the joy hormones like adrenaline and serotonin give you a renewed perspective on the existence and passing time.

Pretty soon, it turns into a dance around a bonfire.

Marco planned to spice up the ordeal by reverse-walking the *Camino Portugués* on the coast to Porto. That was his approach: to differ from others.

Besides, he'd already encountered a few pilgrims who were more worthy than he, from his perspective.

Today, Marco met a German man with a dog and a donkey. The latter had a bad leg because of a worn-out shoe.

Do donkeys belong on the Way of St James?

Apparently, there was another Frenchman somewhere walking the Camino in reverse with five donkeys.

If there was a boundary to establish, where would you set it?

It's preferable to watch and not evaluate individuals.

Society makes it challenging to trust those who are different.

Marco believed that on this Camino, we should celebrate our own individuality, at least within certain moral boundaries.

It's quite liberating when you observe the world around you and refrain from partaking in its craziness.

Does ignoring what doesn't serve you and focusing on what empowers you instead make you more sane?

CHAPTER
SEVEN

"One word frees us of all the weight and pain in life: that word is love."

— SOPHOCLES.

After his six-week retreat in the Peruvian jungle, Marco found inner peace. Daily walks with an eleven-kilo backpack left no space for discord.

Everything seemed to gel with the beautiful scenery, the local cuisine, and the varied architecture of the different provinces along the way.

Another Belgian Marco encountered was on his thirteenth Camino, and he was sleeping outside for financial reasons. An individual with vast knowledge on many subjects, including LSD microdosing, extraterrestrials, and Earth's electromagnetic forces.

There were no dull moments on this Camino.

Marco had encountered this young Italian called Manolo, who was walking with a blond Danish woman with a gregarious smile.

The next day, he crossed his path again, this time walking solo. Marco was very fond of the Italian language, and had worked one summer season near Palermo in Sicily.

Speaking Italian words with decent grammar was fairly easy to him but understanding it was a unique challenge, on account of the speed at which Italians spoke.

It turned out that Manolo was lamenting the death of his father. Marco assumed he had passed away recently.

In fact. he died from a brain tumor at thirty-nine, when Manolo was only five years old, almost eighteen years ago.

Possessing an unfilled void in his heart resulted in squandering his life in an unproductive manner, as Manolo showed by engaging in a continuous three-year drinking binge.

Marco understood the struggles of a twenty-three-year-old searching for meaning in life.

Manolo was crying like a baby despite an exciting first two weeks. The Danish girl's absence was more likely the cause of his sorrows.

Marco shared the story about the dormant five-year-old within us, always ready to awaken. You may know that five-year-old yourselves.

The Vietnamese monk Thich Nhat Hanh talked about embracing and cherishing the five-year-old inside all of us. At five years old, you experience suffering and difficulties. Your parents' lack of empathy or irritability is like a bucket of ice water poured on your heart.

When you identify this little child inside you, you know he needs your care. You may have intentionally ignored him, causing him to suffer. It's time to treasure him, to talk to him with sympathy and compassion. You see that child responding to you and feeling better? And if he feels improved, you'll feel improved, too.

Next, you could imagine your father as a five-year-old and repeat the same exercise.

The young child's voice and the ego's voice often commingle. When you think about it, it makes sense since the ego is projecting your identity, and the neurotic five-year-old fits in like a glove.

How to silence the sound of such a peace breaker, you may ask?

It isn't effortless. Otherwise, we might inhabit a better society and a more peaceful world.

Spend a lot of time doing meditation and yoga or martial arts, calligraphy, or archery to cleanse the subconscious of that neurotic baggage you carry around with you.

In case of failure, living in a Himalayan cave for twenty-five years would probably do the trick.

Marianne Williamson, in '*A Return to Love*' (a must-read) wrote:

"*The spiritual journey is the relinquishment – or unlearning – of fear and accepting love.*"

All of your discontent arises from fear. It's a powerful invitation to surrender to a higher power by rejecting your ego and embracing love.

You're all connected through a fathomless energy that you could call God.

By finding forgiveness first, you could release yourselves from the past.

"Each of us has to find his own way. Nobody can give you a mythology. The images that mean something to you, you'll find in your dreams, in your visions, in your actions; you'll find out what they are after you've passed them. No one in the world was ever you before, with your particular gifts, abilities, and possibilities. It's a shame to waste those by doing what someone else has done."

— JOSEPH CAMPBELL (MYTH AND MEANING: CONVERSATIONS).

Marco traveled around India for two years, including one full year riding a Royal Enfield Himalayan, a motorcycle that lacks power and sounds like a tractor but is as tough as old boots.

After spending so much time on his feet while on the Camino, the mere sound of a motorbike passing by invigorated him.

It's an empowering feeling that borders upon vulnerability when you ride as one with the traffic, the tarmac, and the weather.

Marco bought a 125cc motorcycle in Mexico to practice with gears, having only ridden a moped in his teens. Inspired by the tales of his sister's friend, Anna, he was hoping to buy a Royal Enfield in India.

She had spent years riding around India and had posted all her adventures on Facebook.

If you value your life, you should avoid learning how to ride a bike in India, with its reckless drivers.

Then again, this was the ultimate exercise in mindfulness.

A man and his machine, dressed in survival gear, fighting the elements.

What a beautiful destiny to live and survive the ordeal! Marco became addicted to his initial journey through Punjab.

His ultimate goal was to keep on riding around the world.

He had traveled to North America, Australia, and Canada extensively. There was no need for a repeat.

Asia, Europe, Central and South America, and the mighty Africa beckoned.

Marco's Kundalini yoga training had taught him that there were three minds: the positive, the negative, and the neutral.

To live a peaceful life, one must maintain a calm and stable state of mind, devoid of fluctuating emotions influenced by circumstances.

This state of coherence and equanimity could be the Dalai Lama's preferred realm.

The part of the Camino that didn't disappoint was the suffering required. Marco enjoyed being taken out of his comfort zone. It was fair game to him.

He was asleep at the wheel for an extended period. It was 'time to let go and let God,' so said his yoga teacher's guru.

Allow the Supreme Being – or whatever moniker resonates with you – to bless you with light and glory.

Then, be an observer and watch it unfold. It's a wonderful experience; you must try.

Marco felt excited about walking on this '*Camino de la Vida.*'

Concerning the Camino, there were too many individuals, excessive paved roads, and a lack of empathy from locals. Could it have been a 2022 occurrence following COVID-19?

People were not interested at all in the pilgrims. Maybe they were just indifferent to the sheer numbers of them.

They displayed caution that often bordered upon disdain.

Some travelers, unfortunate enough to sleep outside or to exhibit the marks of bed bugs bites, served as reminders of their unsafe world.

I'll tell you the secret of accomplishing all your goals: Put them on paper, and don't let distractions interfere with your dreams

It could be a half-century or more. What difference does it make? Time is irrelevant in the grand scheme of things.

Marco just remembered that he'd been traveling around South America with a backpack in 1978, and upon arriving in Ecuador, his favorite country on the entire continent, he couldn't afford to visit the Galápagos.

He traveled there with his son in 2016, when they sailed on a luxury catamaran for nine days. He had to wait thirty-eight years for the privilege.

CHAPTER
NINE

"It isn't true that people stop pursuing dreams because they grow old; they grow old because they stop pursuing dreams."

— GABRIEL GARCIA MARQUEZ.

Regardless of the situation, Marco had a fantasy-prone personality. Envisioning had always been his way to escape his shield.

He sensed depressed people suffered from a chemical imbalance and other factors that motivation alone wasn't capable of counteracting.

It occurred to him while having a meal of *cabrito* (baby goat) in a restaurant in Oviedo that despite being a pescatarian or a pesco-vegetarian, he ought to be soft in his convictions.

So he had another sangria.

The inflexibility of mind was the worst evil in this world, he reckoned, especially when it stemmed from ignorance.

Woody Allen describes Oviedo *"as a delicious, exotic, beautiful, clean, pleasant, tranquil, and pedestrianized city,"* and it didn't disappoint.

Marco was having a day of rest after nine straight days of walking.

He had never been more battered. The sensation in his legs was akin to metal spikes piercing his bones while he slept. As a pilgrim, why not strive to imitate Jesus' fate on the cross? That kept things in perspective.

His grandmother Violette used to walk uphill to a little church on a hill in Provence, with chickpeas in her shoes, in order to do penitence.

Marco had hiked on a yatra in Tamil Nadu while volunteering in Sadhguru's ashram Isha in Coimbatore, Tamil Nadu. They walked overnight on a rocky path to a holy mountain, supposed to be done barefoot. Marco, along with many other pilgrims, did it in his shoes.

If you've tried to walk long distances barefoot, you'll understand why.

After a pleasant day of walking, Marco sat down with a vermouth on ice and a twist of lemon. Many years had passed since he last tasted vermouth. It was a popular drink back in France during his teenage years.

Very often, the taste buds carry their own memory. It was enjoyable to relax with a tired body and a clear perspective on life.

Marco had few worries in his world. He could go anywhere he

pleased and stay as long as he wanted within the parameters of a reasonable budget.

The ultimate freedom was the ability to choose your activities and your destination without limitations or restrictions. He told people who were amazed by his lifestyle that he'd paid his dues.

He traveled the world dependent on chance meetings and changing seasons.

His bucket list was an endless parchment of exotic destinations across the seven continents and a succession of physical feats. Quite a sight to behold! He figured it was akin to reaching for the horizon line to see if it stretched further still.

If dying were inevitable, all these thrilling activities would keep him animated and full of vibrancy.

When Marco was a teenager, he was adamant that he wouldn't make it past forty. There he was, in his sixty-fifth year, overflowing with life, full of zest, and, more importantly, brimming with gratitude.

"*Gratitude is the highest yoga,*" said Yogi Bhajan, the man who brought Kundalini yoga to America in the 1960s.

When Marco started doing yoga, his life underwent a drastic transformation, as bitterness, resentment, and greed turned into gratitude through the alchemy of breath.

He couldn't help being born into a family where negativity was *le plat du jour.*

Marco admired young people with old souls.

Despite living for over five decades with the consciousness of an ant (well, they appear to be conscious on a biochemical level), he seemed to attract into his sphere younger individuals with energy, light, and soul galore.

One of the true blessings of our existence is getting older without being burned out and resentful of all the unfair occurrences and the damaged relationships in our lives.

Folks, herein lies the secret:

Pursue the beacon of brightness, the Holy Grail, to make amends and preserve the slender, radiant flame.

However, this stuff doesn't land in your lap one glorious morning.

Keep working at it.

When you believe you've cleaned up your attic (your subconscious), old skeletons have a habit of reappearing in moments of weakness when emotions take control of your psyche.

What a game-changer to manage your feelings and be less reactive to outside events.

Marco wondered how different his life would've been if he'd known all this earlier.

The young can't pick the fruits of old age. Otherwise, it would be like taking an exam with a cheat sheet.

Marco, an imperfect man, felt he was a work-in-progress guided by his mistakes.

From Einstein's hypothetical standpoint that nothing is a miracle, your presence on Earth is going to be a little out of alignment with the marvels of life.

Marco observed that those who held such beliefs fundamentally lacked awareness.

Despite his atheism in early adulthood, he'd always sensed a tangible force governing existence.

However, because his Cartesian mind couldn't comprehend such an odd thing, it was more convenient not to accept it.

Buddha said:

"Do not believe in anything simply because you have heard it.
Do not believe in anything simply because it is spoken and rumored by many.
Do not believe in anything simply because it is found written in your religious books.
Do not believe in anything merely on the authority of your teachers and elders.
Do not believe in traditions because they have been handed down for many generations.
But after observation and analysis, when you find that anything agrees with reason and is conducive to the good and benefit of one and all, then accept it and live up to it."

Marco, with his experience of living in the U.S. for a while, knew that despite the internet's abundance of information, individuals lacked the inclination to seek truth.

The more Marco walked on these endless trails on the Camino de Santiago, the more vignettes from his life kept popping up like fireflies in an Ecuadorian evening sky.

He had been fortunate enough to have had an amazing number of travels and experiences.

Learning from his mistakes was crucial. It was his recurring theme, his way of perceiving and existing.

What's the purpose of life if it lacks the things that make it worth remembering and living?

One day, on your deathbed, you're going to take count.

The night will stretch on, haunted by regrets, resentments, and the ghosts of your past if you don't live out your dreams.
Have you ever met people who always feel bad about their situation and blame everybody else for their predicament?

In the end, the love you take is equal to the love you make.

And then, in a flash, a crazy man ends your fairytale.

Mark these words: Joy and pain are proportional in life.

Certain individuals are oblivious to the law of reciprocation, especially in their personal lives.

"Karma is a bitch," as they say in the States. At one point, you'll need to make amends.

Lately, on this Camino, it was the only rule of the day:

Keep walking and clean, clean, clean.

He played the song '*Love*' by Manu Om for a big portion of the day.

That kept him busy, reminiscing about specific events and relationships from his past and clearing these memories without judgment or resentment of any kind.

Just clean these programs like you would computer malware.

Our subconscious influences our actions. Acknowledging and cleaning are necessary to address this.

It's nothing short of miraculous.

This gem is yours to have, a pearl so rare you ought to share it with your friends. Don't they say that sharing something is like having it twice?

Similar to the hen that laid golden eggs in the fable by Jean de La Fontaine, take good care of such a hen, and she'll keep laying golden eggs. If you slice open her guts, you'll find out she was just a regular hen, after all.

Turn shit into gold.

The mastery of an extraordinary alchemist, a Picasso, a Michelangelo, a Joe Vitale.

Marco cherished his independence. Having been married for twenty-eight years, he no longer required instructions on what to do or how to think.

Loneliness was always present, though, just like carrying a heavy backpack. Eventually, you become accustomed to it, and your back gives you a break.

Would you trade your freedom for a life in chains?

Marco, with all his newfound wisdom, enjoyed helping individuals and counseling them. When issues arose for other people, it reminded him of his past.

He acted like a guru, sharing insight with Camino travelers. He had become a good listener.

By moving beyond your ego and the constant need for validation, you can listen to other people's stories with the primary goal of empathizing and gaining insights from their experiences.

It's liberating to accept the stance of a bystander in the lives of individuals and impart advice from personal encounters.

The rain kept pouring down and although it is an allegory of life, it got on his nerves a little.

Then again, nothing much bothered Marco any longer in this new incarnation.

The immature man who reacted with his emotions *à fleur de peau* (easily set off) was long gone.

He must've been a pain in the butt to those around him.

Time's insight was truly lovely.

Marco always perceived a deep feeling of loneliness in this world, with no individual to turn to for support. He often experienced solitude, like a forgotten attic toy or a voice in the wilderness.

But with his boundless imagination, he managed to escape the clutches of depression, unlike many others in his family.

To combat depression, consider incorporating *pranayama* (breathing) exercises into your routine.

By inhaling positive vibes and exhaling negative vibes, you could promote healing.

There's no scientific explanation for depression because one doesn't exist. Another reason to get on your yoga mat.

How do you combat the deep loneliness that drives you to seek recognition or something to hold on to? At the cost of being trapped in an endless abyss.

When you've learned to love yourself, being alone is no longer a problem since you aren't dependent on the opinion of others to define yourself.

CHAPTER
TEN

"Dance like a snake
On the desert floor
And that girl you shake
Will come beg for more

Dance like snowflakes
On the high prairie
Your sorrows and aches
Frozen in glory

Dance like your feet
Are stuck in the mud
Cling to her spirit
Like dew on a bud

Dance like the sun
Bursting through a cloud
Yell it clear and loud
The night will be fun."

— MARCO, 2014.

Marco could contain the void within the sexual act. That's no different from being addicted to alcohol, nicotine, gambling, sugar, junk food, or cocaine. But far more insidious in terms of the energy exchange.

He found that sex was empowering for his sense of self-worth.

However, dark forces took over his mind, and he lost his sanity in the process.

Marco's craving for sex preceded his desire for a relationship. So, guess which one suffered the most?

Marco liked the company of women who sold their bodies for money while on his travels through Asia, and also in the U.S. and Mexico.

Call them prostitutes or whatever else you might choose. Many women with babies at home rely on such a job to support their families.

They could carry bricks all day long on a construction site with their babies sitting on the sidewalk, like those women in India, for a few hundred rupees. Instead, they choose to use their bodies more maliciously. Who can judge? Men don't have the right perspective to pass on judgments.

When seeking pleasure, a man's foremost desires are companionship and intimacy.

Intimacy needs to outweigh perversion for men.

Self-love is the beginning of freedom, avoiding the company of men. Such freedom comes at the price of isolating yourself from others, and loneliness creeps in a big way.

Marco connected with others and filled the void, using his libido and imagination.

Someone once said publicly: *"You don't pay a prostitute for sex; you pay her to leave afterward."*

After years of unsatisfying intimacy, he yearned to make up for lost time. Ego and sex made for an intoxicating cocktail. In hindsight, sex was the perfect canvas on which to exhibit his lack of respect for women and his longing for approval.

When he was a teenager, he allowed foolish thoughts into his mind about having a small penis or being an inadequate lover. So it was invigorating to prove to himself that wasn't the case at all.

He found it self-gratifying to conquer women and take them home, like a lion who brings its captured prey to its den.

I know this is a terrible analogy that won't endear him to his female readers, so be it for the sake of transparency.

When not dating, he would engage the services of prostitutes to calm his libido, sometimes two at a time.

He liked them young. Do you wonder why older men like younger women?

A man may find himself drawn to a young woman's softness and flawless curves. His goal is to achieve immortality and preserve his youth. So, he projects his fantasies on the young subject.

The compulsion for promiscuous sex defeats men in a mid-life crisis. A closed-hearted man is an even bigger target.

He started to become attracted to transsexuals or *'shemales'*, as they're called. As troublesome as that may sound, it had its own logic, after all.

Soon after his separation from Hazel, Marco went to visit a tantric massage parlor in the old town of Albuquerque. Months later, he came across an article in the paper revealing that the police had arrested the madam and her acolytes after busting the business.

The red-head madam, with the magical touch, stated that as a man matures, he feels compelled to explore the dualities between the masculine and the feminine, going beyond societal norms.

She didn't quite say it that way, but you get the point.

Marco knew many women who experimented with and extolled same-sex encounters. If he were a woman, he would likely do the same.

However, he experienced no pull towards men whatsoever. A sweet and feminine ladyboy from Thailand put those social taboos to rest and then some.

Marco's mental state worsened because of many sexual relationships over time.

Each partner absorbs energy from the other during intercourse.

Marco's yoga teacher highlighted a key distinction between men and women. Men have their sexual organs on the outside, while women have theirs on the inside.

Men, like roosters, must display their libido to the coop.

In heterosexual relationships, the woman receives and absorbs the most energy from a male partner. She becomes the most vulnerable in terms of energy exchange.

Marco studied Pranic Healing in Dharamshala, Himachal Pradesh. It's similar to Reiki but without symbols. His teachers advised him not to shake hands with strangers, such was the potential power of energy transmission.

We refer to individuals possessing dark powers and ill intentions, similar to those in black magic.

Imagine being penetrated by a promiscuous man. You would receive energy from all his past partners in this life and beyond.

This is a hard proposition since all these energies accumulate around the sacral chakra or sexual chakra.

Let's pretend you know nothing about chakras.

We have seven major chakras or eleven major chakras, and many more minor ones in the school of Pranic Healing.

They act as vortexes of energy pulsating and rotating around major organs and are often the precursors of future diseases.

To simplify things, the sacral chakra relates to creativity and expression. All those negative energies, memories, and psychic impressions can either congest or deplete the sacred chakra.

A person with a sacral chakra out of balance will end up confused, uninspired, and susceptible to depression, aggressivity, and malefic tendencies.

So Marco, who indulged in unhealthy sexual relations with all kinds of partners, found himself in a similar predicament.

The heart is the bridge between the low chakras and the high chakras.

The low chakras are all about survival, while the higher chakras correspond to consciousness.

No consciousness can exist when all energies gravitate downwards.

They also follow the path of least resistance.

Love, in its purest form, always transforms from prejudice and anger to empathy and peace.

The Dalai Lama said that if meditation was taught to every eight-year-old, this could stop wars in one generation.

Problems arise when energies follow the path of gravity down the gutter instead of rising up and embracing the Divine.

ELEVEN

"I can speak to my soul only when the two of us are off exploring deserts or cities or mountains or roads."

— PAULO COELHO.

May 2022

Time had passed since Marco started the Camino de Santiago. He had an inner sense that he had strayed from discovering tranquility in his soul.

Traveling alone for the past five-plus years led to his indulging in life's accessible pleasures.

Going on solo adventures resulted in compromising his journey and uncovering his soul's mission.

It had been his quest since time immemorial. He had lost sight of that tiny flame that could lead to the end of the tunnel.

He felt blessed to live such a fulfilling life, deriving numerous pleasures and satisfactions from it.

You could always count on Marco to amuse himself and recognize the many miracles in his daily life.

However, something had always been missing.

It all started on the road in India, from Chandigarh to Dharamshala, Himachal Pradesh.

He was riding his Royal Enfield Himalayan on a hot and strenuous day.

He should've covered this distance in two days, based on his experience.

It was insane to travel over 400 kilometers on a motorcycle in India in just one day.

Indians have little respect or empathy for bikers. Be completely attentive to the task, if you value your life.

You're riding in the middle of dogs, donkeys, cows, horses, vehicles of all kinds and shapes, and 1 million passersby, it seems.

Without warning, they might appear in your trajectory, obstructing your path.

Following the end of the COVID-19 lockdown, he'd spent the entire year riding around India. He had made his way to Sikkim, near the Bhutan and Tibetan border.

The Indian bureaucracy made it difficult to extend his visa, so he put his bike in storage in Siliguri, West Bengal. He searched for greener pastures, so to speak. Nepal was re-opening its borders to tourists, and the trekking season had begun.

Six months later, he reunited with his beloved bike. He shipped it by train to Jaipur, Rajasthan, where he met his brother Bernard, who had come to India for full mouth dental implants.

He was soon back in the saddle, making his way to Himachal Pradesh, where he'd purchased his new bike eighteen months previously.

Being out of practice, a ten-hour ride seemed somewhat preposterous at that point.

He wanted to ride all the way to McLeod Ganj, where the Dalai Lama and his entourage live.

In India, you're constantly weaving in and out of traffic. The road opened up, and he pushed the 411cc plowing beast to its limits. A car zoomed by him, out of control.

It didn't come too close to his bike, like Indians have a habit of doing, nor did it cause him any danger.

Though, in an instant, he felt all the frustration and anger of someone pushed off the road one too many times.

The driver posed a danger by driving erratically on the two-lane road.

So he said to himself: "*Wait until I catch you up in the next traffic jam, I'll give you a piece of my mind.*"

Sure enough, half an hour later, he recognized the compact car caught in the traffic.

As he leaned close to the open passenger' side window, his bike fell to the side. It wasn't unusual for him to lose grip and drop the 200-kilogram bike, not counting the aluminum side boxes and all the luggage.

He was adamant about always riding in full bike gear.

Once he fell, he sprung back up and lunged towards the passenger side door with fervor.

He seized the man's collar, attempting to drag him from the car and assault him.

Realizing his whole body wouldn't fit through this way, he resorted to squeezing his neck, all while repeatedly yelling:

"I'm gonna kill you, motherfucka…"

I don't know how many times he strangled the poor fellow.

When he got tired of it, he exited the car and kicked its left rear-view mirror with his right boot. As soon as the mirror burst into fragments, the man and his machine swiftly departed as if he'd witnessed a legion of spirits.

At that point, Marco stood in the middle of the road with his helmet still on.

His bike blocked the upcoming traffic. He stared for the longest time at the cars and bikes, anticipating somebody beeping their horn so he could pick another victim. It's a common practice in India to serenade others with your klaxon.

Seeing this animal in complete bike gear, raging with such intensity, no one dared make a noise.

Indians are, by nature, peaceful people not interested in physical altercations.

A couple of men close by, no doubt motivated by sheer fear, helped him straighten up his bike, and he departed the dreadful scene.

The absence of any YouTube videos showcasing his act of fury surprised him. He searched the internet for such a sorry spectacle for days afterward.

He had a few hours left to reach Dharamshala. It would be a misrepresentation to say he was in control of his faculties.

Behaving more like a wounded animal, he was searching for a place to hide and lick his wounds. When he arrived in Chandigarh late in the evening, a stupid driver kept beeping his horn at him.

Marco got off his bike to vent his frustration. After a round of insults, he saw a kid sleeping in the back seat and decided to give up on his search-and-destroy mission and call it a day.

What became of the man who spent three months in a Tamil Nadu ashram, practicing yoga and meditation for five hours a day during the COVID-19 lockdown?

What about the sage who mediated by the Ganges in Varanasi at 4.30 a.m. every morning for *sadhana* (daily spiritual practice), for weeks at a time?

Where was the eager student who'd studied Pranic healing with his teachers in Dharamshala for three months or the aspiring Buddhist and Zazen meditator?

All the good energy he had raised was now bound for the sewage pond.

He couldn't recall when he last engaged in a fight. There he was terrorizing the neighborhood like a scene from '*A Clockwork Orange,*' a particularly violent cult film by Stanley Kubrick.

He was used to doing his fighting on the yoga mat and conversing with God by singing mantras.

What could cause a man to lose all his marbles in that manner?

What evil forces led to such aggression, wrath, and desperation?

He thought he'd rid himself of his inner demons, having plied himself with a variety of spiritual studies and new-wave modalities. But there he was in the middle of a crowded street, in plain sight for the world to see:

A psychopath dressed in a biker gang's outfit, out of control and spiraling downwards.

CHAPTER
TWELVE

"We must be willing to get rid of the life we've planned, so as to have the life that is waiting for us. The old skin has to be shed before the new one can come."

— JOSEPH CAMPBELL.

The next day, he received a WhatsApp message from his dear friends Montserrat and Aum, whom he'd met in a Zen meditation center in Tamil Nadu.

"Marco, we have a great opportunity for you in the Peruvian Amazon, near Pucallpa."

What the heck! He was in India, and Peru was 16,000 kilometers away.

Peru was out of sync with his travel plans in Asia.

Then again, Marco was a shadow of his former self. Maybe all along, he'd just been a gloomy figure, astray in the dark?

Next morning, Marco knew he had to go to Peru. He had no alternative.

He sold his bike and flew to Pucallpa.

His friend Montserrat, a precocious twenty-two year old Chilean raised in Sweden, had spearheaded a permaculture project on a property two hours' drive south of Pucallpa.

A Swiss couple purchased that property fifteen years ago. The main purpose was to safeguard that jungle paradise from being encroached upon by civilization. It encompassed thirty-three hectares of woodland with many centenarian trees and a creek running through it. Surrounded by rice fields, it served as a retreat for medicinal plants.

This retreat consisted of twelve cabins for guests amidst a local population of Shipibo workers with their own huts on a couple of hectares of cleared land.

Ayahuasca is a blend of Chacruna leaves and Ayahuasca vines mixed and brewed together. For centuries, shamans in the South American jungle have used it for ritual ceremonies.

For the record, there are around 80,000 species of Amazon rainforest plants, which grow as trees, shrubs, bushes, and climbing plants.

For shamans to have found this particular combination eliminates the trial and error theory.

Legend has it that spirits instructed a Shipibo shaman to venture into the jungle and blend the vines and leaves of those respective plants.

DMT (dimethyltryptamine) is one of the main psychoactive

constituents in the Ayahuasca vines. However, DMT is inactive as a hallucinogen since monoamine oxidase (MAO) breaks it down before it reaches the central nervous system.

It has to be taken with a plant containing an MAO inhibitor – in this case, Chacruna – to prevent DMT degradation.

As it's grown more mainstream in the West, Pucallpa and Iquitos in Peru have become popular destinations for this consciousness-altering medicine.

It's important to note that Ayahuasca isn't a drug but a medicine – unlike psychedelic drugs like LSD and Ecstasy, or any compound made in a lab, for that matter.

A plant like cannabis lowers your faculties and can't be considered as a medicinal plant without its THC compound removed.

The average amount of THC in cannabis has increased more than tenfold over the last fifty years, according to the Potency Monitoring Program conducted by the National Institute on Drug Abuse.

People highlight the fact that cannabis smoking has a long history spanning thousands of years. Today's available strains, however, can be so much stronger that we find ourselves in uncharted territory.

When used ethically and under proper guidance, research has proven that Ayahuasca is safe and non-addictive.

When Montserrat announced that she was going to cultivate trees, plants, and flowers, people laughed at her.

Both shamans declared that this land, a former coca plantation, was barren and incapable of growth. The earth was a mix of pure clay and chemical residues from pesticides and fertilizers.

Montserrat said that the land looked like a dead zone. She admitted to doing nothing during the first week, which amused the locals. She merely strolled and conversed with the land.

Four weeks were the minimum time for a plant diet. Marco figured he had work to do, so he signed in for six weeks.

There are a variety of different plants with their own specific properties.

The owner advised him that Bobinsana would serve him well.

Bobinsana is a plant that opens up the heart. It was precisely what he needed.

Besides, his bladder, along with his sexual chakra, was a mess.

You should try Ayahuasca if you feel such a calling. It will serve you well as long as you keep your mind open and your ego in check.

His first experience with this medicine came when he was working in Baja California in the sales department of a luxury resort.

On arrival in this town, a woman working in marketing at the hotel invited him to a private ceremony. Just the two of them, with a visiting female shaman from Tijuana.

Since he didn't know this young woman, he asked her why she'd invited him. She answered:

"I heard you were a yogi."

The universe works in mysterious ways.

"Yoga wasn't a prerequisite for taking Ayahuasca," he thought to

himself, yet he accepted the invitation. He had always wanted to try the '*Vine of the Soul.*'

Fate decided.

In order to partake in the Ayahuasca experience, one must follow a pre-diet that prohibits consuming meat, alcohol, drugs, junk food, and engaging in sexual activities.

Marco was celibate, a pesco-vegetarian, and a light drinker, not taking drugs or medication, so the timing was excellent.

Vomiting is common among new practitioners as a way to detoxify. The medicine won't be effective until you pass the purging test.

That night, he tried the potion for the first time.

He had the experience of his life. It wasn't the case for the young lady, who wasn't in the best of shape. She smoked weed and cigarettes and drank too much tequila. She spent most of the evening with her face in a bucket, making animalistic sounds.

For the rest of the night, Marco never heard anything from her. He was sitting in a rocking chair, ready for take-off.

Bursting out of the speakers were the sounds of *icaros* (native songs inspired by the spirits of the forest), which helped him chill out.

He journeyed to the '*other side*' and took a long, leisure walk in the 'great beyond.'

Mind you, that night, he transcended his fear of death.

Since he'd consumed a satisfactory number of recreational drugs in his lifetime, he could recognize that he wasn't intoxicated or hallucinating. He was strolling through higher dimensions, just like in a lucid dream.

Everything felt so inviting and serene.

He remembers laughing a lot. The rocking sofa transformed into a magic carpet soaring through infinity.

Steve Jobs, the chairman and founder of Apple, had instructed that 'Autobiography of a Yogi' by Paramahansa Yogananda be given to every single guest at his funeral.

It described his guru's tales about what happened after death. You may be eligible, with a little consciousness gained on planet Earth, to spend 400 to 500 years in one of those ethereal planes.

Marco glimpsed the afterlife and liked it.

It's always up to the healer to decide whether you need more medicine.

He had his second cup, while Gloria had long gone into oblivion.

By then, he was pretty dizzy. The shaman approached him with a third cup a couple of hours later. He didn't want to take any more medicine that night.

She put the cup in his hand. For the longest time, he held it tight, cautious of not spilling a drop. But he had no intention of drinking it.

At one point, he asked the medicine woman why she thought he ought to drink more.

She answered maliciously:

"Porque tú lo mereces!" – Because you deserve it!

Sweet music to his ears, he consumed every last drop of it and then, all hell broke loose.

Mother Ayahuasca, like any loving mother, will discipline you on your journey to enlightenment.

And kick his ass. Did she ever?
How many skeletons did she throw out of his closet that night?

He started throwing up like a man possessed.

Without experiencing Ayahuasca purging firsthand, it's challenging to describe the sounds emanating from his throat, reminiscent of the devil speaking in tongues.

The Kundalini energy is symbolized by a snake rising from below the abdomen and next to the hips. It wreaked havoc inside his belly, like a giant anaconda foraging in his guts.

The shaman was massaging his back vigorously in order for these demonic forces to break loose. He was purging all the bad karma of his former lives within his bucket and was by then more werewolf than human.

It lasted until night, and he escaped the evil spirits as if by magic.

CHAPTER

THIRTEEN

"You have no choice. You must leave your ego on the doorstep before you enter love."

— KAMAND KOJOURI.

Marco's diet with Bobinsana went on seamlessly. Despite the sheer amount of medicine he was taking, he managed to stay in control. That didn't surprise him as much as it reminded him of the benevolent power of those master plants.

Every passing day, he witnessed his heart opening up like the bud of a lotus flower.

The flower pushes its way through the mud, rising towards the sunlight. The epitome of a survivor, it rises from the dark muddy waters in order to find the warmth and nourishment of the light.

Goldie Hawn once said:

"Whether we have it all or we have nothing, we are all faced with the same obstacles: sadness, loss, illness, dying, and death. To gain wisdom, kindness, and compassion, we must strive to grow like a lotus, opening each petal one by one."

He didn't perform any exorcisms or experience the darkness consuming a corner of his psyche. Quite the contrary.

During the ceremonies at night, he would revisit the events of his past with a newfound insight imbued with love and empathy.

All his past troubles took the form of soap bubbles floating in the air, and he had fun watching them bust.

His past troubles mostly came from his egocentric nature. The Oxford Dictionary defines an egocentric as a person who focuses on themselves without considering the emotions or wishes of others.

In his sexual transgressions, he often behaved like an egomaniac: an individual who is egotistical or self-centered.

His noble quest remained to transcend his ego and open up his heart.

Visiting other dimensions was fine as long as he could return to reality and stay grounded.

Psychologist David Londoño has spent seventeen years working with traditional indigenous medicines, both as a patient and student. He's affiliated with non-profit International Center for Ethnobotanical Education, Research, and Service (ICEERS).

David speaks in-depth about the complexity of ego dissolution as related to master plant experiences. In an interview, he explains how our ego is essential and how to develop a healthy relationship with it as opposed to *'losing the ego'*:

"What exactly is ego dissolution?"

"To answer this question, we first must think about the complexity of what the ego is. The ego gives us the sense of having a self. Ego comes from Latin, meaning 'I', and implies a psychic structure responsible for a complex series of functions that are fundamental to psychological health. Among other things, it distinguishes the inside from the outside. It is a boundary that gives you a sense of independence, separation, and individuality."

"For example, the ego helps you to separate your ideas and needs from mine. Imagine losing the boundary of the ego for a prolonged time, not just for a few hours, but for days, months, or years. You would then lose your sense of individuality, and you may not know where your body ends, and someone else's begins. You may not know your opinion on an issue or whether you need to feed yourself."

"If you don't have a healthy sense of individuality, it can be very difficult to function in the world. We need a sense of self for many things: to finish a job, set boundaries with someone, or decide on who we vote for. In principle, the 'I' has all these elements and more."

"In certain experiences with plant medicine, individuals may temporarily suspend their sense of self to some extent. People may feel united or part of something much larger. The sense of identity is broadened. They feel connected to the universe, the cosmos, and others. You become much broader than your individuality."

"Is that what is known as 'transcending' the level of the ego?"

"Exactly. There is a difference between transcending and abandoning or losing the ego. People experience this in other ways, for example, with art, yoga, or meditation. Some spiritual traditions consider it a central theme and view it as a capability or even a goal of the human experience. In this context, the aim is not to lose individuality but to expand and transcend duality."

"However, certain pathologies, like psychosis or depression, can weaken the ego. One way of looking at depression is when someone's ego is in distress."

"From certain points of view, the ego has a terrible reputation and is associated with excessive self-importance. Therefore, many people talk about the importance of "losing the ego." They are referring to reducing the excessive arrogance that is so prevalent in the world. However, these are different things. It is not about breaking or fighting with the ego but about building a healthy ego."

"Sometimes, an experience with consciousness expansion can lead to egoic fragility. For example, an individual may feel invaded by the thoughts of others, lose the ability to choose, or cannot function in the world. There is nothing spiritual about that. It is a problem and, therefore, needs treatment. This differs from a transcendent experience."

"At what point can this state be pathological?"

"If you are having visions or extraordinary experiences within a ceremony, that is not necessarily "pathological." It may be inherent to the healing process that is specific to the ceremony. However, if days have passed since the ceremony and you continue to hear voices commanding

you to save the world as Jesus, it may be a sign of a pathological condition."

"What is the difference? One is time and context. We expect certain phenomena to occur in the ceremony's container. But if they happen outside this context, they are signs that something is wrong. That something needs to be observed and attended to. In traditional Amazonian medicine, practitioners understand certain plants can make a person more arrogant. They handle them with care. Sometimes, it is necessary to have a stronger ego to deal with reality, as with depression."

"On the one hand, there is ego loss. On the other extreme, there is ego inflation, which may happen to someone after an experience with plant medicine. They felt like the center of the world, and their sense of pride increased from an unhealthy point of view. I have often seen people whose narcissism has grown after taking plants."

"In Greek mythology, Narcissus was a hunter who found himself to be so beautiful that he became fixated by his own reflection in a pool. Such was his fixation that he lost the will to do anything else, and he died."

"I know someone with a narcissistic personality structure who, at ceremonies, saw himself as a powerful lion and the leader of the pride. This person felt that the plant was telling him he was a superior being. However, what appeared in his experience was what he already had inside: a feeling of being above others. For this person, it was a message from the plant confirming that he was special, not a mirror of what he had inside. If you can't understand or work with someone to help you understand, it's easy to lose yourself. The plant is showing you your pride and narcissism by seeing yourself as a lion."

"Is there a personality type that is more prone to getting lost in these ways?

"Two personality structures are more likely to enter a pathological situation: one is a narcissistic personality, and the second is a fragile ego. They both can lose the barrier that separates them from the world. This makes it more difficult to function in reality."

"During a plant diet in certain Amazonian traditions, they ensure to strengthen aspects of someone's personality structure before administering the medicine to prevent an experience of ego dissolution. When we don't have an excellent guide, we rarely have access to the wisdom of how to work with them more carefully and wisely. This can lead to going to places we are not prepared for, and we might get hurt."

"The same is true for meditation. There is an entire process of bodily, mental, and even ethical preparation before someone has certain experiences of consciousness. This is because if you voyage without proper preparation, it can do more harm than good."

"In traditional Amazonian medicine, some plants give you a deeper connection with the Earth. The plant Bobinsana, for example, gives you the ability to ground yourself. Botanicals that increase a sense of individuality are for someone who has self-esteem issues..."

Before leaving Mexico permanently, on his fourth Ayahuasca ceremony, his favorite shaman organized a ceremony in a home he rented near the sea.

After taking Ayahuasca, the shaman made rounds in the house with a two-way pipe called a *tepi*.

She used it to blow *rapé* (ground tobacco mixed with a variety of other herbs) into each of the willing guests' nostrils.

Marco's sinuses were pretty sensitive, and he wasn't too keen on letting somebody blow tobacco down his nose.

When he was a little boy, he always had problems breathing. His right nostril remained permanently blocked.

He didn't seek the expertise of a specialist until he was forty, and they diagnosed him with a deviated septum.

A wall of cartilage divides the nose into two separate chambers. It's called the nasal septum. If the wall shifts from the middle, they refer to it as a deviated septum.

His case was pretty severe and required surgery. Under local anesthesia, the surgeon removed part of the bone and cartilage, then reshaped and repositioned the underlying structure of his nose.

The sounds of the bone cracking added a gory effect to the scene. It brought '*Marathon Man*' to mind when Dustin Hoffman is tortured by a Nazi dentist.

A couple of days later, he could breathe in the proper manner. Never underestimate the power of the breath; try breathing with only one nostril for a while. He did it for forty years.

He was also prone to sinus headaches. They came and went without rhyme or reason, turning into migraines.

That's what attracted him to yoga in the first place – to center his attention on conscious breathing.

He could eliminate the headaches that had haunted his younger days. It was a significant accomplishment, necessitating a holistic lifestyle above all.

It always amazed him when people couldn't see the body-mind connection.

Our thoughts, feelings, beliefs, and attitudes have the potential to impact our biological functioning, either positively or negatively.

Our minds can affect how healthy our bodies are.

How we treat our bodies, what we eat, how much we exercise, and even our posture can impact our mental state in tremendous ways.

There's a complex interrelationship between our minds and bodies.

"The brain, peripheral nervous system, endocrine and immune systems, as well as all the organs and emotional responses in our body, communicate through a shared chemical language"

— DR. JAMES GORDON (FOUNDER OF THE
CENTER FOR MIND-BODY MEDICINE).

Researchers have documented the effects of anxiety and depression on the body.

Such ailments and diseases include chronic pain and inflammation, heart disease, diabetes, digestive problems, reduced sexual desire, and a weakened immune system.

Marco had smoked two packs of French cigarettes with no filter for ten years, starting when he was a teenager. He hated tobacco and couldn't stand the smoke any longer, to the point where it'd become detrimental to his social life.

The shaman convinced him that *mapacho* was a sacred plant for the Amazonian tribes and that *rapé* was a tribal sacrament.

He was lying comfortably on his sofa, not paying attention to the dozens of guests gathered in his home.

The shaman expelled *rapé* into each of his nostrils using a bone pipe. As soon as the snuff permeated his mucous membranes into his bloodstream, his head exploded like an engine head gasket.

He didn't remember cocaine being as fierce and violent.

After a while, he settled himself down by taking big rhythmic breaths in a slow and forceful manner, for fear his heart would also burst from his chest.

Unable to move or speak, he stayed on the sofa for an extended period.

That evening, he was in total symbiosis with the atoms spinning inside of his limbs. His ego identity had dissolved into a kaleidoscope of patterns, colors, and sounds. His whole body had melted into the circular motion of the Earth.

In the evening, he went to the bathroom and lay down in the shower, fully dressed. How long did he stay, face down in the drain, making eerie noises and hallucinating the patterns and colors of the ceramic tiles?

In those moments, the demons inhabiting him vanished without a trace. Maybe they followed the pipes to dissolve in the ocean?

That is an essential part of the cleansing and purging procedure. They say that Mother Ayahuasca has a consciousness of her own. She won't steer you in the wrong direction as long as your intentions and those of your shamans are pure.

You just have to trust the process, as the weaving fiber of your deliverance.

FOURTEEN

"Unable are the loved to die. For love is immortality."

— EMILY DICKINSON.

Marco was living in Albuquerque, New Mexico when an old friend came to visit for a few days.

They'd sold cars together in Portland, Oregon. His beloved wife, whom he always described as the most amazing and beautiful person imaginable, had died from cancer a few years before.

Have you ever wondered why the nicest people find premature death in this world?

This question had always bugged Marco.

Since he couldn't find any reasonable answer other than God not existing – otherwise, he would never permit that to happen – he conveniently chose not to believe in God.

It's too easy an argument. The roads are full of low-consciousness pilgrims who share this point of view.

They're probably living a life of great despair, like Hemingway points out in one of his books.

It's a similar concept to the fact that since we're only going to have one life – we might as well treat our body, and consequently our mind, as perishable items.

Don't you see the shallowness of such an argument? It rings hollow as Marco had always been a firm believer of the old adage: *"My body is my temple."*

His uncle Louis, his mother's younger brother, died alone in his apartment in the South of France. The owner of the local bar where his uncle went every day for a glass of white wine, or possibly several, got worried after not seeing him for a couple of days.

On accessing his flat, he found Louis dead. His liver had erupted, most likely during the night.

Louis bragged once of drinking seventeen Ricards before lunch, an appetizer from Marseille based on anise called Pastis, 51% proof. It's the custom in France to serve it in a long glass, three quarters pastis, one-quarter water. A fine habit to carry for decades, no less.

Why do talented men like his uncle – who could build anything by hand, including a sailing boat from scratch – waste their lives and their marriage for a descent into torment?

I'm not sure of the answer, but this is just the beginning of this book, after all.
Incidentally, his ex-wife Sabine recently found her long-time partner – a man devoted to helping others and of great integrity by all

accounts – dead in the stairway leading to their apartment. He had suffocated himself with a plastic bag around his neck.

Depression is that insidious and ugly disease looming around the suburbs of our civilized society, ready to pounce indiscriminately on its prey.

If you don't have first-hand experience of this kind of tragedy, look no further than the tabloids for news of celebrities who ended their lives, and witness the shock and surprise of their loved ones.

Marco's big loss in life happened when his older brother Fabrice died.

He committed suicide when he was twenty-six by overdosing on sleeping pills.

At that time Marco was working in an interim agency in Strasbourg. He received a call from an employee at the agency who said that somebody in his family had passed away.

Please, if you ever have to announce the death of a family member to somebody, say the bloody name straight away.

Before he had the opportunity to call home, don't let him pick and choose whose death he would least likely dread.

He had a sister, six years his junior. The thought that she could've been the one devastated him.

As for Fabrice, there was no way to have anticipated his death.

A year prior, he'd given up drugs and separated from his wicked wife. The last time Marco heard from him, he was studying photography.

Just like Françoise Sagan, who wrote '*Bonjour Tristesse,*' his brother had been shooting Palfium (synthetic morphine) for quite a few years. Marco had been relieved when he learned that he'd gone straight.

They didn't see eye-to-eye when it came to sticking a needle in their arm.

Life was too precious for him to throw it away in a dustbin, together with bloody cottons and used syringes. Mind you, back in those days, prior to Aids, they tended to use the same syringes over and over without even bothering to clean them.

Marco had spent his teenage years, from sixteen onwards, smoking weed and binge drinking, with the occasional LSD trip. However, injecting drugs didn't appeal to him for physical and psychological reasons.

He was seeing first-hand the damage that such addiction had done to his brother and his circle of junkie friends. It wasn't congruent with coping with everyday life and functioning as a member of society.

He wasn't having any of it, which didn't make him too popular with Fabrice and his entourage.

Growing up, Marco always looked at Fabrice with a degree of ambivalence.

When he committed suicide, he associated it with weakness, coming from his mother's side of the family. He has since revised his opinion of him.

Two years separated them, although it could've been a lifetime. He was taller and athletic, with a handsome look and a stern gaze that made him appear inscrutable.

He was an avid reader. 'Thus spoke Zarathustra' by Friedrich Nietzsche was his favorite book. This was well beyond Marco's cognitive abilities, at the time.

Marco has since tried to read it in English, but the translation from German used a lot of old English words. Shakespearean language had never been his cup of tea. Maybe he should try to read it in French.

Fabrice died one year short of Club 27's famous members: Robert Johnson, Amy Winehouse, Jim Morrison, Janice Joplin, Jimi Hendrix. Brian Jones, and Kurt Cobain, just to name the most well-known. These brilliant artists who abused drugs shared a common denominator. They were very perceptive. They didn't take drugs to get high but to tone down the information overload they were subject to.

Fabrice was an old soul, albeit disconnected from the source. His human existence must've been blasphemous to his true essence.

Life as a human probably caused him immense pain.

In any case. one summer between travels, when his morale was pretty low, Marco succumbed to the temptation.

As they say: *"Misery loves company."*

He never enjoyed the high, and he got sick a few times when he contracted bacteremia.

Despite this, in order to gain the appreciation of his brother, who'd been a stranger to him, he did partake in their 'blissed' misery for a while.

With insight, I'm pretty sure he caught Hepatitis C as a parting gift.

Had it been a few years later, with the onslaught of Aids, you certainly wouldn't be reading these words.

It's hard for him to reflect on all this, for he didn't particularly enjoy the experience.

It didn't bring him any closer to his brother, either. I doubt he learned anything from it, apart from gaining a disdain for injected drugs and intuiting that that slow descent into hopelessness didn't fit his DNA.

He was destined for more grandiose things, like a colorful sunset on a white sandy beach in the tropics, for instance.

Marco had never been a big fan of pharmaceuticals.

New antivirals came on the market in 2014 for Hepatitis C, with cure rates exceeding 90% and no side effects. He couldn't resist such a great opportunity.

He started the treatment, one pill a day for ninety days. The price for each pill was $1,000. The insurance took care of every single penny and delivered the pills to his condo with a $0 deductible.

The sweet irony was that he had no job at the time and low assets. He had qualified for 100% coverage from his free insurance despite living alone in a luxury condominium. So much about the myth of poor people in America having no access to insurance.

It was a total success. Hats off to all pharmaceutical scientists.
They haven't discovered an effective drug against cancer yet. Please excuse Marco's skepticism on this matter. Cancer is a gigantic business. Have they purposely overlooked alternative therapies?

Soon, he resumed his travels as a way to escape from his circumstances but mainly to quench his insatiable thirst to discover the world.

Less than a year later, on Fabrice's birthday, he was on a plane to Australia. Through his brother's death, he had tasted mortality himself.

It motivated him to keep exploring the world in search of light to counterbalance all that darkness.

As you grow up with family members, it becomes challenging to get to know them on a personal level due to each individual carrying his own burden of neurosis.

All of a sudden, they're gone from this physical existence, and what are you left with?

Could have, should have, would have?

Buddhists think that all family members are like fallen tree trunks in a river. At one point in time, they'll separate, sometimes for good.

Marco hadn't seen his son Bryce for nearly six years.

How do you make peace with something like that?

Rivers forge their own ways based on circumstances, but there's always the possibility that diverging rivers will reunite.

Maybe we'll commingle again with all our departed loved ones in another dimension and get another chance to demonstrate our love?

It's akin to what Dr. Joe Vitale and Dr. Len call erasing the white blackboard of all the data, memories, and programs.

Back to zero, peace at last, Nirvana.

I'm sorry, please forgive me, I thank you, and I love you.

'I forgives myself', that's the fifth phrase that Joe Vitale uses in his new book, concocted from Divine inspiration.

The pronoun 'I' is the Divine itself, assuring us that all is forgiven without pointing fingers or heaping blame on anybody.

You just have to keep cleaning without discrimination and judgment.

Easier said than done.

They say that we pick our parents, implying that the soul chooses the right mother based on the laws of Karma.

Karma is the most misunderstood word in the dictionary.

Starting to grasp its meaning is akin to being on the spiritual path. You take a couple of steps forward and soon find yourself walking aimlessly backward.

Karma means action. Everything you are made of is karma.

Although you could never escape the *'cause and effect'* phenomenon, you get to choose the path of your destiny.

Karma is more likely the reason souls are reincarnated in a new body in the first place.

This happens during the seventh or eighth months of pregnancy, according to Marco's yoga teachers.

It definitely puts a new perspective on his dysfunctional upbringing.

Then again, in this respect, he isn't really different from the rest of you.

Dysfunction seems like the norm when it comes to everybody's own particular experience.

I'm going to continue, assuming that you believe in reincarnation or that, at the very least, you believe in God.

Mind you, it could be any God.

If you're an atheist, like Marco had been for the better part of this incarnation, I'll understand.

Should you be an agnostic, he'd been there too. I reckon it's a fine place to be: no pressure, no dogma, and no commitments.

FIFTEEN

"In the midst of winter, I found there was, within me, an invincible summer..."

— ALBERT CAMUS.

They say that an infant chooses his parents, along with the latitude and longitude of his birth's location.

When it comes to locale, Marco had deliberately picked the one and only French Riviera.

Nineteen fifteen-seven was the same year that Hitchcock filmed 'To Catch a Thief' with Cary Grant and Grace Kelly. Jacques Anquetil won his first of five Tours de France titles that year on his tour debut.

As far as Marco's parents and their families were concerned, he sure hit the jackpot in terms of dysfunctionality.

He had a knack for these sorts of things, as you shall see.

Growing up within walking distance of the Mediterranean Sea was a treat in itself.

Albert Camus eloquently wrote: *"I always felt I lived in the high seas, threatened, at the heart of a royal happiness."*

He and his siblings used to spend their summer afternoons at the beach.

He remembers his brother Bernard mentioning that the green of the trees and the blue of the sea didn't go together well.

Nothing fit very well in Marco's younger years. But blue and green weren't color combinations to be argued with in his eyes.

Nature and its intrinsic mysteries would become his escape, his *raison d'être* and his muse, for he mainly felt like a lonely soul thrown from a ship in choppy waters, ready at any moment to crash on the rocky shore.

Actually, he didn't understand the concept of having a soul.

He was without an aim or a clue, trapped in a body he didn't care much for. The only things that saved him were a fervent imagination and a scholarly mind.

This was the era of the Fifth Republic.

In December 1958, Charles De Gaulle was elected President of France with 78% of the electoral college vote. As President, De Gaulle helped to revitalize the country and issued a new franc.

He envisioned a strong Europe that would determine the destiny of the world.

If he were to step on French soil fifty and some years after his death, he would be appalled by all the poor policies that had been approved in that timespan.

Immigration is out of control, especially when the immigrants don't get assimilated. The French concept of universalism might be an ideal that's no longer sustainable.

Marco's sister commented recently on France's political situation, specifically the extreme right New Popular Front winning the second round of legislative elections.

"The left fought for work and workers in earlier times. Now it's for a bogus ecology, gender normality, mass immigration, antisemitism, neo-feminism against white, heterosexual men, higher taxes, increased inheritance tax, and a single, dictatorial ideology! It's not what it used to be."

It should be noted that a few things she referred to, originated in the U.S., such as the Woke Movement.

As elsewhere, the sixties were a time of great change and progress in France in terms of the economy and growth.

In the United States, where racial tension, student protests, and new lifestyles and movements developed, there was a lot of unrest, but not more than anywhere else. Once changes were made to the university system, French students went back to classes.

The changes in the lifestyles of women paralleled those in the United States and the rest of Europe.

As for his mother, raising four kids and having to deal with her husband's violence and ill temper didn't look like emancipation to him.

Money wasn't an issue.

His father, in search of validation and to hide from a poor and traumatic childhood, would spend a major part of his days working hard at his business.

To his credit, he did exceptionally well. Starting from scratch and finally acquiring a piece of land and building a hangar on his property, will ensure a comfortable retirement.

Away from work, there wasn't a lot of joy in the household; being a strong disciplinarian didn't endear him much to the rest of the family.

Marco remembers doing the Nazi salute with his two brothers when his dad drove back from work. At around 9 p.m. most evenings, he parked his car in the driveway, only this time with a 'Hail Hitler' greeting.

If his father had been a boxer, he could've spared himself the cost of buying a punching bag since Marco had too much fire inside of him, and his father needed an outlet. They made quite a sparring pair.

Marco was always doing mischievous things and paying the price for it.

What does a clueless father, haunted by many ghosts from his past, do besides vent his frustrations on his youngest son, who always seemed to be in the wrong place at the wrong time.

He was a big, strong man, and you could imagine that his open-hand slaps weren't for the faint of heart.

Actually, in the middle of rewatching *'Game of Thrones'*, Marco could identify with Theon Greyjoy and the abuse he suffered at the hands of his jailer, Ramsey, minus the knife amputations, that is.

It should be noted that Marco kept a butcher's knife in his bedroom.

Many nights, during his parents' fighting, he fantasized about confronting his father and ending their collective misery once and for all.

He never found the courage, though.

Ultimately, his father couldn't control his emotions and was a brute.

Why didn't Marco learn to calm himself down, at least when his father was around? Those beatings would have stopped.

A recurring pattern here comes to mind. Marco always had a defiant attitude, he had to do things in his own way, even when that seemed contrary to his interests. For him, in order to learn valuable lessons, a certain amount of drama was required. Otherwise, those lessons wouldn't stick in his mind.

Sadghuru said: "*Karma is the foundation of life. Transforming these foundation stones of who we are into wheels that will roll and then wings that will fly is the essence of the spiritual process.*"

In hindsight, that made perfect sense. The creative process of turning stones into wheels and then into wings was indeed a daunting task.

From early on, his peers had labeled him as a little crazy. That was just a way to dissociate himself from normality.

You can deduce that he and his siblings were collectively a mess come their adolescent years.

Years later, his sister's thesis for her psychology degree concluded that their father was an authoritarian, castrating father and their mother was fragile with depressive tendencies towards the end of her life.

Hallelujah!

Well, it wasn't a happy marriage nor a household filled with love and compassion.

Marco came to realize in his later years that it made him who he was.

There's no point in playing the victim once you understand that everything happens for a reason.

These are the tests and the obstacles you need to overcome in order to transcend your little miseries and strive for infinity.

At that time, he had absolutely no concept of infinity. To his mind, it was all black or white.

Although he had a strong attraction to colors, he couldn't really discern through the color spectrum.

His Cartesian mind would only see the polarities.

His salvation was a fertile imagination that would take him to the four corners of the world and beyond that imaginary horizon line, where pain usually turned into ecstasy.

Yes, Marco was the ultimate dreamer and on the canopy of his follies and delusions, a kaleidoscope of brilliant hues brightened his days and nights.
He was a lively child despite all that turmoil.

In any case, his mind always came to the rescue with its analytical tendencies to make everything right or wrong.

One spends a lifetime with absurd preconceived notions of our existence that bear absolutely no reflection of reality.
What a waste of energy!

His better memories from his upbringing were of food.

His mom excelled at cooking, while his grandmother's skills in the kitchen were astonishing. With her homemade pasta, mouth-melting sauces, and sageness, the memories of family dinners outdoors still carry the jovial scents of summer.

CHAPTER
SIXTEEN

"It matters not how strait the gate,
  How charged with punishments the scroll.
  I am the master of my fate
  I am the captain of my soul."

— WILLIAM ERNEST HENLEY.

Sunshine and nature were an integral part of Marco's life growing up.

You could say that his imagination and resilience, fueled by his connection with nature, offset his lack of love and attention.

His father, who made a habit of getting rid of his frustration by slapping him in the face with his burly hands, was just repeating the cycle of his youth.

He never admitted to enduring beatings from his own father, but his death at fifty-six from liver cancer confirmed Marco's suspicion of alcoholism as the cause.

He had confessed to his niece that his father used to lock him in a closet.

Marco's grandparents emigrated from Warsaw, Poland, after the First World War. They lived in the north industrial part of France, where his grandfather worked as a miner.

Eventually, they settled near Toulouse in the southwest of France.

His father often told the story of his mother making a mark on the bread with a knife to prevent the children from eating it in her absence. It suggests they were dirt poor.

His grandmother abandoned her family when his father was five. She was always the villain of the tale. I suspect her husband's abuse contributed to her betrayal.

Fortunately, his sister Suzette, who was only twelve, took on the role of raising him and proved to be a veritable saint.

Marco's father had another sister five years older, with blond curly hair, deep blue eyes, and movie star looks. Marco only found out about her in his late-teens.

She got abducted, raped, and strangled by a serial killer who had slaughtered eighteen women before being shot and killed by the police. She had been his last victim and had just turned eighteen.

Liliane was missing for a couple of months before they found her in the Tarn, the local river running through their village. They were dredging the water, and guess who found her?

Yes, I couldn't make this up: Marco's grandfather was the dredger on duty that day.

Imagine this for a moment!

If such trauma wasn't sufficient to drive him crazy or push him to drink himself to death, I'm not sure what would.

Karma hadn't been kind to this family, but he believed he'd chosen his parents by Divine calling.

Now, in this lifetime, he was working towards the recovery of his soul. Hopefully, he won't need to come back for more turmoil.

In the late fifties, seeking help from psychologists or shamans wasn't common for people looking to overcome their subconscious issues and free themselves from haunting demons.

Although shamanism has a long history among indigenous groups, by no stretch of the imagination was this something folks in modern European societies adopted.

Marco wasn't intellectually attracted to shamanism. It felt like a natural progression to his evolution.

On his visit to the Ecuadorian Amazon with his son, he met a shaman and sensed that experiencing Ayahuasca in the near future was inevitable.

Back to his parents. As well-meaning as they were, they continued that cycle of abuse, trauma, and lovelessness into the next generation.

Marco, a young soul who gained consciousness late in life, struggled with his marriage his son's upbringing. But that's a tale for another chapter in this book.

Sometimes, his sister and he would look at each other and remark that it was a wonder they were normal after all that.

Then again, we have to define normal. It has that hint of conformity I'm not too fond of.

More tragedies followed in the aftermath for the family.

His dad's half-brother got killed on his scooter at a railway crossing. His cousin Julianne was riding a shotgun but escaped unscathed.

Julianne's son, who was a hemophiliac, died of Aids when he was fifteen, courtesy of plasma coming from America before the beginning of the pandemic.

His cousin, one year his senior, was in the same predicament, but his infection never progressed to Aids.

Years later, Julianne's husband Romain had a leg amputated after complications with diabetes.

When her son turned two, Marco's sister Arielle became a widow.

Fabrice ended up taking his own life.

Their aunt Suzette's advanced Alzheimer's and senility led to the complete loss of her mental faculties. She was confined to a retirement home and remained in a vegetative state until her passing at 99.

She had outlived her young brother by a couple of years.

As a prisoner of war, her husband André contracted tuberculosis and endured poor health for the rest of his life.

He suffered a heart attack in front of his home and collapsed in the gravel driveway. The paramedics' intervention prevented him from finding eternal peace that day. Following his recovery, he had a tracheotomy and remained connected to an oxygen machine for several years.

The last time Marco saw him, he felt his suffering. His will to live had vanished under the blasphemy of his senseless survival.

His father joined the Navy when he was sixteen, and saw action during the Indochina War.

After the Ho Chi Minh led guerrillas defeated the French in 1954, it became the precursor of the Vietnam War. By then, the Americans wanted to stop the spread of communism at all costs.

Back in France, his father had a bike accident with his Moto Guzzi.

He would be in the hospital for eighteen months. He ended with a big scar running down the side of his face. His leg was badly damaged and burned by the bike's muffler.

That left him with a wound the size of a small coin that never healed and required constant bandaging because of bleeding and pus discharge.

He also had a staph infection and caught tuberculosis while at the hospital.

Marco wouldn't be here today if his mother hadn't been part of a program of correspondence with injured sailors. This was how his parents met.

His father was, above all, a proud man. You can imagine he felt ostracized by others on account of his injured leg.

The physical pain itself must've been the cause of tremendous suffering throughout his life.

The passage of time made Marco realize that we all carry our own cross.

Some carry theirs with more dignity, others end up succumbing to its weight.

Growing up in a family of impoverished, uneducated immigrants, his father's entire existence revolved around seeking validation from others.

However, he found comfort in hard work and providing material possessions for his family. So, where love was non-existent, money acted as the great compensator, at least in his eyes.

Living around some Shipibo families as I am writing this book, I can't help but notice a lot of laughter during the day. Money isn't the root of evil, but neither is the lack of it.

Traveling around the world, it strikes me that the size of people's hearts is often proportional to their lack of funds. Being poor leaves no choice but to embrace the little that you have.

So when Marco's father came home after work late in the evening, he was more bad cop than father.

His poor mother became lost in the chaos. She was too preoccupied with her neurosis to cope with the drama.

His maternal grandmother, Violette, was a sage by modern standards.

She had raised five kids and lost her husband from a heart attack (it could have been a brain aneurysm) while gardening, like Al Pacino in 'The Godfather 3'. He was only fifty-three.

He remembers that his grandpa was a nice man since he always gave him chewing gum. He was six at the time of his death.

I have no clue regarding the problems in this family, in this cycle of life.

When we add our former incarnations to the equation, it can become quite a mess.

On the outskirts of the Amazon, he seeks forgiveness by wiping all data, a process Dr. Len refers to as eliminating the trash and starting afresh from scratch.

By doing so, you could change the world's consciousness, one memory at a time.

Back to Marco's mother's family.

On this side of the Atlantic, you won't find a bunch of individuals more apathetic and neurotic.

His maternal great-grandparents were from Piedmont, Italy, and had emigrated to France, where their children were born.

So, they had already lost the Italian language, unlike his paternal grandparents, who spoke fluent Polish and Russian (at least his grandfather did).

You can imagine that during those years, speaking a language that sounded like German carried a stigma in France. As a result, neither his father nor his aunt spoke a word of Polish.

Her siblings were the quintessential Italian immigrants, working hard in the fields and saving every penny from their labor, while his maternal great-grandfather succumbed to the Spanish Flu.

At 104, his aunt passed away, while her two brothers died at ninety-nine. When she fell and didn't recover from a broken hip, his grandmother passed away at ninety-four.

Anyway, negativity and a grand sense of victimhood ran rampant – at least from his mother and her siblings looking onward, akin to a virus that would infect a computer software.

Where did this come from? I will make no pretense of knowing.

They were decent people with good hearts, yet they blamed their distress on others, while remaining unaware it was of their own making.

Adéle, his mother's elder sister and godmother, embraced her Catholic faith like a frustrated evangelist.

She ended up in a nursing home, having alienated the only one of her three children who had cared for her, along with his wife, for many years. She ended up alone, depressed, and more bitter at her predicament as the seasons passed.

Despite dedicating her entire life to Jesus Christ, why wasn't she happy and content about the prospect of going to heaven?

Marco should be kinder to her memory, thinking that all the prayers she made in favor of her godson paid dividends.

Otherwise, you mightn't be reading these words.

At her funeral, her two younger children left after the church service. They didn't even bother to follow the procession to the cemetery to see their mother buried. They told Arielle they had an appointment!

Marco didn't waver and removed them from his Facebook' contacts and Christmas list at once.

The French have a tendency to be whiners.

It must be the French national favorite pastime, on par with dunking a croissant in your café or playing the '*tiercet*' (horse race) on Sunday mornings.

Sandwiched between his father, who must've been the most critical person of his generation, and his mother, the most negative of hers, Marco was bound to be toast.

It's no wonder he sabotaged his career and relationships with his constant nagging attitude that something was always lacking, feeling entitled to more.

Ah, negativity and self-entitlement are the antithesis of gratitude.

Gratitude gives you a great attitude. You're great and full.

The passing of time allows for endless growth and transformation.

When Marco discovered the holy grail of gratitude, his life transformed into a reflection of this newfound wisdom, shining like a diamond's facets in the sunlight.

Karma in his mother's family has been less tragic but more insidious, like a leaking faucet turning eventually into a flood.

They were dysfunctional, to say the least. However, the overall permeating sense of victimhood on his mother's side of the family took the grand prize.

Victims surrender to circumstances, whereas fighters, like on his father's side, always seem to find the mental force to survive and thrive.

Marco was determined not to give up on his dreams. Despite the challenge of overcoming inherited neurotic tendencies, he believed that with time and effort, he could succeed.

Take his cousin Julianne, Suzette's daughter, for example.

While giving birth to her only son, Fabien, she had a stroke. As a result, she had to undergo years of rehabilitation to regain her ability to speak and now slurs when she talks. Partial paralysis affected the left side of her body.

She smiled outwardly despite her ordeals, drove her own car with modified steering and gearbox, and lived as an independent woman.

After Fabien's passing from Aids, she faithfully visited his grave each day.

With her distinctive duck-like strides, she would cover a total distance of fourteen kilometers, braving all weather. For many years, she never missed a single day.

She amazed Marco with her willpower and persistence. Despite her condition, he couldn't fathom the immense devotion required to overcome such tragedy.

In comparison, his mother complained all her life about her circumstances, and guess what she attracted?

After the divorce from his father, every loser in town.

Bless you mother, I am sorry, please forgive me, I thank you, and I love you.

I suspect you may return soon in a different body to learn the lessons you missed.

His mother always expressed her desire to avoid aging like certain relatives.

Soon after she went to a retirement home, she died at eighty-one from a brain aneurysm, no doubt self-propagated.

The evening before her death, Marco called her at the retirement home, something he regretted not doing often. The receptionist informed him that she was playing poker with other residents, expressing her love for these weekly games.

What would you say to your mother if you knew it was to be your last conversation ever?

Please dwell on this for a while.

Incidentally, today was Mother's Day, and he was too harsh on his mother.

She was the life of parties, an amazing cook and host, and ultimately had the kindest heart. Nobody would've denied these facts at her funeral.

Her younger sister died of leukemia at the age of seventy-three. With a nice pension and bright outlook on life, her will to live was never in question though.

Marco had a crush on her throughout his adolescent years. His fertile mind and raging hormones must've been in alignment with her aura as a sexually disturbed woman.

Another example of transgenerational trauma from his mother's side of the family. In thinking that there were more troublesome cases in this lineage, Marco should have plenty of inspiration to draw from for his next novel.

Their younger brother remarked recently: *"I am the last one left."*

He's Marco's godfather and was born two days before the Dalai Lama, on American Independence Day. Although they haven't seen much of each other in the last few decades, they always shared a bond.

You would be hard-pressed to find a kinder person, artistically inclined and with great sensibility, albeit totally disjointed from his soul.

CHAPTER
SEVENTEEN

"You do not have to raise your consciousness, you have to raise yourself to find access to it."

— SADHGURU.

Marco never felt he belonged. His parents never favored him on account of being the odd duck.

He certainly enjoyed causing trouble, not in the sense that he was a bad kid, just that he needed to let off some steam.

With school being too easy, he resorted to clowning around for attention and validation, seeking laughter.

As he grew into a teenager, he lost interest in school.

America and the Great American West always fascinated him.

Little did he know he would spend over half his life in the United

States. He departed a few months after Donald Trump became president in 2017.

It wasn't a coincidence that Marco left the country. The United States had become too polarized.

His search for the 'American Dream' had been a fine experiment in itself.

But when the smoke cleared, there weren't too many structures worth saving. It had become a barren wasteland, as far as his landscape was concerned.

In his perception, the land of milk and honey held all of society's ills. Trump found the right place to harness the wave of discontent and hatred. He just capitalized on the people's propensity to blame others for their misfortunes. After all, he was a master at pointing fingers and playing the crying game.

Marco had wasted years of his life finding flaws in people.

He had made the conscious decision to no longer partake in these power-sapping activities.

Laura Berman wrote a blazing book titled '*Quantum Love*,' which was on the New York Times bestseller list.

She talks about Dr. David Hawkins, who showed the existence of an energy field generated by various emotions.

He developed a scale called the '*Map of Consciousness*' that assigned distinct frequency values to different emotions, ranging from shame (20) all the way to enlightenment (700+).

Love sits at 500 on the scale, and blame, which shows as guilt on the scale, at 30.

You should note that these numbers aren't linear. Enlightenment, for example, has the potential to be several million times more powerful than shame.

Quantum physics shows that everything in the universe comprises particles or waves, vibrating like strings at different frequencies.

When a vibrational body of a stronger resonance influences another in its field, it's called entrainment.

Laura Berman suggests that raising your emotional vibrations through coherence not only improves your own well-being but also empowers you to influence others.

It functions effectively for couples, families, and even world peace.

One person in a state of pure love could impact 150,000 other people who would entrain in these high frequencies of love.

A Buddha or Jesus in their blissful states would cause the entrainment of several million individuals.

The survival of our species depends on the consciousness of the planet's inhabitants. This could happen in the foreseeable future, but at what cost?

CHAPTER
EIGHTEEN

— BEVERLY SILLS.

Before even making plans for college, Marco dropped a bombshell on his father, who'd dreamed about him becoming a doctor or something equally impressive.

He was done with school and decided to abandon the parental nest. He packed his bag and went to a town near the Spanish border for *les vendanges* (picking grapes) along with his brother Bernard.

Working in the fields, he met a cute and carefree Castellan brunette who hailed from Barcelona. Felisa didn't speak a word of French, and Marco's Spanish was non-existent.

They resorted to communicating with gestures. Under the passion of youth, the hormones kicked in.

Following the season's end in the South of France, they headed to the Cognac region, renowned for its authentic wine brandy.

Marco would ultimately work three consecutive seasons on an estate run by two brothers and their family.

Back in those days, they valued the laborers in the fields.

The mother and her daughters-in-law efficiently operated the kitchen.

The quality of the food was comparable to that of a five-star restaurant.

Chickens, ducks, rabbits, and partridges were raised on the farm. The hosts picked *cépes* (porcini mushrooms) in the forest and used the freshest vegetables and beef cuts from the region. They also made homemade pasta and sweets.

They gave every worker one liter of *eau de vie* per day, besides all the wine they could drink.

Their ability to make work on time in the morning remains a mystery, but they labored hard and played even harder.

Every Sunday, the boss would take one of his prized possessions from the cellar and share it sparingly with his guests. A 100-year-old cognac defies description. A real celebration for the senses.

They would sometimes go to the nearest village bars and cause havoc.

Throughout his travels, Marco never passed up an opportunity to work in the fields during the harvest season. These are among his best memories.

When the season finished, Marco went to live in Barcelona.

Felisa had an apartment and a part-time job as a bar hostess, making good tips.

Before the euro, Spain was dirt cheap. You could eat tapas and drink sangria or absinthe all day but still had enough pesetas left for the rest of the week.

As Franco's reign neared its end, people increasingly demonstrated in the streets.

Life in Barcelona was a lot of fun. Marco was nineteen with not a care in the entire world, except for the petty demons in his own head.

He lived in a foreign country, speaking a different tongue. "*This was a good way to dissociate myself from reality,*" he thought.

Communicating in a language other than your own can make you feel like you're embracing a new identity, which suited him just fine.

At thirteen, Felisa's father kicked her out of their apartment. He instructed her to only come back once she'd found a job. She had little education about the affairs of the world but laughed a lot, even at the silliest things.

In contrast, Marco's anger felt warranted.

The events of your life define your perspective on circumstances that direct your behavior.

So, it wasn't all rosy in Marco's camp. He was sensitive and hid his emotional immaturity under false bravado, relying too much on the escapes granted by alcohol and drugs.

He loved the Spaniards and their carefree attitude about life.

There were a lot of things happening in this town and endless opportunities to partake in all the fun.

They soon rented a house in a small village in Menorca, on the Balearic Islands, for the summer. At that time, it was a laid-back island with beautiful beaches, full of bucolic charm.

Throughout the summer, villages around the island rotated to organize three-day festivals that turned into big fiestas with purebred horses.

People would take their turn hitting the animal, and as the rider forced it to stand on its hind legs, they shouted: '*Olé*.'

Menorquins liked to party. Their drink of choice was *ginebra* and Coca-Cola (gin and coke). Alcohol and sensitivity to horses made a bad pair.

Following one such an event, in the early morning, Marco ended up at the Guardia Civil post. He was half-naked, wearing feather earrings, and had painted his face like a Comanche warrior. He was fully intoxicated.

The Guardia Civil in Franco's times was renowned for being pretty rough and abusive, but they were in festival mode that day. Lucky Marco.

Before the end of the summer, he received his military papers. At the time, *le service militaire* was mandatory in France.

Either he had to report to the 7th Infantry unit in Avignon for a year or provide a valid reason for not doing so.

On his enrollment form, he gave them a simple reason why he wouldn't show up. He wrote in big letters: '*PARANOID*.'

One week before the due date, he was summoned to the military hospital's psychiatric ward in Marseilles.

To make a compelling case, Fabrice had given him a few pills. He was told to swallow a couple just before entering the hospital.

He had no clue about the devilish nature of those pills, but he would soon find out.

The hospital evaluated him for three days before his final consultation with a psychiatrist.

It all seemed like a casual affair. He shared a big room with eight young men in identical situations.

He suspected one could be a spy, so he was intent on playing the game.

Twenty minutes after he crossed the hospital gates, he started to behave unwittingly like a real schizophrenic.

He had fancied himself a good comedian. Now, the lines of reality were totally blurred. He was freaking out.

Out of his mind.

One smart young man was observed in the same room for six months. They knew he was bluffing and were determined to make him pay for it. He was distressed about staying there for the rest of his service.

To his peers, Marco was really crazy, and they reminded him of that fact on numerous occasions throughout his stay. He wasn't in disagreement with them. The whole situation wasn't completely devoid of fun and camaraderie, though.

The psychiatrist agreed with them in his last report.

Marco just remembers his deep, piercing black eyes.

Now, he could return to immerse himself in the blue of the Mediterranean Sea.

Felisa grew tired of supporting the ungrateful young man, and things started to get sour.

He decided to go to Andorra at the end of summer after he landed a dishwasher job in an upscale restaurant.

If I informed you of certain incidents that took place in a working kitchen in a restaurant, they would appall you, especially when the employees feel that they aren't being treated fairly.

To spare your sensibilities, I won't delve into the grisly details of all that happened in this particular kitchen. Let's jump right into one story in particular.

The chef was a big, burly Spaniard, a former foreign legionnaire. Marco, in some ways as insane as he was, had a good rapport with him. They were working their afternoon shift while the owner and his wife were away for a special occasion.

The owner was a decent man, but his wife was mean and condescending towards employees.

They had found creative ways to get even. I promised to keep quiet, didn't I?

It was the executive chef's birthday. He grabbed a bottle of whiskey from the bar, and they finished it in no time, drinking straight from the bottle.

They got plastered, went downstairs to the walk-in refrigerator, and had the most epic food fight ever.

It lasted until all the eggs, tomatoes, and all the contents of the fridge had been turned into projectiles and smashed against the walls and ceilings of the entire downstairs section.

They went at it like psychopaths. The women working in housekeeping cleaned the whole premises to cover up their disgraceful acts.

It took them most of the evening while the two drunks sobered up.

The next morning, the owner fired the entire staff, thirteen employees in total.

I suspect none of them had any problems finding another job straight away since it was the busy season.

Here, Marco still feels a mix of remorse and exhilaration. It was, after all, a gargantuan fight.

Events of this amplitude only happen once in a lifetime. Let's cherish them for what they're worth. That's why he should apologize again to the owner and the entire staff since sensitivity is still not his forte.

He returned to Menorca with a little money in his pocket.

He was expecting to resume his relationship with Felisa. During his absence, she'd found a more promising alternative, a young hippie who made his own jewelry.

She gave Marco his freedom back, and he took it reluctantly.

He stayed on the island for a while. In exchange for housing and money, he assisted an elderly woman with gardening and upkeep, among other tasks.

Eventually, he returned to France, as broke as ever.

CHAPTER

NINETEEN

"The comfort of having a friend may be taken away, but not that of having had one."

— SENECA.

Shortly after, he met a long-haired, bearded individual nicknamed '*Titou*,' from *petitout* in the Provençal dialect, meaning tiny.

They shared an affinity for drinking beer and smoking weed.

Eventually, they made plans to go backpacking together in South America as soon as they could save enough money.

The day arrived when Marco and Titou set off on a seven-month trip across South America.

This journey became an odyssey worthy of Homer, where boys became men.

On a white sandy beach in Barbados, they met two French girls who were intent on backpacking down a similar path.

Their compatibility led to future meetings in diverse locations. It's eerie to reminisce about the ways they used to travel before the internet age.

They would talk about meeting at a later date, and, inevitably, they would all be there, as if by Divine order, sharing the same space for months afterward.

Arianne was a pretty brunette who exhibited the sexual vibes of a free spirit, but her friend Céline was not as attractive and way more prudish and reserved.

By chasing the same butterfly, Marco and Titou got their nets tangled up.

Despite those dynamics, the four of them formed a nice friendship.

In Rio de Janeiro, they met with these two *ingénues* again. They were accompanied by two good-looking Swedes, one of whom was half a meter taller than Titou.

Months later, they trekked the Inca trek together under pouring rain. However, it didn't dampen the experience.

Fast forward to a discotheque somewhere in Bolivia. Drinks were flowing and the music was beyond loud, just how they like it in Latin countries.

Arianne and Marco were dancing together and getting pretty cozy with each other.

As the evening progressed and the alcohol kicked in, he started berating women and the entire *'freaking'* planet.

The owner kicked them out of the bar and threatened to call the police.

What do you expect from a messed up twenty-one-year-old?

It was a constant battle to keep his emotions in check whenever he was sober.

However, with a few too many drinks, he spiraled into a world of paranoia, hate, and frustration.

When Marco woke up the next morning, Arianne was in Titou's bed.

Unfazed, his cunning intellect came to the rescue, as always, by catering to his delusions and ego.

They traveled together for a few days across the Bolivian Altiplano, a vast plateau at 3,650 meters of altitude.

They journeyed in the back of an open-end truck. The cold weather made the two lovers act like teenagers in heat.

Marco remembers making eye contact with Céline from time to time and cracking a wry smile.

Two years later, upon returning from Canada, Marco found out that Titou and Céline were now living together. They eventually got married.

On a subsequent visit to spend the night at his friend's, they had invited Arianne for the evening.

This time, he couldn't resist her charms.

They became infatuated with each other. She welcomed him into her mother's house, where she lived. You could tell Marco was in her good graces.

Two weeks later, he woke up and left like a thief in the night. He went to work in Germany to earn some Deutsche marks.

However, he was becoming too attached to the young woman. That was his way of protecting himself from the pain in his heart.

A recurring pattern that would resurface in the future whenever somebody came too close to his soft spot.

Céline soon gave birth to a beautiful girl that they named Zoé.

Titou had an addictive personality and kept abusing alcohol and drugs.

Despite buying a beautiful house near Aix-en-Provence, it failed to tame Titou's inner demons.

They eventually divorced, and Titou left for a place he had always talked about, French Guyana, to start a new life.

Years later, Marco learned that he'd died in a car accident. He'd just turned fifty.

Driving back early in the morning from a sailing outing with friends, he crashed into a tree.

He was alone at the wheel. Marco remembers that his friend was a skilled and responsible driver. Who knows if he had drunk too much El Dorado, the famous Guyana rum, the night leading to the accident?

They had had some intense experiences together, yet they hardly knew each other.

What a shame that these two closed hearts never opened up to one another.

Throughout our lives, we struggle to communicate with those we hold dear.

Sadly, we can only realize and convey our empathy and compassion for their pain and sorrow after they've passed away.

There won't be a second chance in this life either to tell them that we loved them.

With all his travels, Marco had made a lot of acquaintances but very few friends.

Céline became his best friend. She was a bit of a saintly figure to him. They had some great laughs and a genuine affection for each other.

Although she never discussed religion, she had a profound fascination with religious books.

Instead of working in the private sector for a bigger paycheck, she dedicated her life to helping others in need and became a nurse.

Once she retired, she would always talk about going back to India, where she'd been backpacking with Titou.

With a house in the country paid off and a modest pension, she envisioned taking better care of herself in her retirement years.

New legislation in France, however, had delayed her retirement by two years.

She once confided to Marco that, like many women who prioritize others, she was tired of neglecting herself for all these years.

Marco was working in Mexico when Zoé messaged him that her mother had died of leukemia at sixty-five, after a short illness.

It broke his heart. If somebody didn't deserve to die at this stage, it was Céline.

Regrettably, she'll never have the chance to hug and embrace her two granddaughters, who were born a few years after her death.

From a Christian perspective, she deserved to be in heaven.

Marco saw it differently. A soul is pure energy, forever ablaze like an Olympic torch.

Regardless of whether people are dead or alive, their energy will keep radiating around the cosmos.

We just need to draw from the energy of our beloved departed ones and perpetuate their presence within us.

Inside our hearts, we must allow them to shine like the countless facets of a diamond that capture the sun's light and wear it proudly on our chest like a *boutonnière.*

While we may not share a bottle of *rosé, "the sky's the limit,"* as they say.

Dissociating ourselves from simplistic concepts of heaven and hell is indeed refreshing.

CHAPTER

TWENTY

"Just as one candle lights another and can light thousands of other candles, so one heart illuminates another heart and can illuminate thousands of other hearts."

— LEO TOLSTOY.

Before Marco went on his three-month retreat in Peru, he flew to Cusco.

Over the past decade, the Salkantay trek had emerged as a superb Inca trail alternative.

Fortunately, you don't have to book the trek months ahead of time. It's longer, harder, higher, and simply spectacular.

In one section of the path, you have a different angle view of Machu Picchu and are near the original Inca trail.

Marco chose this spot to make an altar for his friends, burn incense, and reminisce about their adventure together forty-four years ago. He hadn't been able to contact Arianne. They last met at Céline's soirée ages ago.

This woman, once so gorgeous, hadn't aged gracefully. "*So much about fantasizing about the past,*" he thought.

She had black teeth, a botched belly, and a pale yellow complexion that reeked of liver disease in Marco's eyes. Could she be possibly dead by now?

Just in case, Marco set a place for her at the altar. He couldn't help thinking that he was the last musketeer left, still swinging his sword at life decades later.

That filled him with pride and gratitude. He wouldn't trade his life for anything.

With no desire to return, he moved away from the United States almost six years ago.

Having spent three decades getting a taste of the American Dream, he realized the experiment was over.

It's normal to look at earlier periods with a little nostalgia.

You're not the same person you were when all these prior events occurred. Your experience and newfound wisdom have polarized the lenses through which you see and perceive things.

The problem is when people identify themselves with the sum of all that happened to them and the persons they interacted with.

Nostalgia can become the very thing that clouds judgments and distorts reality.

Still, when the focus is on negative or hurtful things, it soon takes its own one-way path towards mayhem.

CHAPTER
TWENTY-ONE

"So you want to tame me
Make me all yours to be
Sing me sweet lullabies
Clip the tip of my wings
Put me in a gold cage
Turn me into a sage
Above all other things.

I hear the wind swirling
And the tide calling
I'm like the finest sand
In the palm of your hand
I am not who you think
I have space in my heart
For other birds to sing.

So you want to tame me
    And feed me sanity
    We would walk on that beach
    And watch the red sun sink
    On that turquoise sea
    A rainbow within reach
    Beyond that safe harbor,

A cover of pine trees
    And your dinner parties
    My mind in a fishbowl
    And my senses gone awry
    I am not who you think
    I have space in my soul
    For bald eagles to soar.

So you want to tame me
    And take my will apart
    I am not what you thought
    I have space in my plot
    For other seeds to grow
    It is not what it seems
    I have space in my dreams

For her sweet love to flow."

— MARCO, 2013.

Marco and Hazel had overstayed their tourist visas in Australia by more than three years. They decided it was time to leave for the States.

Upon seeing their passport stamps at the Perth airport before their departure, the immigration officer called his supervisor. The man in charge took them to an office where two men interviewed them.

They inquired about their whereabouts and self-support during these years with curiosity.

Marco said they'd been exploring this awesome country of Australia together all along.

His father sent him allowance money whenever needed.

The two jovial officers glanced at each other with a wry smile on their faces. One man stamped their passports and said: *"Good on ya, mates, 'ave a good one."*

These were the good old days before computers, social security numbers, and photographs on the driving licenses.

Marco had various jobs, including construction worker, taxi driver, photographer, janitor, bartender, cocktail server, painter, and field worker. His taxi driver's license, which had his photograph on it, was in Steve Henwood's name (a gift from a fellow backpacker upon leaving the country).

He would often mention to people that his mother was French and his father British. Otherwise, his name of choice was Marc Dubois, a name he found more exotic.

Hazel had her fair share of occupations as well.

Soon after arriving in France, they planned to get a marriage license.

Marco was only interested in getting married in order to get his green card for the *'Land of the Free and the Home of the Brave.'*

That wasn't a very romantic way to treat the noble institution of marriage, nor his girlfriend.

Sadly, he didn't care about anyone but himself, oblivious to the impact of his actions.

For some obscure reason, probably the trauma from his upbringing, he didn't want his parents involved. His brother Bernard was living in Bordeaux with his girlfriend, and they were out of town.

Their apartment was available, and it stood 500 meters walking distance to the *mairie* (mayor's office). They took this as an omen and arranged to complete the paperwork.

French bureaucracy can be capricious, and that's putting it mildly. The two old women in charge of the administration disliked the marginal couple at once.

Over the next few days, they made their lives difficult by always requiring some additional documentation they didn't have. They seemed, in a subtle but sadistic way, to enjoy the process.

On the fourth day, it became obvious that they had no intention of granting them a marriage license.

Marco was pretty temperamental back then.

He got enraged and started running up the stairs, yelling at the top of his voice:

"Where's that 'fucking' mayor? I want to speak my 'fucking' mind to him."

He ran the entire length of the hallway until he saw a sign on a door that he didn't have time to read. He stormed through it like a man gone bonkers.

A man in his early thirties was sitting at a desk and asked in a surprisingly poised manner: *"What's going on?"*

Two policemen entered the office with handcuffs and guns in their hands.

The man quickly stood up, put himself between the officers and Marco, and asserted:

"That's fine. I will handle it."

The officers left and the gentleman instructed him to take a seat, calm down, and please explain the situation.

Ten minutes later, they were laughing like longtime pals.

When Marco used the term *'old bitches'* to describe the two women, the mayor's aide cracked a sarcastic smile and acknowledged that they were overly zealous in their work.

They soon descended the stairs together, accompanied by the policemen, who had remained behind the closed door throughout the duration of their conversation.

Hazel felt a sense of relief when she realized that her future spouse had avoided arrest.

The mayor's aide instructed them to come back the next morning.

Two days later, the assistant to the mayor and his girlfriend were their witnesses as they were sworn in as husband and wife. On each side of the official were the two old women who Marco didn't spare one of his murderous gazes for a split-second.

Hazel must've been asking herself why she was getting married to this maniac in the first place.

The wedded couple and their observers ventured out for drinks afterward.

Their marriage would last twenty-eight years, which, in hindsight feels like an eternity.

Given that Bordeaux's mayor was Jacques Chaban-Delmas, who served as Prime Minister under President George Pompidou, Marco could've landed in the penitentiary.

Instead, they left for America two months later. The year was 1985.

CHAPTER

TWENTY-TWO

"Passion will move men beyond themselves, beyond their shortcomings, beyond their failures."

— JOSEPH CAMPBELL.

Ronald Reagan was half-way through his two terms as president. *'Back to the Future'*, the iconic film with Michael J. Fox. was the top-grossing movie of the year.

Everything appeared simpler living in the States, from buying a new car to getting a credit card in the mail. There were signs that said 'Help Wanted' at every street corner.

Individuals were friendly and easy to interact with, as opposed to Europe, where individuals always appeared so aloof.

Over seven years, Marco and Hazel pursued their passion for overseas travel, explored the country, and earned trade school degrees in photography and culinary arts, respectively.

The Great American West lived up to expectations.

Having grown up watching Western movies, Marco fancied walking in the footsteps of his heroes. Traveling from the East to West coasts, they spent months camping and trekking in the various National Parks.

With the spectacular scenery and an abundance of space and opportunities, one could easily envision oneself as a pioneer.

Marco, like always, faced difficulties in managing his emotions, especially when he was contained within the enclosed space of a car and they were lost.

He must've been an annoyance for those around him. Nothing seemed to bother Hazel as she was the stoic one, keeping everything bottled up inside.

They moved to Portland, Oregon, in 1992, and he started a career in sales. When he wasn't employed in canneries during the summer in Alaska, he worked as a photographer for most of the last nine years.

When you're a kid, you rebel against your parents and do the opposite of what they envisioned for you. As you get older, you unconsciously mirror them.

Marco's father had started his career selling cars and eventually built a successful caravan dealership.

So Marco became a car salesman, an occupation he would keep for thirteen years. Many years later, the director of a time-share resort in Albuquerque told him that he was the salesperson with the most natural talent that he'd worked with. The man in question possessed ample experience in his field.

I don't know whether he was stroking his ego or not. Although it was flattering, Marco had a hard time embracing the concept.

When you're busy fighting the demons inside your head, you see success as a balancing act to your problems. Eventually, you lose the balance and start self-sabotaging.

He was like a jigsaw, alternating between tremendous highs and tremendous lows.

If these last statements defined his sales career, so be it. He never enjoyed working. He was always envious of those individuals who possessed a genuine passion for their profession.

When they said: *"Find something you love to do and you will never work a day in your life,"* it unfortunately never applied to him.

Hazel never complained once about her job, not even when she was sick or seven months pregnant. That was a trait he really admired in her.

It didn't help that Marco would be employed for twenty years in industries where ethics were too often at the bottom of the list.

When your income relies entirely on commissions, you must prioritize making a sale over truth or empathy.

It used to bother him when he was selling cars that the *'assholes'* always got screaming deals while the nicer people ended up getting taken to the cleaners.

Marco was the ultimate pre-judger. He had mastered that inexact science when he was selling cars.

Since he could pick his victims, he'd designed an elaborate way to disqualify the clients he deemed unworthy or a waste of time.

He was often right in his assumptions.

On account of a wrong-shaped nose or the way they dressed or strolled, he'd walk by prospective buyers without flinching.

Often, their shoes were the determining factor.

He once read that most women pick a potential partner based on these three factors: their teeth, their nails, and their shoes. So maybe he was onto something.

Despite his laziness and judgmental attitude, he achieved decent success.

The power to create your own reality was still unknown to him. However, his negative attitude often yielded negative results.

Imagine if he had embraced positivity and gone with the flow?

Combining highly competitive individuals and big egos within a team can create an explosive mixture that shatters your moral compass. What are you left with?

Sometimes, you come out of a fight unscathed. Other times, you take a beating.

It's a good thing that Marco retired four years ago. By then, he was so hopeless that he could no longer sell ice to Eskimos.

He had read '*The Four Agreements*' by Don Miguel Ruiz.

It appeared that he was employing the principles outlined in the book.

Upon reviewing the set of four agreements, he was way off the mark.

1 - Be impeccable with your words.

While committed to speaking with integrity, both to clients and to himself in his inner dialogue, his twenty-five years in high-pressure sales contradicted the statement.

2 - Take nothing personally.

Marco always took everything personally, as he perceived it was all about him.

Things that other people say have no relevance to you. It's always about them.

3 - Don't make assumptions

You know what they say: "*When you assume, you make an ass of you and me.*"

Marco took an additional step beyond assuming.

He also judged by forming an opinion about the intention according to his own moral correctness (or lack thereof). This was a slippery slope.

4 - Always do your best

Guilt and growing self-judgment come from not doing your best.

By not enjoying what is happening right now, one is living in the past and only half alive.

This leads to self-pity, suffering, and tears.

There was also a fifth agreement:

5 - Don't believe in yourself or anybody unconditionally

It's hard not to believe in yourself without being delusional when you only listen to the voice of your ego.

As far as believing others, do a full investigation before trusting someone unconditionally.

When it came to following the *'5 Precepts'* in Buddhism, he was completely off track.

In order to uphold the precepts, you must commit to abstaining from killing living beings, stealing, sexual misconduct, lying, and intoxication.

They're meant to develop the mind and character within the Buddhist doctrine in order to make progress on the path to enlightenment.

TWENTY-THREE

"Bad times have a scientific value. These are occasions a good learner would not miss."

— RALPH WADO EMERSON.

Marco and Titou experienced their fair share of stressful situations while backpacking around South America for seven months.

Brazil was a tough country to navigate.

They were so happy to cross the Paraguayan border after six weeks in Brazil. When you travel on a tight budget, you end up in the worst parts of town that most tourists avoid.

That implied staying in the most inexpensive hotels possible, with no space for discrimination or better judgment.

When arriving in a new town, Marco would leave Titou in a bar or café with the backpacks and go searching for a hotel. Since the price was always the determining factor, they ended up staying in some real dives.

Once in Belem, they found themselves obliged to lock themselves in their room while local prostitutes banged at their door most of the night. These women didn't give up easily, but the two travelers resisted more for financial reasons than moral ones.

In Recife, Marco's brand-new trekking shoes with shiny red laces were stolen one night.

They arrived late in town and made the not-so-intelligent decision to sleep in a park.

In a Bahia hotel at the edge of a *favela* (ghetto), fights and gunfire kept them awake till dawn.

Walking in the city one afternoon, they got harassed by a group of kids begging for money.

Titou got impatient with them for being too aggressive and brushed them off.

Soon afterward, a young man approached Titou with his right hand outstretched for him to shake.

As soon as Titou took his hand, he struck him across the face with his left hand, employing a wooden stick he concealed behind his back. The blow missed his eye by half a centimeter and opened up a big gash near his eyebrow. Blood kept pouring out.

At that point, the attacker crossed the road, and the three of them engaged in a rock-throwing battle until they grew weary of it. By then, blood had completely covered Titou's face and clothes.

They tried to stop cars passing by but to no avail.

In the end, they found themselves obliged to pay a significant sum for a taxi that would transport them to the hospital.

The entire night was spent waiting for a doctor to sew up Titou's face, as the emergency ward was filled with an eclectic cast of injured individuals. It was a pretty traumatizing experience.

Titou needed eight stitches, and the next morning, his face swelled up like a soccer ball. But not the Brazilian version of the *'Jogo Bonito,'* the beautiful game.

Of course, when you take drugs, you end up associating with the least desirable characters.

In oppressive countries like those in South America, this presented some challenges, and they experienced many sordid situations.

Now imagine being innocent or stupid enough to carry your little stash of weed across borders!

One of these two *'brilliant'* globetrotters carried a bag of marijuana in his underpants across the Bolivian border, no less.

Oddly, the customs officer asked them if they wanted to buy some dope later on. Maybe he was testing them, but that was certainly peculiar.

They spent the night in this tiny border town.

Marco was in charge of the passports, the traveler's checks, and the cash in a pouch that he carried around his shoulder. I don't know why he hadn't found a more inconspicuous way to do so.

Anyway, he'd placed his money pouch under his mattress and their stash of weed next to it before going to bed.

At 2 a.m., three police officers stormed into the room, accompanied by the hotel manager. They started to search their backpacks for drugs.

Law enforcement individuals and army personnel in those countries are never subtle or chummy.

When they asked Marco to show them their passports, he reached under the mattress to retrieve his pouch.

I can't explain why none of the three policemen toppled their mattresses at this point. However, it wasn't their destiny to end up in a Bolivian jail.

You might assume Marco learned a valuable lesson that day, but that would overestimate the cognitive abilities of a twenty-one-year-old.

Titou had even fewer excuses. He was four years older.

Santa Cruz de la Sierra was one of the world capitals of cocaine production in those days.

There, you could find cocaine that was 80% pure, mixed with acetone instead of ether. Marco wasn't an aspiring chemist, but it had the reputation of being the best.

Upon arriving in this charming little town in the Amazon lowlands, a friendly foreigner greeted them, recommended a hotel, and invited them to a local drug lord's house for the evening.

It was a beautiful colonial property, and there were about twenty foreign guests that night, all of them males.

A private chef brought sumptuous dishes to a big communal table throughout the soirée. French wine and cocktails were flowing freely.

The genial host, with wild curly hair, serenaded them on his grand piano, playing Beethoven's symphonies as a concert pianist possessed.

He would disappear behind a closed door for a while, presumably where the lab was located.

Then, he would come back with a big pot of cocaine, similar in size to a big yogurt container, and a wooden spoon. Going around the table, he would take turns shoving an ample amount of white powder under the nostrils of each guest.

Despite his inability to utter a single word that night, Marco had mastered the most intricate laws of the universe.

These debaucheries continued for the next two nights until an iota of common sense surfaced out of nowhere in the cerebral cortex of these young fools.

They came so close to becoming recruiters for this drug lord, and that would've been a sure descent into hell. In the early hours of the fourth morning, they skipped town.

It surprised them that nobody pursued them to collect their dues despite those days of free treats.

CHAPTER
TWENTY-FOUR

*"I never saw sad men
Who looked with such wistful eye
Upon that little tent of blue
We prisoners call the sky."*

— OSCAR WILDE.

A little Ecuadorian village in the mountains near Ibarra, three-and-a-half hours' drive from Quito, became famous in the seventies.

Bob Dylan, members of Pink Floyd, and Joan Baez traveled there to experience the local delicacies, *hongos* (magic mushrooms), that were abundant in the fields.

A woman by the name of Aida had opened a hotel in this little village near the volcano Imbabura.

This was a destination prized on the itinerary of the two backpackers.

They became friends with a young man from the French part of Switzerland who arrived on the bus from Quito.

They proceeded to the fields to collect mushrooms after leaving their backpacks in the room.

The magic mushrooms in Ecuador, unlike other parts of the world, are big and white, full of water, and the flesh inside is bluish.

They filled a couple of bags with these delicacies and took them back to their room.

Aida had warned them beforehand to be cautious of the police.

Marco lifted a ceiling tile in his bedroom and spread out the mushrooms in the space above to dry. For dinner, Aida made them her famous mushroom omelet, and their spirits soared.

There was a local brass band playing in the village. They sat on an outside patio and ordered a jug of *chicha*, a type of fermented corn beer that was the staple alcoholic beverage in the Andes.

They laughed uncontrollably and marveled at the multi-chromatic terraces that lay before them like puzzle pieces. The fireflies illuminated the sky like fireworks on the 4th of July, while the distorted horns created the most hypnotic sounds.

The following morning, they returned to the fields.

This time, they were picking and eating mushrooms as they walked. They were getting high when a car with three plain-clothed policemen stopped on the dirt road adjacent to the cow fields.

They had time to throw everything away before the men reached them.

It must've been pretty obvious what they were up to, though, with their fingers smeared in blue and with blue streaks running down their cheeks.

The policemen drove them to their hotel, turned their room upside down, and questioned the owner about them.

They jumped back in the jeep and drove one hour high into the mountains before they arrived at the local jail.

Marco, the sole Spanish speaker, instructed his friends to stay quiet and not discuss magic mushrooms or drugs to avoid self-incrimination.

They needed to continue speaking French and assume everyone would understand, much like many French tourists do when abroad.

It was great thinking since they were separated at the jail and led to separate rooms for questioning.

For a couple of hours, a few men took turns playing the good cop, bad cop routine.

They started out being very casual and friendly.

They only wanted Marco to tell them they were having fun in the fields that day. "*It was no big deal,*" they said. "*All the foreigners came here for the same reason, and it* was *common knowledge. Simply be honest with us, and we'll let you go.*"

Marco had watched his fair share of *films policiers* (detective films) and dramas featuring foreign penitentiaries. He wasn't buying any of that.

He made it clear to his captors that he and his companions had no interest in hallucinogenic and dangerous substances like magic mushrooms.

They were just walking in the fields that morning and enjoying the scenery.

One officer got agitated and threatened Marco a few times, while others were more laid back.

The jail was set like a Spanish hacienda, with a big outdoor space surrounded by dwellings that served as the prisoners' cells. A running track took up half of the outdoor area.

When the guards got tired of questioning them, their little group met again outside, and they ordered them to run.

The altitude was nearly 3,000 meters, and it wasn't long before they started slowing down.

One officer held a wooden stick in his hands, and he struck them on the back as they passed him at each new turn. This lasted for quite a while.

Titou, possessing a short fuse, wanted to retaliate, but Marco told him to shut up and keep running.

Marco didn't see it coming when another guard threw a half-meter piece of barbed wire at his feet. That caused him to tumble on the track face-first.

He sported a significant bandage below his wrist, courtesy of a spider bite that got infected. A few days prior, he visited a doctor who inserted a drill into his wound to aid in the release of pus.

He used his wrists to soften his fall and avoided any cuts or injuries. Regardless, the pus had stained his bandage. He remained on the ground, feigning excruciating agony.

The ruse worked, and that put a stop to this sinister exercise around the track.

After a while, a guard escorted them to the outside showers next to the track.

Someone ordered them to strip down. The wind was blowing, and it was bitterly cold.

The guards stared at their naked bodies, fully entertained, while they were forced to stay under the freezing water for a long time.

Marco couldn't help wondering what perverted ideas ran through the guards' minds.

By then, it was time to parade the three backpackers around the various cells.

A gathering of ten or twelve women was loitering around the corridors.

One guard asked Marco to pick a woman of his choice.

He had never witnessed a more terrifying display. They looked like a bunch of lepers missing half their teeth and with ugly scars on their faces and maimed bodies.

Marco suspected they were suffering from an untreated venereal disease such as syphilis or gonorrhea.

He swiftly answered that he had no fancy for any of them.

Another guard he hadn't yet encountered approached him to inquire if he preferred men instead.

When he glanced at the muscular black man, who resembled Apollo Creed from the '*Rocky*' movie, he almost soiled his underpants. He replied with a resounding: "*Heck no.*"

Marco didn't lose his virginity that day.

At that point, the sun had set, and the guards had thoroughly enjoyed their time with their captives.

The same officers gave them a ride down the valley to the nearest bus stop, and they shook hands like best of friends when parting ways.

The following morning, the young travelers took the earliest bus out of town.

Two months later, Marco and Titou were having lunch with a couple of backpackers somewhere in Colombia.

One of them had met two German men who were imprisoned in the same jail for six months for a similar offense.

He wanted to know more about their tale, but the men remained tight-lipped regarding the specifics. You could imagine why.

A sad and tragic story suddenly flashed through Marco's mind.

Only when things happened to him on a physical level did they have an impact on him. This would be a recurring pattern in his life.

The body retains more memory than the mind, maybe that's why.

Despite how scary and gruesome this episode was, he apparently hadn't learned much from it.

When Marco met Felisa in the south of France, her boyfriend was in jail in Tunisia.

That didn't bother him at that time, but in hindsight, she should've supported her friend in need instead of hooking up with the first vagabond who came along.

Samuel was a brilliant political student at the University of Barcelona.

During the summer break, he embarked on a solo trip to North Africa for a couple of months.

Hashish, known as *kif*, was permitted in Morocco. Men smoked it in a long, skinny pipe with a narrow clay bowl called a *sebsi*, often accompanied by drinking mint tea.

King Hassan II, believed to be a descendant of Mohammed, owned half of the country's cannabis fields.

Unaware of the country's draconian laws on drug consumption, the young man was promptly arrested with a couple of grams of *kif* upon crossing the Tunisian border.

He spent one year in a jail near Tunis. His parents had to bribe the government with the sum of $100,000, which was a fortune in those days, for his release.

Before leaving Spain, Marco met Samuel at a party. He was, by all accounts, a broken man.

He had been repeatedly beaten and raped throughout his tenure in jail.

CHAPTER
TWENTY-FIVE

"Never travel faster than your guardian angel can fly."

— MOTHER TERESA.

Marco and Titou were hitchhiking in the Columbian mountains, about four hours away from Medellin.

It was Friday afternoon, and a convoy of five vehicles stopped to offer them a ride.

They were a group of mine engineers going home for the weekend.

They operated army jeeps that had undergone conversion for civilian use, with a back cargo space that remained open.

Since all drivers were alone, the backpackers split up. Marco joined the first vehicle and Titou the last.

The workers were in festive spirits as they maneuvered their small

SUVs through the tortuous roads in the Andes. They made repeated pauses for beers and shots of aguardiente, a sugarcane-based liqueur with an anise flavor.

Several stops later, Marco's chauffeur, who had maintained pole position, fancied himself to be Mario Andretti, the former racing driver.

As he entered a curve at too fast a pace, he slammed on the brakes, resulting in the vehicle spinning in circles. He got ejected straight away. The jeep seemed to take forever to complete a full turn-and-a-half.

It settled in the right-side ditch, facing the direction they came from.

Marco exited the car unharmed and ran fifty meters toward the unconscious driver, lying face down on the tarmac.

He moved to his right and stared in horror at a 200-meter drop. In the fading light, he discerned a river flowing through a canyon.

After Marco's long period of introspection with death itself, the other jeeps arrived at the scene.

Titou later informed him that he stood there motionless and white as a ghost.

The driver suffered severe injuries. The group successfully rescued the jeep from the ditch. Fortunately, it had not been damaged. Titou assumed control of the wheel and proceeded towards the nearest hospital in Medellin, a few hours away and 1,200 meters altitude lower in the valley.

The injured man lay in the back on blankets. In an effort to console him every time the jeep hit a bump, and he screamed in pain,

Marco held his hand and applied a wet cloth to his forehead. It was a lengthy ride into a dark and haunted night.

They arrived at the hospital right before dawn. The two travelers parted ways with their companions straight away.
They would never know the extent of the man's injury.

When they first landed on the South American continent in Venezuela, they proceeded to drive to the Amazonian capital on the Trans-Amazonian highway, a 4,000-kilometer patch of dirt cut through the jungle.

Once they reached Manaus, the capital of the Brazilian Amazon, they took a small boat to Belem on the Atlantic coast, nearly 1,500 kilometers away.

They slept in their hammocks for seven days and ate fish head soup each evening, the local delicacy!

The budget vessel stopped at every village along the river. Late one afternoon, as they docked at a deserted place, Marco asked the captain whether it was safe to go swimming, to which he responded with: "*Sem problemas*" (no problem).

The warm water was as dark as a moonless night.

A crowd had started gathering on the dock, and everybody started laughing hard, visibly entertained. Becoming suspicious, the two brave young men exchanged a glance and promptly swam back to land as if they had a fire in their pants. They'd both seen videos of piranhas devouring an entire cow in record time.

That reminded Marco of a weekend spent on the shore of the Murray River in South Australia. He was visiting a young man who'd given him a lift while hitchhiking in Saskatchewan, Canada. He lived in Adelaide with his parents. His father's occupation as a taxi driver proved convenient for exploring the city.

They drove four hours north of the city to the wood cabin of a friend. The following morning, they took a ride on a small boat along the river.

Soon, it got stuck in shallow waters. When the two Aussies didn't take action to help, Marco stepped forward and proceeded to push the boat out of trouble.

Before doing so, he inquired about the safety of the situation. He stayed for a few minutes, wading in the muddy waters.

When they returned to the cabin, his friends told him that the Murray River was notorious for its black venomous snakes. Australians have a dark sense of humor.

Marco wasn't amused. If you had to pick piranhas or snake bites for your demise, which one would you choose?

CHAPTER

TWENTY-SIX

"We consume our tomorrows, fretting about our yesterdays."

— PERSIUS.

One month after the accident in the Colombian mountains, they returned to France because they were running out of money.

Over the past few months, they'd a few close calls. Both reached a consensus on expressing gratitude to their guardian angels, who had accompanied them on their journey.

They learned and experienced substantial growth.

Marco wanted to keep traveling forever though. His enthusiasm remained unaffected.

It felt validating to be a survivor.

Soon after returning from South America, Marco traveled to Canada. He spent six months on Prince Edward Island.

He worked on a tobacco farm, and then later picked cabbages and Brussel sprouts.

Prince Edward Island is notorious for the quality of its magic mushrooms.

When he left the island, he had a big bag of psilocybin mushrooms that had dried in an oven by a local.

He visited the network of his buddies in Montreal and Quebec City.

In February, he spent the carnival there. It was 17 degrees below Celsius. Marco spent most of the carnival indoors, he didn't know it could get so cold. During that time, he bartered some of his mushrooms for hash, grass, and synthetic mescaline.

While traveling to visit a girl-friend he'd met in Peru in Lac St-Jean, he hitchhiked through the Laurentides National Park.

The previous vehicle had left him stranded in the middle of nowhere, and it was snowing heavily.

The scenery resembled a wintry postcard scene. Despite not being dressed for such a harsh winter, he was enjoying the moment.

As a car pulled up, Marco thought he was lucky somebody would stop in his weather. He soon recognized a member of the Canadian Mounted Police by his baggy pants and Stetson hat.

The law enforcement officer asked for his passport.

After glancing at his backpack partially covered with snow, he asked in a casual manner:
"If I were to peer inside your backpack, would I find any drugs?"

Marco answered nonchalantly:
"Not at all, officer. You're welcome to take a peek if you wish."

The trooper kept his gaze fixed on Marco for what felt like an eternity.

He then wished him good luck and left.

If Marco was shaking, it wasn't from the cold. He hadn't even bothered to hide his stash of drugs. It sat atop the backpack. If the trooper had opened it, it would've been the first thing he saw.

Perhaps the young man had nerves of steel, but as they say: *"You can't fix stupid."*

When spring arrived, Marco hitchhiked across Canada all the way to Vancouver, BC.

Back then, hitchhiking was the perfect method to travel.

For one thing, it cost nothing. You'd meet some interesting people, they'd invite you to their home, and sometimes they'd even offer you a job.

Upon his arrival in the United States, he abandoned hitchhiking.

There were too many disturbed individuals around. He calculated that he'd hitchhiked over 42,000 kilometers on four continents in his nine years of backpacking. Enough to circle the world at the Equator.

A significant amount of time was spent sitting by the road though.

Once in the Northern Territories in Australia, he got stuck for twenty-four hours at the same spot, with his head buried under cover on account of the flies.

He encountered some frightening moments along the way, but nobody ever attacked or robbed him.

After spending a few days in Vancouver, Marco continued towards the Yukon Territory. The prospects of finding work were better farther north.

In the 19th century, the Yukon experienced the biggest gold rush in history.

It was a mythical land the size of California with 45,000 inhabitants.

Researchers have recorded 7,000 grizzlies and 10,000 black bears, along with other predators like coyotes, wolverines, and wolves in the area.

Marco was standing on the road in the middle of nowhere. A jeep with Colorado plates stopped to give him a ride. The driver and his friend, both Americans, were on their way to Alaska for the salmon fishing season.

Inside the car were two French-speaking Canadians they'd picked up on the road, among them an Indian from the Mohawk tribe.

They arrived in Whitehorse on a Saturday.

The two Americans offered to sell their jeep to the Quebecois. They no longer needed the vehicle as they'd found work on a fishing boat.

Marco was a little suspicious and advised his friend to wait until

Monday to report the sale. The buyer couldn't resist the tempting $500 price and ignored his advice.

They camped outside of town and spent the following few days cruising around in their yellow jeep, playing cowboy in the Far West (two cowboys and an Indian, to be exact).

At a local agency, they found work taking inventory at a supermarket.

The Indian chose not to work and remained at the camp.

They started out the next morning. At lunch-time, they jumped in the jeep to grab some lunch.

Suddenly, a police car came speeding up behind the jeep with its siren blasting. Another police car blocked their way ahead. One officer was on one knee with his shotgun aimed at the jeep.

The two officers in the car behind shouted for them to exit the jeep with their hands raised above their heads.

Marco had seen a lot of American movies. Making a sudden move now would've been ill-advised unless one desired a hasty departure from this world.

The police officers forcefully pushed them against the rear panel of the jeep and handcuffed them.

Someone had declared the vehicle stolen. Once inside the station, things got cleared up when the officers realized smarter individuals had duped the young men. The atmosphere turned more convivial.

Marco possessed a Quebecois working ID that a backpacker he met had given to him. The details and reasons weren't very clear, but that was convenient.

There wasn't any photo on it, and as it turned out, the man wasn't wanted by the police.

Marco didn't trust the other Indian who was traveling with them.

Previously, passports were highly valuable, fetching up to $10,000 on the black market.

He had taken his passport with him to be safe. Otherwise, he would have been released like his friend.

Now, the authorities caught him lying and working unauthorized with a tourist visa.

They confiscated his passport. The two exonerated thieves returned to their tent without a mode of transportation.

It was now an immigration matter. They arranged for an adjudicator from Toronto to fly in and render judgment on Marco's case.

Marco wasn't the boasting type (although this may be open to debate from readers). He reckons he spends time in jails in six different countries.

He never stayed the night in any of them, though. That should tell you that he was either innocent, in the wrong place at the wrong time, or that he had extraordinary skills of persuasion.

The adjudicator arrived in town a few days later. He seemed like a distinguished man at first sight. Ten minutes into the proceedings, he stopped the inquiry and told Marco: *"Let's go out for lunch!"*

They left the police station, walked to a nearby restaurant, and had a tasty meal and a couple of 'cold ones' each.

When they came back to the station, they were the best of friends.

They agreed that if Marco could show that he had a minimum of $1,000 within ten days, the adjudicator would forget about the entire episode. He could then cross the Alaskan border, which was 500 kilometers west, without a red mark on his passport.

Give it to those Canadians. They were hospitable hosts, considering the circumstances.

Marco, due to his extensive travels, had been broken countless times.

More than anything, he hated financial assistance. It felt so degrading to him.

To his credit – aside from banks and credit cards – he doesn't to this day owe a penny to any individual he borrowed money from.

You have to draw the line somewhere, don't you?

In Peru, his bus got stuck for hours due to a flooded river. He befriended Marc, a Parisian who was traveling with his friend Denis on a different bus.

They promised to meet again farther north, and when they did, they had a ball.

Marc, a highly educated man, held a lucrative job in Paris. He was the only person that Marco called.

Although it was a substantial sum of money, Marc agreed to help his friend in need.

They planned for the funds to be sent to a particular bank in Whitehorse. It was supposed to take five working days at the most.

After one week, Marco went to the bank every day. His friend had confirmed that the money had left his account and that there was nothing else he could do.

Marco got another week of grace from the authorities. Still no money.

It took another couple of days before the Canadian government deported him back to France.

The scenery around Whitehorse was magnificent. A couple of days away from the summer solstice, the days were graced with twenty hours of sunlight. It felt like an enchanted land, straight from the pages of a glossy travel magazine.

The locals were friendly. Marco hated the idea of returning to France. He would've done anything to stay in Canada.

Finally, he was on the plane to Vancouver. An immigration officer met him at the airport.

The airline had scheduled to refuel the plane in Montreal without passengers disembarking.

The officer was supposed to embark with Marco all the way to Montreal to ensure that he wouldn't exit the aircraft.

After Marco promised him he wouldn't do such a thing, the officer bid him farewell and released him to go alone.

When the airplane landed in Montreal, it stayed on the tarmac for an hour while some passengers departed and others came on board.

He had his backpack inside the plane.

He was well-acquainted with Montreal, and, with it being the beginning of summer, it was the ideal time to be in Quebec. Even though they'd canceled his tourist visa, he could've easily returned to work on Prince Edward Island.

Why didn't he exit the plane that day? The thought had tortured him throughout the flight. Was it because of a promise he made to the man in Vancouver?

No, he'd broken enough promises before.

His sole desire was to quickly flee the plane and run away as far as he could. The last thing he wanted was to be back in Paris.

Glued to his airline seat by some unknown force, he didn't make a move on that particular day.

He dreamt of immigrating to Canada when he was younger. He saw his dream shatter into a thousand pieces in front of him.

By all calculations, it would take him thirty-four years from this moment forward before he gained a trivial amount of consciousness.

Wasn't there a faster, less painful way? Who was the sadist directing this play?

Six years later, by some twist of irony, Marco flew to Alaska with Hazel for the salmon fishing season.

They would end up working three summer seasons in the Bering Sea and on Kodiak Island.

This time, he had an American green card. He received it in his mailbox two and a half months after his arrival on the continent.

Upon arriving in Paris, he stayed at Marc's apartment for a couple of weeks before leaving for Germany to find work.

Just a couple of days before his departure, Marc received a letter in the mail.

The money in Canada had been sent to the wrong financial institution, located just across the street from the intended bank. Marco had passed the bank daily, but how could he have known?

TWENTY-SEVEN

"Be where your enemy is not."

— SUN TZU.

Before he became interested in yoga, Marco had studied different martial arts.

It had a calming effect on him, allowing him to let off steam.

Soon after arriving in New Mexico, he enrolled in a dojo where they taught an obscure Japanese martial art.

The sensei, named Aloha, was a long-haired Hawaiian of Japanese ancestry.

By all accounts, he was a skilled fighter. Despite his laid-back personality, it was wise to remain in his good graces.

Having a small group of students, he would exaggerate their

combat abilities, always stressing that this was no ordinary dojo and the techniques they were mastering were lethal.

Sparring wasn't included in the curriculum due to its classification as too dangerous.

Marco studied there for three-and-a-half years, along with his son Bryce, who'd eventually enrolled in the kids' club.

Two months before his black belt test, he was practicing some simple punching techniques with a couple of white belts.

He brushed against the face of a tall, lanky new student and barely noticed.

The student didn't complain, and the training continued with no interruption that evening.

The next day, Marco received a call from Aloha.

Apparently, the white belt student had a black eye, and his girlfriend had threatened to sue the dojo.

Aloha vented his frustrations on one of his oldest and most loyal disciples.

When he finished berating Marco, their relationship had been irreparably damaged.

Marco's ego suffered badly; nonetheless, he felt his sensei had been too vindictive towards him. He had unloaded his entire bag of complaints on his unfortunate *protégé*, emphasizing nothing but his many defects.

A few days later, Marco walked by an MMA training facility and stopped to talk to the manager.

He offered to let him come in for a free trial the next morning.

When he drove home the following day, after taking a long shower, he felt a deep sense of disgust towards himself.

Each student in the gym, including a teenager as thin as a pair of shears, would've beaten him up in a real fight.

At Aloha's dojo, they never practiced kicks or fighting on the mat.

When Marco asked why they weren't training in grappling, Aloha's answer was a resounding:

"Don't get on the ground!"

A Brazilian Jiu-Jitsu practitioner who'd learned some basic techniques could soon wrap you up like a pretzel and get you to submit with ease.

Marco believed he could defend himself, but it was an illusion. Nothing more than a glorified concept perpetuated by his former teacher's ego.

He paid the full year's tuition that day because he was given a significant discount.

He never saw Aloha again and began practicing at his new center three or four times a week.

It was hard training. Marco felt the sport was for young men, but he loved the sweat, competition, and comradeship.

But he kept getting hurt. He pulled an intercostal muscle in his chest that required a full month of recovery.

Two days after resuming training, he strained the same muscle on the other side.

He decided then and there that it would be the end of his Jiu-Jitsu training. He had been a member for eighteen months, and he had stayed at home with various injuries for six of them.

It was a humbling experience, but he'd acquired a lot of skills.

It was time to let go. Be aware of your restrictions. This is all part of growing.

Marco liked to push himself to the limits.

Despite his stubbornness, he was usually happy to move on once he learned the lesson. *"There's no point flogging a dead horse,"* as they say.

He would turn to yoga, a more mellow form of releasing the 'crazy.'

CHAPTER
TWENTY-EIGHT

"Travel light, live light, spread the light, be the light."

— YOGI BHAJAN.

Soon after returning to Albuquerque from Denver, Marco joined a Kundalini yoga studio.

That was the beginning of a love affair.

Oddly enough, this relocated studio was two kilometers away from his former home, where he had lived for ten years.

By then, he and his ex-wife Hazel had been separated for four years.

He seduced and discarded a few women along the way, spent all his money, got ejected from his condo, and was sleeping in his Lexus.

When consciousness emerges from the labyrinth of your mind after a long period of darkness, how could you possibly stay unaware?

A couple of months later, Marco enrolled in the Kundalini yoga teaching program.

He wrote about his experience in this article:

A COURSE IN SELF-MASTERY

"My birth name is Marco, and I was born and raised in the South of France. However, the name I was given at birth never aligned with my destiny.

The 3HO organization gave me my spiritual name, Taj Simrit Singh, based on my full name and date of birth. It means: 'The fearless lion who is the embodiment of the splendor and radiance that flow perfectly from meditating on the name of God with every breath.'

Three and a half years ago, my life changed forever when I started practicing yoga every single day.

You've heard the old saying? "When the student is ready, the teacher will appear."

Sevak Singh, my teacher, has been teaching Kundalini yoga for forty-four years in his home base of Phoenix, Arizona, and in other parts of the world. He's a tall Sikh, impeccably dressed in white cotton clothing with a matching turban. He has a long salt-and-pepper beard that gives him a wise aura.

It took me just moments, upon meeting him to realize that I was in the presence of a dignified man. Sevak's words resonated with me.

I recall the first time I heard him say early in his course, "You're not your mind." This prompted a sort of epiphany for me, as for as long as I could remember, I'd been operating solely through my mind. I'd always thought that I was uniquely my mind: that strong and stubborn mind of mine, the very one that got me in and out of trouble throughout my life.

Within two months of meeting Sevak, I enrolled in a Level 1

Teacher Training Course in Kundalini Yoga. Yogi Bhajan said: "Nothing in this world happens by accident. It's all part of a master plan."

It's a short one-and-a-half-hour drive from Phoenix to Gisela, a small community south of Payson, Arizona. I was flying along in my car, headed to my first four-day retreat at Heart and Soul, without a care in the world. I was working for an on-call agency in Albuquerque and sleeping in my Lexus. I saw this as a chance to shift this mindset.

Heart and Soul is on a two-and-a-half acre property that Sevak purchased five years ago in Gisela, a hamlet of 500 souls scattered around an irrigated valley. The Black Mountains and Tonto Creek frame Gisela, and the Tonto National Forest surrounds it.

For the next six months, our group of 10 students would get to call this little piece of paradise home. As a bonus, our four-day retreats each month coincided with the full moon.

There we were, as if we'd descended from the heavens on a zipline and had landed right in the middle of this land. On one side of the retreat, there was a giant mulberry tree with a solitary swing hanging from one of its branches. Beyond that was a gate that led to the River Road; we'd pass this gate many times throughout our stay.

A leisurely ten-minute walk along a dirt road, flanked by an assortment of prefabricated homes, led us to Shanti Om three times a day for breakfast, lunch, and dinner. Shanti Om is the haven of peace that Ram, a close friend of Sevak, built for his semi-retirement home.

The west side of the property housed our ashram, a cozy house with three bedrooms equipped with bunk beds, a kitchen, a living room, and two bathrooms. Right across from the ashram was a renovated yoga studio covered with corrugated iron sheets. A heater and a swamp cooler helped tame the elements.

There's just something magical about an immersion course that takes you across the winter, spring, and summer seasons.

I'd always been in rebellion against the mere existence of God. My main purpose for being there wasn't to find God or unravel the universe's mysteries. It was to rediscover myself amidst a collection of long-lost objects.

Sevak described 'the journey of our souls' as the path they take through many reincarnations, potentially totaling 3.8 million variations.

During his classes, Sevak was fond of saying that if there was a magic pill that could take you through your journey, he'd be all for it. The fastest way through which he could identify — the 'Learjet' that can enable a person to merge with the divine and experience a complete symbiosis of body, mind, and soul.

Yogi Bhajan brought Kundalini yoga to the U.S. in 1969. Numerous authors have covered the history of this type of yoga. Throughout thousands of years, masters taught Kundalini Yoga in secrecy, risking their lives as the punishment for teaching it was death within a year.

Yogi Bhajan passed on his teachings for thirty-five years, until his death in 2004, and left an incredible legacy for this world. He used to say that you must be a lighthouse and spread your light on others. He didn't want disciples, but he wanted to train other teachers to pass on his teachings to future generations.

Kundalini yoga incorporates asanas, other physical exercises called kriyas, pranayama (breathing) exercises, and mudras that involve placing your fingers and hands in various positions.

The practice involves using mantras written in Gurmukhi, a language derived from Sanskrit that originated in the 16th century in

Punjab, India. These mind projections that Kundalini yoga music can sing or accompany can transport you to another dimension.

When Yogi Bhajan arrived in California in 1969, by Toronto, he landed right in the middle of the hippie culture of the West Coast. He noticed right away that many young individuals were engaging in drug experimentation and challenging societal norms. However, he had an intuitive sense that drugs only offered a temporary solution to a deeper, ongoing problem. He knew the proper solution to counteracting the world's ills lay in his ancestral teachings.

Soon afterward, he founded the 3HO foundation mentioned above, with 3HO standing for Happy, Healthy, and Holy. To quote Yogi Bhajan, "Happiness is your birthright."

Kundalini yoga gave me the road map I needed to be whatever I aspired to be, as long as that was in sync with seeking the well-being of others. This is called seva, which means selfless service.

If you want to break free from your ego and radiate like a beacon of light, focus on serving others and showing love, empathy, and compassion towards them. Otherwise, you won't align with your soul's purpose.

Through Kundalini yoga, I learned we have 10 bodies, and among them, three minds: the negative, the positive, and the neutral mind. It dawned on me that the path to prosperity lies in the neutral mind. One can only access this sacred place when they are not preoccupied with conquering or surviving, but accepting whatever comes without overreacting.

This is called surrendering, and therein lies the real secret of the practice. It's not a secret in the sense that it's hidden or hard to find — it just requires a certain level of awareness and steady practice. Awareness itself won't get you there unless you're willing to do the heavy work.

For me, however, the real magic of Kundalini yoga lies in the mantras. Guru Nanak, a Sikh guru and a traveling musician, wrote most of these. There are multitudes of artists who've put these mantras to music.

There is a belief that everything in the universe originates from sound. In the 1960s, scientists learned the sun's surface is made up of sound waves. The sun has up to 10,000 frequencies rippling along its surface.

It's not surprising that by tapping along to this sound current, you can develop the ability to cross the gate to the infinite or whatever you want to call it. When it's resonating at its most awesome primal force, you can call it God. In Kundalini yoga, true to beliefs in Sikhism, we hold the belief that there is one God that cannot be found externally but resides within each individual.

During my first weekend at Heart and Soul, I found God, but not in a born-again sense. No need for death or rebirth. It turned out my experience was subtly organic. Little did I know God was the spark of life and glory that inhabited every organism in the Universe. My senses were always attuned, amazed by the world's wonders. However, I lacked supreme intuition, which required detachment from my egoistic self and remained dormant in my gut. I fought against God's existence out of rebellion, frustration, and pain.

Throughout Sevak's self-mastery course, I realized I was the one who created my own limitations. We spend our entire lives inside a little bubble populated by the things that hurt us and cause us pain. We end up, by working against our conscious minds, recreating stories and scenarios that take us to what we were hiding from. No wonder we're lost in a conundrum of self-victimization and self-sabotage.

Are you aware that we possess three brains: The 'mind' brain, the 'heart' brain, and the 'gut' brain? "You are not your mind," Sevak's voice kept echoing through my being as a reminder of this idea, like the wind hurling through a canyon's wall.

One morning, we'd just finished listening to Japji (Sikh prayers), doing yoga exercises, and chanting mantras during two and a half hours of sadhana. I wandered outside the yoga studio on this cool and moist February morning, in a bit of a trance.

The night-long rain left the fields wet, resembling a carpet of clouds under my feet. The sun hadn't yet risen, and the light of the full moon had dressed the pale dawn with yellow and orange hues. The countryside was wrapped in blankets of fog, and I sensed that I had been transported inside the pages of a fairytale book.

When I made eye contact with that lost wandering soul in the far corner of the field, I didn't flinch at all, for I recognized it as my own. It had come back home at last. In a flash, I woke up from the inertia that had possessed my physical body. I felt ever so light, with God pulsating in every one of my 30 trillion cells.

My gaze took me effortlessly for a jolly ride along the river, over the hills, and into the infinity of the universe. I'd been a monochromatic cocoon before turning into a colorful butterfly. All the nectar of this world was within reach of my proboscis. I felt so rich and so free.

Yogi Bhajan has also said, "Gratitude is the highest form of yoga." I felt, for the first time during this incarnation on Earth, great and full. I'd always sensed God permeating inside my being and all around me; I'd just lacked the intuition in my 'gut' brain and the love and compassion in my 'heart' brain to acknowledge and dwell in it.

The monkey in my 'mind' brain could find himself another host, for I had grown tired of his pompous act!

"Wahe Guru..."

TAJ SIMRIT

TWENTY-NINE

"Death the last voyage, the longest and the best."

— THOMAS WOLFE.

The main purpose of life must be to evolve. Why else would we exist, enduring life's constant heartbreaks?

To end up where we'd all started, with the self-awareness of a newborn?

Marco's father was soon a victim of COVID-19. For five years, he'd been living in a retirement home. He was confined to a wheelchair and suffered from Parkinson's disease. He had an active mind though, and still dreamt of traveling the world.

Marco was in an ashram in Tamil Nadu when he heard the news from his sister.

To him, his father's death was both a blessing and a liberation. He would dread ending up in a nursing home and witnessing his own physical decline. He figured he would prefer to die as his buddy Titou did in Guyana, and meet his maker head-on without suffering.

CHAPTER
THIRTY

"And the day came when the risk of remaining tight in a bud was more painful than the risk it took to blossom."

— ANAIS NIN.

While in Kathmandu, Marco had befriended a young man and his family.

The father was doing astrological and palm readings from an office inside their humble apartment in Thamel.

Before Marco's departure, the father took a reading of his moon, beginning with his left hand.

He informed him of his beneficial moon, promising good health and a prosperous life for twenty-five years.

Marco questioned why he wasn't checking his palm. Throughout that time, his focus remained on his chin. Apparently, the moon is located beyond an individual's chin.

When Marco probed him about women, without taking his eyes off his chin, he simply answered: "*No.*"

That would leave him five years short of the number 88, which symbolizes fortune and good luck in Chinese culture.

If he were to pass at that age, he would join the likes of Thomas Jefferson, Sigmund Freud, Andrew Carnegie, Voltaire, Victor Hugo, Paul Newman, and Tina Turner.

Distinguished company.

From a pragmatic perspective, Marco wouldn't mind becoming a centenarian.

As long as the body and the mind were sound.

He drew inspiration from Dan Buettner's book: '*Blue Zones.*'

The National Geographic explorer has led teams of researchers across the globe to uncover the secrets of the '*Blue Zones,*' geographic regions where a high percentage of centenarians live.

The recipe for longevity is deeply intertwined with community, lifestyle, diet, and spirituality, as Dan Buettner discovered.

For over twenty years, he studied communities in Sardinia, Italy; Okinawa, Japan; Nicoya Peninsula, Costa Rica; Icaria, Greece; and Loma Linda, California.

He also added Singapore as the sixth Blue Zone in 2023.

The people eat whole foods and have plant-based diets. The five foods in every Blue Zone are whole grains, greens, tubers like sweet potatoes, nuts, and beans.

Some individuals eat meat in moderation, and those on the coast supplement their diets with fish.

Marco had long overcome his fear of death.

He couldn't blame those who thought life was limited to one existence.

In this scenario, fearing death would be justified as the end of their Descartes' best representation: *"I think, therefore I am."*

A couple of insights had started to creep into his head of late.

When life is so joyful and effortless, why desire its end?

You start projecting into the future all the things you have yet to accomplish and all the places you have yet to discover.

Since you're no longer in the present moment, a little anxiety appears. It's a Catch-22 that keeps you from being at peace.

Furthermore, the old concepts of: *"Why are you on this planet in the first place? What is your purpose?"* resurface, and you're as clueless as ever.

You're caught in this conundrum while intending to lighten up.

Marco wasn't hitting the panic button yet.

Deep down, he knew he had to make a bigger difference in people's lives.

All the hedonistic activities that filled his days weren't worth a 'sack of shit' in this particular trade.

The impetus to keep moving forward and searching for answers –
encompassing that unfathomed energy force – would become his
fountain of youth.

CHAPTER
THIRTY-ONE

"It's never too late to be what you might have been."

— GEORGE ELIOTT.

Before taking his last breath, Marco's father told the nurse that he was about to embark on the most amazing voyage ever.

This insight was a miracle for someone who didn't believe in life after death.

The American researcher Dr Rick Strassman investigated the effects of DMT (Dimethyltryptamine), the active ingredient in Ayahuasca, by giving high doses to volunteers over five years.

He later hypothesized that the pineal gland releases DMT when a person is near death and that DMT connects us to the spirit world.

You could read more about his work in the book 'DMT: The Spirit Molecule.'

From his ashram in India, Marco thought consciousness had reached his father at last, before his soul elevated.

Marco was in the perfect environment to behold this happening. At last, the father and son made peace.

His soul – no longer trapped in his crippled body – was liberated to explore 'the great unknown' as described by Joseph Campbell.

Marco saw it unfold by looking at the South Indian sky in the evening. It was a beautiful bonding experience, with the person he needed bonding with the most.

Yogi Bhajan said that we'd solve half of our problems if we forgave our parents.

Marco's mother had been easier to forgive. She had never been abusive, physically or psychologically.

Keeping sane was impossible with the multitude of ghosts haunting her. It was undeniable that she was doing the best that she could.

Her death, nine years before her former husband, turned out to be the defining moment in Marco's poor existence of late.

He witnessed his most despised qualities originate from his maternal lineage.

With her passing, Marco understood that he carried the burdens of his own past and those of his parents.

To break the generational cycle of pain, questioning is essential.

Transgenerational trauma affects future generations because of the traumatic events endured by their ancestors.

The primary mode of transmission is the psychological and physiological effects that the trauma experienced by members of a family has on subsequent generations in that group.

Despite having difficulties controlling his anger, Marco never physically harmed Hazel nor Bryce, proving that you have the power to put an end to this transgenerational trauma.

His life will forever be altered by his mother's unexpected death.

Hazel responded in a very detached and cold manner to his mother's passing.

Despite supporting him in his decision to fly to France for her funeral, she didn't utter a single word of comfort or sympathy.

Maybe she unconsciously knew that Marco no longer needed a mother figure and that he was about to break the chains that bound him?

Overall, it felt like a heavy fog of negativity and victimhood had dissipated, and everything around him started to take on a different hue.

THIRTY-TWO

"Only the descent into the hell of self-knowledge can pave the way to godliness."

— IMMANUEL KANT.

Marco was sitting at a table next to the kitchen in his Albuquerque home.

He was talking passionately about a National Geographic cruise to Antarctica. Hazel had her typical gloomy outlook on life, and she asked him bluntly: *"Why do you spend so much time discussing going to Antarctica? You will never make it there."*

As a dream buster, she had no equal. Would you be willing to marry such a person?

Her good heart and commitment to morality were evident.

She never denigrated nor begrudged anybody. Marco never heard her complain about her situation, regardless of the circumstances.

Despite her many qualities, why did she have to be such a drag?

Would you rather die having never experienced the intricacies of life?

What if you let your imagination fill the void between your dreams and aspirations, and pure fantasy without the input of reason?

Wouldn't it be in itself the ultimate therapy for the existential malaise of our times?

Suddenly, a thought occurred to him:

"*Someday, I am going to divorce that* 'cunt'."

Even after twenty years of marriage, he never considered it. No way, this couldn't possibly be part of his inner dialogue?

Like a gong, this haunting thought reverberated in his head.

These uttered words turned instantly into an indelible obsession as if they'd been tattooed on his forehead.

It took five more tortuous years before these thoughts turned into deliberate action.

When Bryce was born a few months before September 11, Hazel and Marco had been living together for eighteen years.

You could call him a miracle child.

His existence in flesh and blood serves as evidence that his soul has a real purpose.

I can only hope that this book will be the catalyst for his inner transformation.

When Marco was in Mexico, he had a numerology reading by one of his old teachers in Arizona. She mastered Jyotish, the Divine light of the Veda.

This is the name for Vedic astrology, which arose during the Vedic period in India between 1500–500 BCE.

It describes how the planetary patterns at the time of our birth give valuable clues to help you understand your life's journey.

During the numerology reading, she asked Marco for his ex-wife and his son's birth dates.

She knew nothing about them at all, nor did she ask.

She told him things about them that blew him away.

Either he knew but couldn't convey them, or he discovered them as she spoke.

She informed him that Hazel harbored a dislike for men because of her father and other matters I am not at liberty to disclose.

Bryce would have self-worth issues during his life.

He would, despite his intelligence and perceptivity, always lack in *amour propre* (self-esteem).

So, you can imagine that the separation of his parents, his mother's overbearing presence, and his extra sensitivity would compound these tendencies.

He needed to realize that he was already a perfect being of light, beyond his self-induced feelings of unworthiness.

That would be the biggest challenge in this life.

Six months after Marco and Hazel met, she became pregnant.

Marco was clueless about Hazel's thoughts, but he wanted no involvement with children. She wasn't very keen either, so she had an abortion.

Having kids appeared to be nothing more than a hindrance.

The same line of thinking continued until they decided they were ready to give a shot at parenthood sixteen years later.

When they decided it was the right time, Hazel had an ectopic pregnancy.

She required surgery that meant she would lose one of her fallopian tubes. Instead, she decided on a new drug that had come onto the market. It made her really groggy for a week, but she recovered quickly.

Hazel was tough as nails and never complained. Since she interiorized everything, she was next to impossible to read.

Bryce was born two years later. His parents were three or four months short of turning forty-four.

At forty, a woman's ability to have babies drops by about 80%, making this a remarkable occurrence.

He arrived seven weeks early and required steroids to develop his lungs. They are the last organs to develop at around thirty-seven weeks.

Otherwise, he was healthy. He spent six weeks in an NICU (neonatal intensive care unit).

The doctor and nurses at the University of New Mexico's

Children's Hospital in Albuquerque were *"angels of the first degree"*, like in the Van Morrison song 'Tupelo Honey.'

For Marco, it was the greatest lesson in compassion and humility.

Their exceptional commitment to their jobs turned fear and worries into hope and solace.

Marco loved being a dad, and Hazel was a natural mother.

Since they had different schedules at work, they took turns at babysitting.

The first few years went smoothly.

The couple's dynamic changed after years without children. Marco didn't mind that his son had replaced him as the king. He had loved nobody in this manner before.

Hazel became protective of Bryce, like a she-wolf to her pup.

From an early age, he displayed the traits of a gifted child. With great intensity, he learned rapidly and was in a perpetual mode of observation.

Hazel thought that her son's sensitivity and high perceptibility made him weak and prone to be hurt. Protecting him from harm and ensuring his well-being became her obsession.

She must've believed she was the only person capable of safeguarding him from the dangers of this world.

That wreaked havoc on the relationship between the parents. Marco was passive in dealing with this situation.

Truth be told, Hazel had always been in control of everything in their marriage, except bringing home the bacon.

They decided Hazel didn't have to work. Marco was making decent money in sales and, a handful of times brought some insane checks back home.

That lasted six or seven years. Then things unraveled.

Who knows what Hazel did at home while Bryce was at school?

Granted, the house was always clean, and she knew her way around the kitchen.

She loved to read, her literature of choice being Italian romance novels.

In light of the fact that Marco was neither Casanova nor Romeo besides their common Italian heritage, you could find her attenuating circumstances, couldn't you?

According to John Gray in 'Men are from Mars, Women are from Venus':

"Men primarily need trust, acceptance, appreciation, admiration, approval, and encouragement.
And women need caring, understanding, respect, devotion, validation, and reassurance."

Based on what they failed to provide each other, Marco and Hazel were millions of galaxies apart.

A child is supposed to fully develop their personality by age seven.

Bryce was often the mirror copy of his mother.

You couldn't blame him the least; his mother was projecting all her fears and insecurities onto him.

By then, Hazel was the sole protector of her son, and Marco had become the enemy. He could sense a growing hatred similar to that of his wife in Bryce's eyes.

This battle wasn't fair. He would lose his sanity in the process.

When someone you love is taken away from you and there's nothing you can do about it, a relentless pain takes hold of you and never lets go. It starts to erode your heart like rust corroding metal.

Hazel had metamorphosed into a bitter and unattractive woman overnight. Of course, her transformation had been more gradual.

What became of the intelligent, fun, and lively woman he once knew?

She didn't give a shit about her appearance any longer and had put on weight.

She had transformed into a fearful and resentful woman.

Years later, Marco realized it was more likely the menopause. They had never mentioned this word while together.

She was stubborn and would've denied it.

Marco was into sports: tennis, golf, martial arts, soccer, hiking, you name it.

Hazel had never set foot in a gym in her life.

Eventually, Marco realized she hadn't seen a doctor in a decade, not even for a check-up.

The woman I'm referring to earned a bachelor's degree in nursing in three years while working part-time.

Her demons had taken hold, though she would be reluctant to admit it.

Hazel was the oldest of four kids. Her father had been a fireman in Boston.

After getting injured at work, he struggled with lifelong back issues, which required him to take pain medication. He was also dealing with diabetes and obesity.

Living with him was likely a challenge.

Hazel had never opened up to Marco about her relationship with her father.

Let's say that all the siblings in her family exhibited signs of a dysfunctional upbringing, especially her only sister.

He had a heart as big as his frame and had built his entire house pretty much on his own. He also had a caustic sense of humor, which appealed to Marco, so they got along well.

When Hazel was sixteen and still going to school, she got pregnant. While living at home with her parents, she managed to hide her burgeoning belly under baggy clothes.

Her father found out one day when she was eight months pregnant.

In 1970, abortion became legal in New York, three years before the Supreme Court decision of Roe v. Wade decriminalized it in 1973.

Abortion became illegal past 24 weeks unless the mother's health was at risk or the fetus wasn't viable.

Her dad forced her to abort. Soon after that, Hazel left school and her parent's home behind.

You could imagine the toll it took on this young woman.

In such a harsh world, she had to mature quickly and rebuild her life, all while caring for herself at such a young age.

Tears surface as I type these words. Much pain and suffering are frozen in this moment in time.

Now thawing, they transformed into flash floods capable of sweeping away everything in their path.

Hazel was resilient. She rebuilt her life as best she could.

Years later, she underwent another abortion. This time, it was her own decision.

Memories of loss and betrayal were never far away, always lurking, ready to strike again at any moment.

As time passed, Marco understood her sorrows within the limitations of a man's palette of emotions.

Being part of this story hurt him, as an observer and, ultimately, as the villain.

Does he possess the authority to disclose such personal information?

For the sake of transparency, would he be adding fuel to the fire?

In all likelihood, when she glanced at Marco, she was projecting her hatred for her father, the one who'd murdered her unborn baby.

Other demons would soon join the procession.

She anchored all her resolve and priorities on the tiny figure of Bryce the moment the doctor cut the umbilical cord.
What a weight it must've been on his frail shoulders!

She breastfed Bryce for two-and-a-half years. He slept in the marital bed between his parents.

In the car, Marco was the mere *chauffeur*. Hazel always sat in the back seat in proximity to her son. She ensured her chick's safety by staying close to the nest.

Marco bought a bicycle for his son. Following a few falls, Hazel stored the bike in the garage for good. The list goes on and on.

Of course, Marco perpetuated his own misery.

He became a mere spectator in educating his son. The years kept passing by, like the frames of a third-grade movie.

Hazel was in charge of everything, and Marco often took the path of least resistance.

The wiring of men is different. They are easy to please.

A tasty meal after work, a soccer match, a couple of beers, a *fellatio*, and some nice desserts. That will do the trick.

It should be noted that Hazel was a great cook and pastry chef.

That made for a convenient partnership.

Marco had a sweet tooth. He had always indulged in food, and sugar was both his escape and his nemesis.

He was pretty lazy and didn't lift a finger at home.

He was unaware of the bank balance or credit card debt. If the swimming pump stopped, he was ready to go buy a new one. Whereas Hazel would spend the entire afternoon repairing it.

Hazel filed her own taxes at the year's end to avoid the cost of hiring an accountant.

Yet, she overlooked the creative deductions his co-workers concocted. She had high moral standards.

While Marco was a contrarian, Hazel abided by the status quo.

She was, in fact, a bona fide control freak.

Bryce was a gifted child. An intelligent and sensitive kid.

Due to the lack of spiritual consciousness in that household, I hesitate to label him as an indigo child. Perhaps, once he figures his shit out, he'll be on that path?

People believe that indigo children possess special, and sometimes supernatural, traits or abilities.

As mentioned, he was very perceptive.

On September 11, Hazel and Marco were camping outside of the Cascades National Park in Washington State.

They were having dinner that evening, and the news was on.

They avoided the TV, not wanting to see the troubling images.

Bryce cried non-stop for three hours that evening. It was like he was soaking in all the pain and horror.

Marco had sworn to himself that he would only speak to his son in French, not a word of English. He intended for his son to be fluent in French.
That lasted for six years.

I talked earlier about this age when kids start to have their own personalities. That coincided with the incident in the kitchen when Marco got his face tattooed, as a figure of speech.

Bryce started to ignore him and refused to speak French. Perhaps he was simply a kid not wanting to stand out from his peers at school, but I doubt it.

When speaking French, they had an intimate connection. Hazel was now the outsider.

This interaction didn't fit into the dynamics at play among these three characters. Poor Bryce had no choice but to align himself with his mother.

It was the beginning of the end.

Marco gave up like he'd already given up on pretty much everything else, apart from his thirst for freedom.

The French language, known as *la langue de l'amour*, fell out of favor.

It was fully warranted. Love was scarce in this tale.

Hazel had won another battle, this time with the full participation of her son.

Whether it was conscious, or unconscious didn't make any difference.

This house felt like a prison and Marco wanted out.

He hadn't love nor respect for his jailer. Frankly, he despised her more and more with every passing unit of time.

Days passed, and years lingered. It was a slow and painful descent into no man's land.

Some days, he envisioned waiting until Bryce finished high school.

It would require six more years, with the aura of a twenty-year solitary sentence.

There was a French school in Albuquerque that had a French baccalaureate program.

Bryce could've gone to pursue his studies in France, not a bad thing considering the weaknesses of the American school system.

Marco got vetoed on both fronts with his noble idea.

Bryce became a student at the Albuquerque Institute of Math and Science, a charter school designed for gifted kids. This school welcomed anyone to enroll.

The challenging level and homework, averaging three hours a night, deterred most kids from participating.

It was a perfect match.

Hazel, as usual, ensured timely completion of the homework.

Bryce spent his evenings and half the weekend in his bedroom, studying.

Marco kept his work, his sporting activities, and the remote for his HD TV.

He never set foot in the kitchen except to grab another beer.

He still slept in a king-size bed with his wife. It was awful.

The eerie silence and the lack of intimacy would've tempted any man to cut his wrists and drown in his own blood.

It became the American nightmare. This home was devoid of laughter and anything else that resembled fun.

Hazel never listened to music and didn't have any friends.

No one would dare spoil Bryce, the apple of her eye.

Marco would arrive home late after work and sometimes stay in his car for twenty minutes.

He felt nausea at the thought of seeing her. She made him physically sick.

So, while blasting music on the stereo, he'd replay various scenarios in his head until he found the courage to enter the lioness' cage again.

Her cooking, usually so healthy and delicious, had also started to taste bland and insipid.

His disdain for Hazel had taken hold, like the seeds of a lotus flower germinating in the mud.

It would take a decade for lilies to flower from this container of contempt and resentment.

Following her husband's death, Hazel's mother adopted the lifestyle of a snowbird. In order to escape the winter in Massachusetts, she bought a home that was 200 meters away from her daughter and son-in-law.

She tagged along with them on vacation for the next six years.

Regardless of her always being nice to Marco, who knows what discussions occurred in private between Hazel and her?

It was too close for comfort. Ultimately, he wanted to end his marriage with both the mother and the daughter.

The big impediment is that most of our thoughts originate from our subconscious.

According to neuroscientist and author Dr. Joe Dispenza, the human brain receives 400 billion bits (47 megabytes) of information every second.

Of those, we're only consciously aware of 2,000 bits (0.0002 megabytes).

Those who have access to more information are the gurus of our civilization.

Many of us are left with choosing (albeit unconsciously) the neurotic thoughts that match the drama surrounding our stories.

Marco explored the world, eager to learn new modalities and gain knowledge.

It was becoming clear that his mind wasn't the answer.

Now, he was in the lowlands of the Peruvian Amazon, ready to rise like a phoenix from its ashes.

The heart center is the bridge between our three lower and three higher chakras.

He knew the fire ceremony belonged at the altar of his heart.

THIRTY-THREE

"The only devils in the world are those running around in our hearts. That is where the battle should be fought."

— GANDHI.

Since Marco had experimented with Ayahuasca in Mexico, he knew deep inside that the solution to his predicaments lay somewhere in South America.

One needs to hear the calling of medicinal plants, however faint it may be. There's no other way.

Three major things could hamper your experience: your ego, your fears, and the Judeo-Christian demonization of the sacred plants.

Please don't let your ego convince you that you're not hearing the call. That clever fellow will do anything to sabotage your evolution.

Now, if you have bipolar disorder, schizophrenia, or depression, and you take psychotic medication, it would be wise for you to completely avoid Ayahuasca or use extreme caution.

You also don't want to read too many internet stories.

As Ayahuasca has become more mainstream, it's had its share of dishonest and abusive operators.

The key is to do your research before you embark on your journey to the Amazon.

As I share Marco's experiences with you, please remember that I'm not suggesting, in any way, that you should abandon your spouse or career in order to reinvent yourself in the jungle.

Marco was a lost soul in tattered clothes. He needed mending.

His first six weeks in Peru were nothing short of a transcending experience.

The Shipibo-Konibo is an indigenous tribe along the Ucayali River, in the Amazon rainforest in Peru.

Their shamans offer master plant (or tree) *dietas,* which go way beyond the traditional Ayahuasca ceremonies.

This is a traditional process of connecting with the spirits of the plants, enabling the plant to share its teachings and wisdom with the students, who are referred to as *pasajeros* or passengers.

Plant *dietas* require a strict nutritional diet and a commitment of four weeks.

There are a variety of different master plants to choose from, based on your particular situation.

Marco was advised to do a *dieta de Bobinsana*. Since he'd heard the calling loud and clear and time was on his side, he signed in for six weeks.

Bobinsana (Calliandra angustifolia) is a tree that produces bright pink starburst flowers.

It's a powerful shamanic plant, deeply respected among the indigenous people of the Amazon.

This beautiful, divine, and feminine master plant is famous for its ability to open your heart to love. It also has strong spiritual cleansing and balancing properties and will help strengthen and protect your energy field.

When dieting Bobinsana, you'll also receive a lot of healing, growth, and wisdom in areas such as your immune system physical, mental, and emotional traumas.

In cultivating self-awareness, respect, love, connection, gratitude, humility, peace, patience, kindness, truth, and empathy, you'll enhance various aspects of your life.

From an energetic perspective, these herbs will introduce a heart-centered sense of calm into your being, allowing you to reflect and stretch your roots.

With the complex demands that many people face in the world these days, it's common for the emotional body not to receive proper attention.

For this reason, Bobinsana is often recommended as a first *dieta* to help you open up your suppressed emotions and connect more deeply to your heart's innate wisdom.

Three months minimum was required for a tree diet.

André van de Braak, a professor of comparative philosophy of religion in Amsterdam, wrote in his book 'Ayahuasca as Liquid Divinity':

"You are not drinking a plant that allows you to see spirits. You are drinking spirits in a liquid form. Ayahuasca is a spirit, millions of spirits, turned into liquid for you to drink. When you drink those spirits, you are actually choosing to host them into your body. That's why you have to diet. Prepare a space acceptable enough for them to be in and comfortable enough for them to get to work. That's why diets can be very strict sometimes. You are actually inviting people into your body, and these guys are trees."

Marco was already thinking about returning to the Amazon to do a tree diet.

Inviting spirits or trees into his body wasn't an issue for him, as long as they supported his soul's growth and psychological health.

A doubt had been cast in Marco's mind halfway through the retreat regarding the topic of authenticity.

Workers were on the roof of one of the *tambos*, replacing the Nipa palm leaves.

When spotting a boa swimming in the creek, one of the men proceeded to kill it using a long spear.

They severed its head with a machete, abandoning it by the creek.

Aum happened to walk by a few minutes later, and the boa was still alive with its head half chopped off.

He swiftly put an end to the snake's misery by fetching his machete from his tambo.

Marco had always associated Ayahuasca with snakes. The available literature was sufficient to support it, along with the Kundalini energy, which was depicted as a snake uncoiling from the bottom of your spine.

During one powerful ceremony, he had enchanting visions of snakes parading around the *maloca*, adorned with headdresses made of wildflowers. A vibrant spectacle he attributed to the synergy between Ayahuasca and Bobinsana.

The following night, he found himself alone with both shamans. After taking the medicine, he saw the opportunity to have an intelligent conversation with them regarding the incident with the snake.

"Why do you let animals suffer in this manner?" asked Marco, a little perplexed.

The shamans raved about the boas not being animals but monsters. In the darkness, they came and took away their little ones. They were the devil incarnate.

"What about their souls?" retorted Marco.

"Boas don't have souls," responded the male shaman.

Marco went on to ask him: *"Do other forest animals have souls?"*

He replied in an empathic manner: *"No."*

This same man boasted about having lived alone in the jungle for ten years studying medicinal plants. Now Marco was smelling a rat!

Soon, the conversation turned to human beings. *"What about our souls? Where do we go after death?"*

This experienced Shipibo shaman claimed that no one possessed a soul, whether they were humans, animals, or plants. After we die, we either ascend to heaven or descend to hell.

He was adamant about reaching heaven while the boa was already burning in hell.

Oddly enough, it sounded like a weekly catechism class Marco attended when he was a kid.

He was cognizant that Franciscans and other missionaries had been evangelizing to the indigenous population since the 16th century.

Still, that point of view was far too witless for him at this stage, especially given the circumstances.

Snakes are sacred in Hinduism, Buddhism and Jainism, especially the Naga or hooded cobra. Anacondas aren't too far behind, in Marco's eyes.

In Christian and Islamic myths, they represent evil. The serpent tempts Eve to eat the forbidden fruit, resulting in Adam and Eve's expulsion from heaven.

At the end of the six-week retreat, his friends Aum and Montserrat had a few days off.

They wanted to keep their options for the future open, while they longed to connect with an authentic and powerful shaman.

So, they embarked on a three-day trip and visited a couple of retreat centers.

They met Darwin when he came to the retreat. He performed a couple of ceremonies with them.

They liked him. He had a powerful voice and a good heart.

They were particularly interested in his mother, Maestra Juana.

Isa Yaka was born into the Shipibo community of Pahoyan, one of the most powerful Shipibo healing lineages in the Peruvian Amazon. She is sixty-eight years old.

She has a husband and eight children.

For many years, she's studied with her uncles, Papa Pascual, and Papa Benjamin, as well as with her aunt Manuela.

All of them are members of the highly respected Curandero family, the Mahua family.

Juana began her first Noya Rao *dieta* with her father, when she was fifteen years old, and has dedicated her life to the path of healing ever since. She once dieted Noya Rao for four straight years.

She sang a couple of *icaros* for them in an enthralling voice.

Marco asked Darwin which would be the best tree for him to diet.

He looked back at him a little bemused as if he'd said something sacrilegious, and answered without a hint of hesitation: "*Noya Rao.*"

Nine months later, Marco was back in Pucallpa for a three-month retreat with Darwin and his mother, Juana. The long quest to open his heart fully was well underway.

It was also time to finish the book that he'd started at the beginning of the Camino de Santiago, a year and a half prior to that.

He had found out that walking twenty-two kilometers and

writing a book on the same day was not too compatible. Hence, he had put the project on the shelf until further notice.

Now, the opportunity to do a three-month master tree diet with Noya Rao was going to be realized. He would take advantage of all the privacy and the free time that he had to write for a few hours each day.

The dynamics between Noya Rao, Ayahuasca, and his life story promised to be compelling.

People have traveled the world to get their hands on the extremely rare master tree of pure light, Noya Rao.

It's the most sacred tree in the Shipibo tradition because of its ability to connect you with Divine realms and beings and fill you with pure love and light.

It's the king of all master plants and holds all of their worlds within its sacred universe.

With the right guidance, this tree provides a beautiful journey to what some call 'enlightenment'.

Noya Rao encompasses the wisdom of all the other master plants. Together with Bobinsana, they form an enchanting symbiotic relationship.

The existence of the Noya Rao was forgotten, while the Shipibo-Konibo oral tradition lost influence and disappeared because of European colonization that began in the mid-1600s.

The tree hasn't yet been classified botanically. It grew legendary as it disappeared from the landscape and from the collective memory of most for many years.

These retreats aren't for the fainthearted.

However, after tasting from the silver cup, it will compel you to return, not out of necessity, but because you've glimpsed a clarity beyond this world.

Imagine a giant tree living in the Amazon rainforest, its branches climbing to the heavens and its roots reaching down to the center of the Earth.

Let's plug this solitary tree into the wood-wide web (the concept of an interconnected forest has evoked comparisons with the internet), and add to it all the animals and insects that visit the tree or make it their home.

The tree, along with the network of fungi that binds all trees and plants, is an integral part of the miracle of creation, just like its fruit, flowers, and seeds.

Have you ever walked in the forest, sat, and meditated next to a giant tree?

Have you tried leaning your head against its trunk and listening to its heartbeat?

Doesn't this tree contain, in its entirety, all the codes of the universe?

What if you could discover the secrets of life by merging with a tree? Your blood and the tree's sap intertwined, your parasympathetic system in harmony with its wisdom?

Entrain your own energy to the pure, powerful energy of nature.

The Japanese call it *Shinrin-Yoku*, which stands for bathing in the forest.

Welcome to the Shipibo Noya Rao diet.

Darwin claimed that his Noya Rao had been macerating for two years, although Marco came to realize with time that the Shipibo could blur the lines of reality.

He had been drinking a glass every afternoon for the past six weeks.

Then there were the Ayahuasca ceremonies, fifteen times a month. Two days on, two days off.

I believe it created a direct pathway to God Himself, compelling all the elves and forest spirits to take residence in your consciousness.

He was only halfway through his diet, and the seeds of this sacred tree, which only existed in small numbers, were slowly taking root at the heart of his being.

The Mahua family and other Shipibo shamans have been guarding this tree, but they keep their location secret for obvious reasons.

I understand if you're skeptical, but please don't tell Maestra Juana. As I said, she started a Noya Rao diet at fifteen and has helped many with their diets for over twenty years.

In addition, Darwin told Marco that forest workers had seen light escaping from the tree canopy at night.

During the day, however, they couldn't find the source of this light.

Even if you were to walk through the jungle at night, which isn't a good idea, and miraculously came across a Noya Rao, you wouldn't see the luminescent light coming from the leaves – unless you'd already dieted the tree or had the purest of hearts and intentions.

I had read articles about bioluminescent fungi in the Amazon, but that wouldn't explain anything about the legend of Noya Rao.

That makes the story almost mythical and adds an element of exclusivity to this tradition.

On the one hand, Marco didn't mind.

He hadn't come all this way to remain inside the square box of his mind.

Darwin had shown him enough evidence of this tree's existence to convince him he was privileged to be there and take part in this experience.

It's a blessing to be able to sit down with these maestros of the Mahua lineage.

Most of the younger generation have lost interest in the healing arts, preferring to belong to the Western world with its attractions and temptations.

They're not connected to plants and spirits from an early age. The Shipibo-Konibo tradition of medicinal plants, in its original form, may no longer exist soon.

Every day, loggers and cattle farmers cut down 10,000 acres of virgin rainforest for timber and grazing.

Researchers suggest that there may be tens of thousands of plants in the Amazon basin that are yet to be discovered.

How many of these plants could cure physical ailments, let alone the psychological illnesses of our modern age?

Since Marco was on his own quest in Peru in order to open his heart and learn forgiveness, he couldn't help making parallels with 'The Celestine Prophecy' by James Redfield:

"You see, the problem in life isn't in receiving answers. The problem is in identifying your current questions. Once you get the questions right, the answers always come."

- Give credence to serendipity:

"The first insight occurs when we become conscious of the coincidence of our lives... These coincidences make us feel there is something more, something spiritual, operating underneath everything we do."

Marco learned to go with the flow and look for the messages behind every event, encounter, and coincidence.

- Embrace the energy of nature:

Researchers estimate that there could be 390 billion trees in the Amazon. Here, he was doing a diet of Noya Rao, a rare tree that hadn't been classified yet.

-Reconnect and focus on spiritual growth instead of economic growth:

He had lived the American Dream for thirty years. Only it had turned into a nightmare.

He had traveled for three years in Asia, trying to gain a little consciousness. Now, he was ready to leave his ego on the curb and commingle with the spirits of the forest.

- Understand and let go of the past:

"According to the manuscript, we all must spend as much time as necessary going through this process of clearing your past."

The Peruvian government declared Ayahuasca a National Treasure in 2008.

He never second-guessed whether he was in the right place, for he knew in the deepest recesses of his heart that he was where he belonged.

-Find your purpose and go after your mission:

Each of us has a spiritual purpose or mission, which we may not have been fully aware of. Bringing it into consciousness can propel our lives forward.

Marco hadn't found his purpose yet, at least not at the beginning of his diet.

It had been a lifelong process. His task now was to synthesize the information from the Gods and allow the seeds of Noya Rao to sprout inside his heart. Some say it could take up to five years for these seeds to turn into saplings.

CHAPTER
THIRTY-FOUR

"It is said that before entering the sea
a river trembles with fear.

She looks back at the path she has traveled,
from the peaks of the mountains,
the long winding road crossing forests and villages.
And in front of her,
she sees an ocean so vast,
that to enter
there seems nothing more than to disappear forever.

But there is no other way.

The river can not go back.

Nobody can go back.

To go back is impossible in existence.

The river needs to take the risk

of entering the ocean
because only then will fear disappear,
because that's where the river will know
it's not about disappearing into the ocean,
but of becoming the ocean."

— KHALIL GIBRAN.

Patanjali wrote the first book on yoga in the 2nd century BC. The Yoga Sūtras of Patañjali are a collection of 196 Sanskrit sutras (aphorisms) on the theory and practice of yoga.

In the Indian tradition, the sutras describe the means of attaining spiritual power and occult abilities.

Siddhayah (spiritual accomplishments) arise from birth, herbs, incantation, asceticism, and contemplation (section 4, verse 1).

The Yoga-sūtra and Hindu Yoga and Tantra texts describe siddhis (paranormal powers) possessed by a Siddha, an ascetic who has received enlightenment, as ways of knowing and acting. These powers include flying, enhanced vision, invisibility, and a profound understanding of one's body and the cosmos.

Since Marco was sometimes conflicted in his beliefs of self-realization, he found a little validation in seeking spiritual powers in the Amazon. He believed that the paths of asceticism or contemplation could take many lifetimes. He was running out of time.

Throughout the spiritual and religious history of humanity, many cultures have used herbs (psychoactive plants) in this way.

We shouldn't overlook the potential role it plays in bridging the conscious and the unconscious. By keeping in mind the principles of non-attachment and achieving a natural state of mind, herbs can be utilized to help remove barriers.

Archaeological evidence has been found of the use of San Pedro and Ayahuasca for magical-religious purposes in pre-Columbian cultures, as early as 1500 BC.

Strands of human hair from a 3,000-year-old burial site in Spain contained traces of three different alkaloid substances that were known to cause altered states of consciousness.

THIRTY-FIVE

"Everything is either an opportunity to grow or an obstacle to keep from growing."

— WAYNE DYER.

Marco had applied for *Sadhanapada*, a seven-month program designed by Sadhguru at his ashram in Tamil Nadu, starting in July 2024 and leading to *Mahashivatri*, a festival of worship for the Hindu god Shiva.

Last time at the ashram, he submitted his application, but the program got canceled because of COVID-19.

With tens of thousands of people applying, he knew his chances of being chosen were slim.

Especially since the program didn't cost a cent and the participants would benefit from the support of Sadhguru.

Each year, they apparently select up to 1,200 dedicated individuals from over thirty different countries.

He didn't quite fit the demographics, which minimized the odds of being selected.

His intention was to keep applying every year. The universe would favor his application if it was to be part of his master plan.

This would be his greatest life challenge.

He couldn't think of anything harder that required more energy and dedication.

Marco knew the layout of the ashram.

A typical day will keep you occupied for thirteen hours. That included eight hours of service, three hours of yoga, and walking long distances around the ashram itself.

Now imagine adding another four hours daily to that schedule, with more yoga and meditation and various other supervised activities.

Marco was living an active lifestyle filled with *farniente* (do nothing in Italian).

Would he be willing to sacrifice his comfort for 3,672 hours of supervised calls to action?

By all accounts, they turn the lights off at 9.30 p.m., and the *Sadhanapada* members wake up between 3.30 a.m. and 4.30 a.m. every day for 216 consecutive days.

It's a rigorous program on a strict schedule and they keep you on a tight leash.

"Exactly what this snarling rescue pet needed!" (to paraphrase Robert Downey Jr. during his Oscar speech for best-supporting actor).

Who said you can't teach an old dog new tricks? Marco was the living proof you could change your paradigms.

He was already planning to get in yoga shape before July.

He aimed to keep his mind occupied and his body engaged during that stage of his life.

Since this book kept dragging into the future, Marco had the opportunity to volunteer at the ashram for a few weeks after writing these last words and not having been accepted into the program.

While scrutinizing the new group of *Sadhanapada* participants for the longest time in the pouring rain, he had the uncanny feeling that he was already an active part of the experience.

The rain appeared to be falling in slow motion, making him wonder whether the scene was indeed real or whether linear time had been frozen in its tracks.

He also concluded after elaborate calculations that his odds of being selected in future programs were only 0.25%. This dismal percentage put a smile on his face.

It occurred to him that your presence in physical form may not be required to impact future events concerning the same time frame and location.

Could you create an experience solely in your mind and watch it ripple on the surface of time like a stone thrown into a bottomless pit?

The past, present, and future would loop endlessly, thus having no start or finish.

It shed light on the concept of making amends for his past, and filled Marco with hope and contentment. Plus, it opened new possibilities for his atonement.

As an added bonus, he would no longer be obligated to wake up at 3.30 a.m. every morning. That would be a relief!

At times, he found the messages at the ashram overly self-serving, especially within the specter of potential abuse of power.

Marco couldn't be blamed, as he had a lingering sense of *déjà vu* in his gut, similar to a kid who'd burned his fingers on a stove and quickly learned his lesson.

Not being a hardcore devotee, he had the luxury of observing things and retaining the right to be critical.

Without a doubt, the whole enterprise operated like a well-oiled marketing machine.

The guru's talks were characterized by an overall theme of devotion. In one of his videos, he stated that it was crucial to follow a one-track path solely with your mind, which could be heartbreaking at times.

In his eyes, this was akin to heresy.

Marco was aligned with Paulo Coelho's quote:

"Remember that wherever your heart is, there you will find your treasure."

He wasn't about to betray his passions and parade shirtless around the ashram for a couple of hours like a member of the Red Army, mechanically repeating : "*Shambho, shambho...*"

Now, repeating this exercise three times a week for seven months would indeed break his wings.

He fancied himself as a free-flowing butterfly, pollinating colorful flowers. He had worked too much on opening up his heart to be single-minded on an ascetic path, devoid of creativity and compassion.

An intensive program of nineteen days called '*Devi Seva*' was about to start in the temple of Linga Bhairavi, and he was fortunate to have been selected for it.

He had to do a bit of convincing. They probably underestimated his ability to keep up with the kids from Gen Z.

Bhairavi is the all-encompassing, creative, and primal force of the universe. As the consort of Shiva, the embodiment of the Divine Feminine had 108 names, including Durga, Parvati, Bhargavi and Annapurna.

Now Marco was in his territory. His quest to honor the divine feminine and expiate his misogynistic tendencies, had been his long-time pursuit.

What a glorious opportunity to share the new-found bounty in his heart with the Goddess he knew as Adi Shakti.

Back at his first yoga festival in the mountains of New-Mexico, he had one session with a clairvoyant. When he probed her about the future woman of his life, she bluntly answered: "*You should focus on Adi Shakti instead.*"

He didn't ask much for himself. With a much grander scale in mind, he focused on forgiving all the people in this world who abused women.

An average of nearly ninety rapes a day were reported in India in 2022, according to data from India's National Crime Records Bureau (NCRB).

Now imagine all the assaults that weren't reported.

Throughout his travels, Marco had a sixth sense for women who'd been abused sexually. He could see the reflection of his closed heart in their gaze.

He intuited that most of them had never forgiven their assailants.

Marco, in his efforts to help the victims of sexual crimes, spent a lot of his time asking Bhairavi to help them forgive themselves, first and foremost.

It was no simple achievement to understand the magnitude and the significance of such an endeavor. If anyone did, Adi Shakti was the one who had the ability to bring it off.

"Kundalini Mata Shakti, namo, namo."

"I bow to the Divine Mother of all Peace."

Marco was exhilarated by the devotion he witnessed at the temple during his *Seva.*

The attention to details pertaining to the running of the temple's activities and performing of all the rituals left him bedazzled.

All the colors, the scents and the sounds emanating from the temple merged into a pink aura of love and grace.

Kali, also known as Uma on her benevolent side, had, as always, triumphed over the wickedness of men.

Soon, it was time to depart from the ashram.

It's crucial to acknowledge the delicate balance between devotion and fanaticism, as well as between rhetoric and manipulation.

The danger lies in the influence that a powerful and charismatic, all-encompassing guru could have on their disciples. If history could teach us a lesson, it would be wise to avoid tunnel-vision thinking and develop a sense of detachment.

Be more like the Buddha.

THIRTY-SIX

"We are all in the gutter, but some of us are looking at the stars."

— OSCAR WILDE.

Marco met a young man named Andrew at the Kundalini Yoga festival in Florida. He had just graduated from a teacher' training course in Bali.

They soon became good friends.

Marco shared his desire to travel to India and study Sattva Yoga in an ashram near Rishikesh.

During a two-day yoga festival in Albuquerque, he had the chance to attend an impressive class taught by a long-time student of the guru.

Fast forward five years. Marco was in his rented house in Corsica one evening when Andrew contacted him on WhatsApp. He hadn't heard from him since Florida.

Marco had spent three days at the ashram near Rishikesh after the COVID-19 lockdown. He had taken a couple of classes, but the ashram had suspended all the teacher' training courses. The guru hadn't been to the ashram in a year.

It turned out Andrew had followed Marco's advice closely. He had gone to the ashram on three different occasions to study with the guru.

He had also learned the Indian horoscope science Jyotish, the *'Eyes of the Vedas and the Light of the Divine.'*

They agreed to do a reading online a few days later.

Andrew's knowledge and wisdom impressed Marco.

While talking about his birth chart and planetary positions, Marco realized the person he was and the person he was becoming. It was eerie.

He had a strong and passionate energy to live life.

There would be challenges around sexuality that also involved addictions.

He needed to regulate his emotions and would be confused about his sense of purpose.

His Moon was in Scorpio, always moving, searching, and transforming instead of settling down.

He was blessed to have a sharp insight and intuition.

Andrew reiterated that Marco had been in his Rahu period for several years. He had been busy expanding his consciousness and reconnecting to his heart.

We are born with our inherent traits and tendencies, but we have the power to rise above them.

You just need a little awareness.

Even though everything is written in the stars, we retain the power to shape our own story.

We aren't mere individuals but threads woven into life's tapestry of existence.

THIRTY-SEVEN

"Only in the agony of parting do we look into the depths of love."

— GEORGE ELIOTT.

Marco saw his son after the New Year.

They agreed to meet in Fort Lauderdale, Florida, and spend one week together in the Everglades.

He had invited him a few times from different locales around the world.

For a variety of reasons that Marco couldn't control, Bryce had failed to show up every single time.

Six years had passed since their last encounter.

He was just a few months shy of turning twenty-three.

He was in the early stage of his fourth seven-year period of consciousness. This marks the legal drinking age, leaving home for college, and making it on his own.

In the meantime, he'd graduated with a Bachelor of Science degree in accounting.

During a residency program with a law firm in Houston, he realized that filing taxes for wealthy people wasn't his destiny. Nor was socializing with his co-workers at the firm in order to score points for future promotions.

During his stint at college, he'd created an online poker club. According to him, when he plays poker, the probability of victory is 60%. It becomes more math than luck.

It dawned on Marco that he was rebelling against his mother by turning his back on conservative activities.

He inherited his anti-corporate America stance from his father, which wasn't a bad thing.

They had been strangers to each other throughout his adolescent years.

Erasing the past is impossible in this dimension. I can only hope that this book will be the catalyst for a deeper relationship between father and son.

I wrote this story to foster empathy for everyone involved, beginning with Bryce, rather than ostracizing his mother from his life.

In their hearts, I wish they'd find the resolve to forgive Marco.

Only by rising above the lingering feelings of betrayal and anguish, would they seek solace in the spirit of forgiveness.

"In the hope of seeing you again soon, my son, and share some laughs."

THIRTY-EIGHT

"Illusion is needed to disguise the emptiness within."

— ARTHUR ERICKSON.

The GR 20 is a long distance hiking trail that traverses the Mediterranean island of Corsica, diagonally from Calenzana in the north to Conca in the south.

The 200-kilometer trail follows the granite backbone of mountains that divides the island in two. It comprises sixteen stages among peaks that soar over 2,000 meters in altitude.

People hype it up as the toughest trek in Europe.

Unless you completed two or even three stages every single day, it wasn't that extreme, but being fit and fearless of heights would be advisable.

In the genuine sense of the word, it was spectacular, offering sights and smells that defied the imagination.

Marco found Corsica's beauty and ruggedness astonishing.

He had never been so in tune with his surroundings and in awe with nature. The physical challenge added sparks to the fire.

The diet in Peru had sharpened all his senses and magnified all his perceptions.

He fell in love with Corsica. His faith in France had been restored since being here.

Knowing the island's history, he should be cautious not to offend the locals with such a statement.

The setting was perfect for reading 'A Return to Love' by Marianne Williamson, an American author and political activist.

As of now, she remains a Democratic Party candidate for the 2024 U.S. elections.

The book contains her reflections on 'A Course in Miracles' by Helen Schucman. It shares her insights in applying love in the search for inner peace.

A glorious concept that meshed perfectly with the rugged landscape.

Akin to opening a jewel box full of gems; I will only share a few with you:

"Our deepest fear is not that we are inadequate. Our deepest fear is that we are powerful beyond measure. It is our light, not our darkness, that most frightens us. We ask ourselves: "Who am I to be brilliant, gorgeous, talented, fabulous?" Actually, who are you not to be? You are a child of God. Your playing small does not serve the world."

"There is nothing enlightened about shrinking so that other people won't feel insecure around you. We are all meant to shine, as children do. We were born to manifest the glory of God that is within us. It's not just in some of us; it's in everyone. And as we let our own light shine, we unconsciously give other people permission to do the same. As we are liberated from our own fear, our presence automatically liberates others."

"Our self-perception determines our behavior. If we think we're small, limited, inadequate creatures, then we tend to behave that way, and the energy we radiate reflects those thoughts no matter what we do. If we think we're magnificent creatures with an infinite abundance of love and power to give, then we tend to behave that way. Once again, the surrounding energy reflects our state of awareness."

CHAPTER
THIRTY-NINE

*"I would rather live my life as if there is a God and die to find
out there isn't, than live as if there isn't and die to find out
that there is."*

— ALBERT CAMUS.

Marco was talking with a British expat who'd built a hotel
and restaurant on the Panamanian Pacific coast sixteen
years ago.

Of Malaysian descent, he was a reputed chef in the area.

Marco liked teasing him. Even though he believed it was pointless
to reason with such a stubborn man, he continued to do so.

Soon, the conversation went to energy, souls, and doing good
deeds.

He was a likable fellow but excessively stuck in his ways.

Marco enjoyed provoking thoughts in people to shift perspectives and stimulate awareness.

Often, their ego got in the way, that was their self-defense mechanism.

Marco discussed the possibility of achieving peace in a different dimension, based on Einstein's premise that for every action, there is a reaction and the law of Karma.

The host proceeded to question the purpose of good deeds in this life with a hint of sarcasm, suggesting he could do them in future lives if reincarnated.

Marco's response was uncomplicated.

He had no desire to return, regardless of the shape or place, to understand the lessons he'd struggled with in this life.

A mere ninety years seemed absurd when faced with the prospect of eternity. The small taste of eternal peace he'd experienced far surpassed those earthly pleasures that kept human beings in delusion.

CHAPTER

FORTY

"To err is human, to forgive is divine."

— ALEXANDER POPE.

Recently, Marco was having dinner with his brother and sister. To speak kindly, Bernard's understanding of life is in alignment with his simple and unenlightened lifestyle.

It was no surprise that their wine consumption was excessive on that particular evening.

Marco always liked to bring new concepts into the discussion. Despite his doubts, he believed he could eventually speak in a way his brother would understand. If you don't challenge the people with whom you share the same blood, what's family for?

Bernard, feeling cornered at one point, declared: *"I have my convictions."*

240

When Marco asked him to elaborate, he reiterated that he held onto his convictions — as if they were something valuable to be locked away in a trophy case. According to the dictionary, a conviction is a strong opinion or belief.

Marco acknowledged, in a simple statement, that his convictions weren't grounded in reality and compared it to digging his own grave.

Bernard finds grace and salvation in being a musician. He is equally skilled in playing the piano, guitar, bass, and drums. Had he possessed the gumption and creativity to transcend his limited view of existence, he could have been a one-man band.

Later in the evening, Bernard began to rave about his ex, calling her names.

Despite the fact that they'd been divorced for over twenty years, it still lingered in his mind and clouded his judgment.

Marco stated that he should've forgiven her and moved on with his life a long time ago.

Bernard mentioned her drug addiction and psychotic personality while facing all the hurdles she placed in front of him regarding their son.

He would never forgive her under any circumstances.

During all this time, Bernard's love life had been non-existent. Are you still wondering why?

By constantly dwelling on negative thoughts and verbalizing them, he'd been subjecting himself to punishment all along. In both instances, he chastised himself for both the harm done and his obsession with not relinquishing that pain.

He refused to acknowledge the connection between his attitude and his current situation.

Arielle tried to support Marco in this argument but it was all in vain.

FORTY-ONE

"I am not an Athenian or a Greek, but a citizen of the world."

— SOCRATES.

Marco prefers not to disclose his place of origin.

People often wonder about this question first. It's an automatism and a way to put a label on somebody based on pre-set impressions that's customary in North America.

Besides, he spent enough time in India, where everyone you met wanted to shake your hand, even more so during COVID-19. There were fewer foreigners traveling around, and they asked you the same five questions over and over:

"Where are you from?"
  "How old are you?"
  "What do you do for money?"
  "Are you married?"
  "Are you traveling alone?"

Marco's mind danced with innovative ideas as he dodged these queries.

He claimed to be a nomad, belonging to no country.

When pressed about a specific place of birth or passport, he would retort: *"I have a nomad passport."*

A lot of folks would appear confused, that was the whole point.

Sadhguru describes a nomad as somebody who *'was no(t) mad'*, a person who kept moving on and didn't settle anywhere.

Marco said that he was ancient. He traveled in the company of God, and his money came from the sky. This wasn't too far from the truth.

He discovered it was a good way to create an enigmatic persona.

He was, after all, different from others and the non-conforming type.

In India or other Asian countries, solo travelers always spark curiosity, since most people there travel with family or in groups.

Marco will be completing a two-year cycle by soon returning to India, where he'll be able to examine the various aspects of his life that prevented him from finding peace and start making adjustments.

You could encapsulate the previous two years in a time capsule and send it to outer space, circulating in orbit.

It probably wouldn't land back on Earth for a few decades, such was the transformative power of those past events.

FORTY-TWO

"A nation will not survive morally or economically when so few have so much and so many have so little."

— BERNIE SANDERS.

Marco saw a street post that said: *"It's not paradise if the people can't afford to live here."*

This has become a serious concern in the touristy or crowded places around our planet.

Real estate keeps rising in prices. The old supply and demand paradox.

The cost of living is out of sync with the wages.

Starting in America, and slowly spreading throughout the world like a plague, the middle class has been steadily shrinking.

The rich continue to amass fortunes while the poor remain destitute. This is the curse of a capitalist system gone astray.

When you travel, you have to take care of the main three considerations: accommodation, food, and transportation. It can become expensive and tiresome.

Marco had it all figured out, though.

A camper van with a motorcycle in tow would solve these problems. Having a house on wheels and returning to his gypsy roots, could there be a more suitable option for him?

When he was in Costa Rica for the first time, he rented a Toyota 4×4 with a foldable tent on the roof for six weeks. That was a thrill he can't wait to replicate.

In 2026, he plans to upgrade his way of traveling. Skipping hotels and restaurants would be a great change, allowing him to slow down if desired and to cook his own food.

An optional raising roof will give extra space, in case friends or family members want to tag along.

He intends to travel all around Europe and venture as far east as Mongolia.

Once he is done, he fancies traveling from Mexico all the way down to Patagonia and returning to Europe from South Africa upwards.

His first shaman in Mexico had told him about some of his former lives.

He had been a rugged explorer in Africa, with deep and piercing blue eyes. That would be a return to the source, as such.

Unfortunately, the only thing he wished he'd inherited from his father were his blue eyes.

He had also experienced various other lives such as a Shaolin monk, a snake charmer in India, and Merlin's apprentice.

When Marco attempted to learn the flute, it became evident that he couldn't recall any of his previous lives, as opposed to Sadhguru, who claims to remember three of his former lives.

His martial arts teachers would also vouch for that fact.

Recently, Arielle was teasing Marco about how he followed in the footsteps of their father.

Furthermore, she mentioned that he had an insatiable thirst for high-risk sports activities, women, and exotic travel. Or could it be: travel and exotic women?

"The apple doesn't fall far from the tree."

FORTY-THREE

"No tree, it is said, can grow to heaven unless its roots reach down to hell."

— CARL JUNG.

Despite Marco rehearsing his separation for over five years, Hazel probably never saw it coming and seemed in total distress about it.

She made a few attempts to take control of the situation and restore some common sense to her husband, who had clearly gone astray.

When everything failed, her demands became a little delusional.

Money was a concern like in any divorce, but the main issue revolved around the custody of Bryce. She dreaded leaving him in such irresponsible hands.

Marco wasn't too keen to let that woman get all her wishes. Ego and frustration had a lot to do with it, with an added touch of revenge to spice up the ordeal. Mainly, he fantasized about reconnecting with his son.

He set a meeting with a divorce lawyer in Albuquerque who his friend Danny had recommended.

From his office, you could see the Sandia mountains stretch into the distance.

Robin would've been difficult not to like. He was a middle-aged Zimbabwean of European descent who had immigrated to the States. He carried himself with a confident yet laid-back demeanor and had a British sense of humor.

After enduring a long and unhappy marriage, he divorced his wife. Shortly after, he discovered the woman of his dreams.

As convenient as this story would've been for his sales pitch, it turned out to be true.

When Marco met his second wife months later at a party, they had the aura of a blessed couple.

Marco was sold when Robin drew on a piece of paper:

DIVORCE = FREEDOM.

He was a no-nonsense kind of lawyer, savvy, with a lot of experience.

Weeks passed before he met Hazel for their first clients and lawyers' meeting.

Hazel's lawyer, in contrast to Robin's detached reliance, seemed overly nervous and aggressive.

Was it because Marco was behaving like an immature jerk, or because she was identifying too much with her neurotic client?

When they took a break outside, and Robin was lighting a cigarette, he turned to Marco and deadpanned: "*You have been married to 'That Thing' for twenty-eight years?*"

Truth be told, Marco behaved like a 'prick' in the months following his separation.

He cut down all communication with Hazel and let his bad temper run the show.

In her book *'The Dark Side of the Light Chasers,'* Debbie Ford has an enlightening exercise that pairs our defects with a first name starting with the same letter.

You have to turn that defect into a quality opposite each grouping.

I'm sharing Marco's list with you, hoping you'll be able to relate to it.

- Arrogant Adam
Learn how to be humble

- Aggressive Allan
Be more friendly and laid back

- Bastard Benoit
Become a better person, open up your heart

- Condescending Cori
Show respect to others

- Critical Chris

Don't mirror your defects onto others

- Destructive Daniel
Become creative

- Dirty Dick
Learn integrity

- Egomaniac Eloy
Transcend your ego

- Inconsiderate Ignacio
Have empathy and be of service to others

- Jealous Jeremy
Don't be a five-year-old spoiled kid

- Judgmental Jude
We are one; who are you to judge?

- Mean Martin
Be kind

- Negative Noah
Change your inner dialogue, look for the silver linings

- Perverted Peter
Work on sex addictions

- Selfish Sasha
Do good for people

- Sarcastic Sam
Show courtesy

- Unfaithful Ulysses

Be loyal

- Violent Victor
Equanimity, self-love

It's a shock at first when you write your list.

It can be demoralizing to read about yourself in such an unflattering way. Then, you slowly realize that this is all part of your evolution.

There's real magic in this alchemical process.

It would take nearly a decade before Marco learned how to embrace his darker side.

In 'Psychology and Alchemy', Carl Jung wrote:

"One does not become enlightened by imagining figures of light, but by making the darkness conscious."

FORTY-FOUR

"Love is my lifelong obsession, joy, adobe, and torment."

— DEBASISH MRIDHA.

Prior to his journey to Mexico and his initial exploration of medicinal plants, he'd reached out to a retreat center in Ecuador.

The retreat had hundreds of glowing reviews.

He felt it was a foregone conclusion that he'd go there someday. It was one of those certainties that shone in the sky among the stars.

He had returned to the Galápagos islands, this time to go scuba diving on a Liveaboard. It turned out to be a magical experience.

Imagine being on a boat for eight days, cruising to the farther-out islands. They dove three or four times a day, sometimes among a group of Hammerhead sharks.

He had another month before starting his three-month diet in Peru.

He booked a twelve-day retreat at that center before hiking the Salkantay trek near Cusco. He figured that they would be good precursors to his Noya Rao diet.

Marco had heard about the Eagle and the Condor prophecy that spoke of human societies splitting into two paths: that of the Eagle and that of the Condor.

It's difficult story to trace and it originates from many indigenous groups, including the Shipibo of the Peruvian Amazon, the Quechua of the Peruvian Andes, the Shuar of Ecuador, the Hopi of New Mexico, and the Mayan of Mexico, among others.

The mind, the industrial, and the masculine are represented by the Eagle in certain versions of this prophecy, whereas the heart, intuition, and the feminine are embodied by the Condor.

The start of a 500-year period, where the Eagle people would dominate and almost eliminate the Condor people, was foretold by the Eagle and Condor prophecy in the 1490s.

You don't need to look further than the decimation of indigenous tribes, the devaluation of their ways of life, and the severe damage done to the Earth's ecosystem since the era of the conquistadors.

According to the prophecy, in the next 500-year period starting in 1990, there's potential for the Eagle and the Condor to unite, soar together, and elevate humanity's consciousness.

The prophecy only speaks of the potential, so it's up to humanity to activate this potential and ensure that a new consciousness may arise.

The prophecy stated: *"When the Eagle and the Condor come together in harmony, there will be peace on Earth."*

Of course, Marco, being more pragmatic and self-centered, was mainly interested in his own peace of mind.

He had repeatedly seen human beings unable to dissociate themselves from their experiences and struggling to find peace.

That appeared to be the major impediment to their happiness.

The retreat was nestled in the Andes mountains of Ecuador. It sat on fifty-five acres of peaceful pastures, manicured gardens, and pine forests mixed with eucalyptus.

Good spirits roamed freely throughout the property.

Several buildings with different architecture and all types of accommodation dotted the property, ranging from dormitories to more elaborate private quarters. Most of the buildings were adorned with psychedelic paintings made by the guests and the volunteers.

As soon as he arrived at the center, he felt an uplifting energy permeate the grounds.

But being no fan of big groups, he could see straight away that that would be a challenge.

There were thirty guests. The vast majority had no experience with the medicine and were burdened by their reasons for being there in the first place. Let's say that some guests carried a heavier burden than others.

It was designed as a psychology immersion course fueled by medicinal plants. Once Marco got on board with this reality, it would be smooth sailing. He bonded with a few guests straight away, and that made it all worthwhile.

Marco was staring at the sacred fire, lying comfortably on a floor cushion and wrapped in a blanket. This was his second Ayahuasca ceremony at this retreat.

Often, people with little experience in medicine try too hard to process their experience through their minds. The secret is to let go.

The humming sound of the shaman's flute imbued the numinous space inside the *maloca.*

Suddenly, the fierce energy of the fire opened a path back to Marco's own heart's memory. It was happening organically, without the input of rationality.

"You haven't forgiven Hazel yet. How could you expect to find peace? How would you expect to attract your soul mate until you forgave your ex unconditionally?"

It was the voice of insight and intuition.

Marco didn't hear it as a soothing voice but felt it instead, sending his heart tumbling down like a house of cards.

He realized he still felt resentment towards his ex-wife. He wanted to believe he had forgiven her for making him so unhappy.

He just wasn't able to forgive her for taking sole possession of his son. That alone had torn his heart to shreds.

He would need to raise his thoughts of her to a new frequency of love.

Without pure, unconditional love, his life purpose will stay stuck in its tracks for lack of traction.

Marco understood his purpose for coming here seven years after initially reaching out to the retreat organizers.

During the twelve-day retreat, they had three Ayahuasca ceremonies, two San Pedro ceremonies, and one *temazcal*. This is a sweat lodge ceremony conducted in an igloo-shaped hut constructed from volcanic stone, wood, or concrete.

Once inside, they pour water onto burning hot volcanic stones to produce heat.

At the center, the purification included giving both Ayahuasca and San Pedro and was scheduled at the end of the retreat. As you can imagine, it was pretty intense.

He had never tried San Pedro before.

He was eager to experiment with mescaline, the psychedelic proto alkaloid found in both San Pedro (native to the Andes) and Peyote cacti (growing in Northern Mexico and the Southern United States).

The ceremony started at 5 p.m. and continued until 11 a.m. the next day. Most of the guests took the medicine two or three times throughout the night.

Possibly because he'd taken a lot of medicine the year before, Marco was all set with the first cup and stayed high for eighteen hours.

The intention always overrides the amount of medicine. More isn't always better.

The American founder of the retreat was the shaman, walking around with an eagle feather she used for smudging (the burning of sacred herbs, typically sage, sweet grass, cedar or tobacco, and the ritualistic use of the smoke for cleansing, purifying, and connecting with the spiritual world) and a big cigar of *mapacho*.

She had set up the entire ceremony as a psychiatric ward of sorts.

Fellow guests took their turn sitting in front of the fire, confessing how they'd lost their power.

Marco wanted to roam the forest like a wild beast and escape other people's problems at all costs.

They had to stay near the *maloca* at all times – except for going to the bathroom fifty meters away – for security reasons.

He ended up staying most of the night outside, sitting alongside the smokers, observing things from the outside.

It turned out to be a long, challenging night.

He realized, for the first time in his life, that he was an empath.

An empath is a person highly attuned to the emotions of others.

There was so much trauma boiling under the roof of the *maloca* that night.

It felt like a pressure cooker with a deficient release valve.

It was ready to blow at any moment and spray its contents all over the Ecuadorian night.

Finally, coming to terms with the fact that he needed plenty of space — energetic, emotional, and physical — was an epiphany of sorts.

The more he gained from his spiritual exploration and development, the more sensitive he became to other people's negative energy.

In truth, the negative energies displayed in relation to his sexual compulsions were quite evident.

According to the Cambridge Dictionary:

Compulsion is a very strong feeling of wanting to do something repeatedly that is difficult to control.

Power over something comes from controlling it.

Peace and control seemed hopelessly intertwined in this particular predicament.

Regarding negative energies, we're dealing with the type that can cling to your soul. These psychic impressions can be incredibly potent and destructive.

Besides, he had yet to learn how to channel that potent sexual energy into the higher realms.

Even a little awareness can greatly correct current tendencies.

Simply reacting to tendencies leaves you in a deep state of enslavement.

We have the power and ability to transform habit into choice and compulsion into consciousness.

Only it might just take a lifetime.

The key was to learn how to shield himself from the energies that weren't in tune with his well-being.

To compound the problem, he was hard of hearing, especially the high-pitched frequencies of women.

He would've enjoyed sitting on the couch and talking about his power. It wasn't a matter of having lost it but rather of being in the process of regaining it.

When they called his turn, he refused. He promised himself to take a hearing test once back in civilization.

Having said that, slight hearing loss could benefit you in group situations. It's a proven method to ignore meaningless speech. Trust me, it works.

He still felt he could've learned something valuable from the interaction. However, wisdom had its own pathway.

FORTY-FIVE

"To awaken, sit calmly, letting each breath clear your mind and open your heart."

— GAUTAMA BUDDHA.

How could you stray from spiritual bypassing altogether?

That is a pertinent question indeed.

Marco had inherited the tendency to be indiscriminately judgmental from his father. When you judge others, you put yourself above them.

This is a slippery slope, as far as your ability to not compare yourself to others, to show empathy, and to stay humble is concerned.

Yogi Bhajan talked about the 3 Cs to avoid:

"Compare, Compete, and Complain."

You could see that Marco was doomed in this respect.

The spiritual ego is the worst ego of them all, assuming you'd want to categorize and rank the different types of ego.

Throughout his travels, Marco had frequently experienced it.

People will often feel and act superior to their peers based on their experience, expertise, and knowledge.

Add a little consciousness to that mix, and their sense of self-entitlement could go through the roof.

Marco had seen it in yoga studios, in ashrams, in retreats and, God knows, in countless places where people gathered, regardless of the locale or the occasion.

Worse of all, he'd catch himself leaning in that direction and have to make adjustments to regain a sense of equanimity.

Of course, foreigners were often the biggest culprits.

Presumably, this could be a result of the colonial superiority complex.

As an aside, Marco found that after years of data analysis, approximately 20% of the population smelled bad (as in really bad).

Consider yourselves fortunate, provided that you have access to clean water.

In 2021, the World health Organization (WHO) and the United Nations Children Fund (UNICEF) estimated that 2 billion people worldwide lacked access to clean water.
In any case, make sure to shower and apply deodorant, plant-

based if that's your preference. Maybe your olfactory senses are deficient, but other people have a strong sense of smell.

Marco is convinced that he was a bloodhound in some former life. He could sniff out odd scents from a distance.

Having body odor doesn't make you more spiritual, or does it?

John Welwood coined the term 'spiritual bypassing' in the mid-eighties.

What I described above is merely the tip of the iceberg. What we often fail to see is that people use spiritual practices and beliefs to avoid dealing with painful feelings, unhealed wounds, and development needs.

No matter how many layers of spirituality they adorn themselves with, they won't find peace until they resolve their issues and lingering traumas from the past.

If you don't acknowledge and deal with your shadow side, all the masquerades in the world won't change your true nature.

Ann Stuart wrote: "*You can dress a pig in satin and lace, and it's still a pig.*"

The psychoanalyst Carl Jung first developed the concept of the shadow. He used the term '*shadow self*'. This is the part of our unconscious mind that holds repressed aspects of ourselves, including those that are deemed evil, unacceptable, harmful to others, or detrimental to our health.

A personality comprises two components. The way we interact with the world is impacted by our conscious personality, known as the '*Persona*.' Our unacknowledged aspects are symbolized by the second component, the '*Shadow*', which contrasts with our conscious self. Within us lie the aspects of our psyche we avoid and feel ashamed of.

Discover your shadow by observing others and noting qualities you dislike. Avoiding and suppressing disliked qualities of yourself can lead to a distorted perception of others.

The second San Pedro ceremony, a few days later, was one of the most profound experiences of his entire life.

Marco took part in the opening ceremony and was allowed to stay outside until morning.

He found a clearing above the *maloca* and wandered all evening. He set up an altar next to his blankets and used it as a home base.

He would go back and check the action in the *maloca* as he pleased.

He was as high as a kite and wandered the forest barefoot for a few hours, collecting myriad things under a crescent moon.

He foraged the forest floor like a starving animal and went back to his camp from time to time to build his altar with the riches he'd gathered.

Huachuma, also known as San Pedro cactus, represents the divine masculine. It's a grandfather figure, teaching us to make peace with time and understand that certain lessons require a lifetime to grasp.

Some believe that a plant teacher is an enlightened being, an avatar spirit, manifesting as a plant, tree, vine, cactus, or mushroom. It guides us in raising our consciousness in times of confusion and adversity. When ingested sacredly, with honor and intention, its spirit can heal us and guide us along the path.

Shamans collectively believe that our attachment to a culture that conditions us is the source of much of the sickness in this world.

A culture that teaches us to identify with an array of mental concepts and disregards our timeless connection to the Earth, the sky, and all the elements.

Marco, from his cozy vantage point, could see the mountains rise above the tree canopy. He was standing below a tall eucalyptus tree, his arms spread wide apart in order to embrace all the wisdom of the universe.

The sweet and minty scents of the forest assailed his nostrils, and he could feel the earth spinning beneath his feet.

His chest radiated an intense heat as if it'd been seared by hot coals.

His heart had transmuted into a treasure chest of sparkling and multicolored crystals, beaming all their radiance back to the sun. He sensed that this orgasmic energy, going back and forth in a seamless loop, was LOVE in its purest form.

Abuelo (grandfather) Huachuma was the alchemist.

Meanwhile, someone had frozen linear time. God: the Generating, Organizing, and Delivering force that ruled the megaverses, took care of that.

When it all stopped, Marco was in tears.

Tears of joy fell from his eyes like raindrops from the infinite sky. He had never experienced anything more transcending before.

The sun was now hiding behind the mountains.

Marco had never felt so weightless in his life, not even in accelerated free fall while skydiving.

He had been repeatedly told not to stray too far from the *maloca*.

He always had been a contrarian, but in this case, he couldn't possibly stay put.

Closing his heart to love had been his curse in this life, he deduced.

That was all in the name of self-preservation. But at what cost?

So he went wandering into the night. He had no headlight, and it was pitch dark.

He had finally found his purpose in life.

His new quest would be to crack open the treasure chest in his heart and share the jewels inside with others.

He was cognizant that more hard work would be required.

Rumi's words were echoing in the dark forest:

"Why are you knocking at every other door? Go, knock at the door of your own heart."

Marco had traveled around the world in his search for inner peace.

Now he knew exactly why he had come to Ecuador.

He remembered what Yogi Bhajan had said:

"Nothing happens by coincidence. It's all part of a master plan."

He had planned to be in Peru in ten days to start his diet. The stars couldn't have been more aligned.

He figured he would get the headlight that he'd left in his bedroom.

He took a different path at the risk of ending up somewhere else. He couldn't care less.

The medicine was still strong.

He'd felt the electromagnetic energy field of his heart. It vibrated as if a violin bow were drawn over his nerves. He entered a small chapel-like structure on one side of the property.

It was set up as an altar to Gaia, the primordial Earth goddess in Greek mythology.

He had returned to his mother's womb.

He stayed there, lying down on a big mat for the longest time. It was such a cozy feeling.

When a volunteer found him later, sitting on a sofa inside one of the buildings, he was so relieved. He had been looking for him for a few hours and was concerned about his welfare.

Marco told the young man he was wrong to worry; there was no chance he would ever go astray again. He had seen the spirit rise from his wretched heart. He had finally tasted peace. It had been a long journey.

CHAPTER

FORTY-SIX

"When you want something, all the universe conspires in helping you to achieve it."

— PAULO COELHO.

Marco's sister was pondering the point of writing your life story.

"Leave the past behind and move forward," she said.

The problem with that statement is the inability to move on without making peace with the past and forgiving others, especially yourself.

The thought of reviewing our entire previous experiences is often overwhelming, yet it's an important part of the process.

Our history is a blessing that guides and teaches, and it carries as many positive messages as it does negative.

Seek blessings for the events in your life and find gratitude.

You'll experience what it feels like to be blessed.

If you don't let go of blame and resentments, you'll remain trapped by the past and continue to define yourself by your experiences. That's a scary proposition, a familiar curse of our ages.

Writing a book is both therapeutic and offers a unique perspective. Make amends by seeing through the filter of love, not judgment.

Past heartbreaks and tragedies were mere precursors to your evolution.

Take in the good, and release the bad.

I am sorry, please forgive me, I thank you, I love you. I forgives myself.

Finally, yoga, ho'oponopono, and medicinal plants working in symbiosis.

Peace at last. Who thought it was a niche market?

Marco could often identify with the main character in Paulo Coelho's book 'The Alchemist'. Santiago is a Spanish shepherd boy from Andalucia.

He didn't have a clear vision of a hidden treasure at the base of the Egyptian pyramids.

However, he believed in the interconnectedness of everything in the universe and trusted that his soul held the answer.

If only he could discover his true purpose in life and make acquaintance with his 'Personal Legend.'

Along the hazardous way, he would have to listen to his heart by taking risks and believing in himself and his abilities.

Incidentally, publishers translated '*The Alchemist*' into eighty languages. Total sales exceeded 150 million copies.

I was reading an article titled 'Writing books is not a good idea' by Elle Griffin.

It wasn't comforting for a new writer. Editors are interested in writers who already have an audience. The typical self-publisher sells an average of 250 copies.

In 2020, according to Bookstat, which looks at the book publishing market as a whole, 2.6 million books were self-published, and a mere 268 of them had sales exceeding 100,000 copies. That's only 0.01% of books.

Even at the highest end, only eleven books sold over 500,000 copies. This is insignificant compared to the fact that the top ten Netflix films in 2020 received over 68 million views in their first month.

The brilliantly made 'The Queen's Gambit' broke Netflix records with 62 million views in the first four weeks of its release.

Whereas 98% of the books published sold fewer than 5,000 copies.

The act of writing a book should be driven by passion, or seen as a testament to one's determination.

When you have to rewrite your novel a second time, it becomes a challenge to replicate the initial writing. The ideas and words take a shape of their own, and they don't follow the writer's wishes or direction.

Marco realized that his attachment to the end result caused him to lose half of the contents of his manuscript. The message carried its weight in humility.

C.S. Lewis wrote:

"Humility isn't thinking less of yourself, it's thinking of yourself less."

CHAPTER
FORTY-SEVEN

"We travel, some of us forever, to seek other states, other lives, other souls."

— ANAIS NIN.

As Told By Maestra Juanita (written by Elio Guesa):

The setting for Maestra Juanita's legend is a small Shipibo village to the north of the Ucayali river.

"In this isolated village was a young boy who lived on his family's farm together with his mother and brothers. At the river's edge, there was a majestic tree known to the villagers as Noya Rao.

Witnesses saw fish turn into birds and fly away.

The young boy would disobey his mother and run into the jungle to avoid working on the family's farm. There, he would spend his days playing beside the tree and in the river.

One day, his mother became worried as the boy had not returned by nightfall.

As the days passed, he never returned. Despite desperate attempts, they never found him. For years, his mother called out his name.

The villagers believed he turned into a beautiful bird and flew away."

CHAPTER

FORTY-EIGHT

"Know that your work speaks only to those on the same wavelength as you."

—JEAN COCTEAU.

During the last six weeks of his diet, he was writing for an average of three hours each day.

He would drink Noya Rao daily and take Ayahuasca every other evening, around 8.00 p.m.

After singing *icaros*, his shamans would fall asleep by 2.00 a.m. and stay in the *maloca* until sunrise.

Marco stayed till 3.30 a.m. or 4.00 a.m.

He would sing an eclectic mix of Kundalini mantras, Spanish and French songs, Hindu mantras, and a couple of Shipibo songs that Darwin had taught him. He enjoyed singing lullabies to his shamans. Since he discovered his singing voice, it had become a tremendous source of Divine inspiration. It was impossible for him to sing mantras while staying in the mind.

It forced him to operate from intuition, from the heart.

In Sanskrit, 'Nada Brahma' means the sound of God, suggesting that the energy of sound created the entire universe, in essence becoming the sound current of Creation.

Plato stated that the cosmos is constructed according to musical proportions.

Pythagoras called it the 'Music of the Spheres', believing it fills our inner ears and that we're in contact with it from the moment of our birth.

In '*Journey to Ixtlan*' Carlos Castaneda wrote:

"First, you must use your ears to take some of the burden from your eyes. We have been using our eyes to judge the world since the times we were born. We talk to others and ourselves about what we see. A warrior always listens to the sound of the world."

Several spiritual masters teach that the '*essence of divinity*' is in everyone, and then we explore this inner space through meditation.

Darwin had reiterated that Marco's singing during the ceremonies created an awe-inspiring experience as if the sky had burst open, and he could witness a vibrant spectacle.

Then, Marco would retire to his *tambo*, first making a stop outside under the stars, drinking tea and smoking mapacho.

He would then proceed to his hammock and write until he was too tired to keep his eyes open.

When someone stole his iPad, he also lost about 160 pages of his upcoming book.

Under Ayahuasca's influence and other master plants, he had experienced a beautiful space. How could he return to that cocoon and let his words reemerge?

It would be hard for him to judge his own work.

He was the only one who'd ever read his words. He would often alternate his own perception of them, between sublime and mediocre, between a masterpiece and *'human excreta.'*

Who will ever witness the enchanted nature, or the lyrical nonsense in those words?

Since he was the one who wrote them, he figured he could replicate those writings. He misunderstood everything.

As Marco's friend suggested, he would rewrite his book under a different consciousness this time around. It may have been a blessing for his readers.

He found his words had taken a direction of their own, and he had a hard time controlling them. Maybe he was channeling?

Before he finished this last thought, his former shaman from Mexico sent him a message. He hadn't heard from her in five years. She wrote him, out of the blue, knowing nothing of his situation, that:

"Everything that is for you just is. Nothing, nor nobody, intervenes with the will of the Celestial Father."

I couldn't make this thing up, trust me. Not even for literary glory.

Marco knew now the challenge that was presented in front of him. Like a phoenix from its ashes, he was bound to rise.

Hazrat Inayat Khan said:

"There can be no rebirth without a dark night of the soul, a total annihilation of all that you believed in and thought that you were."

When somebody asked Michelangelo from whence he was getting his inspiration, he answered that the sculpture already existed in the block of granite.

He just needed to uncover it.

I feel someone robbed Marco of his work because of his attachment to it. It stroked his ego to imagine himself on The New York Times Best Seller list or on The Oprah Show.

The wraith of spiritual ego loomed on the horizon, like a holocaust of sorts.

Marco had often seen it throughout his travels. Stephen Hawking wrote:

"The greatest enemy of knowledge is not ignorance, it's the illusion of knowledge."

The Divine Creator was in a fierce mood that day and aimed to teach him an existential lesson.

Marco was mad at the thief. He cursed him and even used his imaginary black Pranic powers to wish him dead.

A few days later, he forgave him for his transgressions.

God knew Marco had his own cross to carry.

CHAPTER
FORTY-NINE

Allow me to recount the most shameful episode of Marco's life, bar none.

It happened in Barcelona, at a different time than when he lived there with his girlfriend.

He encountered a French backpacker, and together they roamed the city, with nothing but bad intentions.

They were both broke and needed cash.

They plotted over a coffee to target a woman on the street and snatch her bag.

The fact it wasn't Marco's idea doesn't exonerate him in the least.

He always resisted schemes from less desirable characters he met along the way. Not this time, though.

He followed through with the plan. End of story.

They hunted to find the perfect prey. The pathway was calm as a woman in her late forties had her purse tucked under her arm.

His partner in crime was supposed to do the grabbing and run away.

Marco's role was to protect him if someone obstructed his path.

He snatched her purse as planned. The woman began yelling with such anguish that Marco stopped dead in his tracks as he started to run after his accomplice.

She was imploring from the top of her voice: *"Chicos! (boys) Chico..os! Chico...os!"*

In that moment, he yearned to erase this unfortunate moment and transform this gruesome reality.

Snatch that purse back from the thief and return it to this lady in distress. Forget the entire episode and regain their dignity.

The thief was up ahead, and Marco had to fulfill his part of the bargain.

She must've been very poor. Otherwise, why would she be so distressed?

Perhaps she expected a beating from her husband for her carelessness?

No one obstructed them, although Marco sensed potential opposition along the way.

People aren't too brave, even less when a situation doesn't concern them directly.

Ten minutes later, they had lunch and drinks with the money in her wallet.

In pesetas, it amounted to around thirteen dollars. Before making some racist comments, they threw away everything else, including a card that recognized her as being Jewish.

He never shared this story with anyone. He finds it quite despicable.

That woman's haunting cries still echo in his head, as if she were repeating them in front of him now.

Later that same day, he separated himself from this dubious individual. He had other schemes planned that Marco didn't approve of, that left him soaking in his own shame.

First, take responsibility and then seek forgiveness.

It's always in that specific order. It's a life-long process.

The longer you keep a dirty secret inside without asking for forgiveness, the more harm it does, and the fresher the memory. It's ironic how it works.

This is the second time I've told this story, and I hope that the price won't need to be paid twice.

Call it karma, if you wish. Newton's Third Law states that for every action, there's an equal and opposite reaction.

So, another thief stole Marco's iPad, and he had a field day. I thank you and I love you.

The circle of ho'oponopono ought to be in full swing.

Erase the data, erase the memory.

Deeply rooted in the container of gratitude and forgiveness, love could ultimately bloom, forever interwoven with grace.

Oprah Winfrey said:

"True forgiveness is when you can say thank you for the experience."

Your liberty is in jeopardy but the shackles that keep you restrained are of your own creation.

CHAPTER
FIFTY

> *"You have to participate relentlessly in the manifestation of your own blessings."*
>
> — ELIZABETH GILBERT.

On realizing that life's trials are hidden blessings, Marco chose to shift his focus to the lessons they held, rather than their implications.

That, in itself, took an enormous weight off his shoulders.

Every single event in our lives is tied to the evolution of our souls.

It simplifies creation's unfathomable complexity. It also implies that human beings, as well as animals and plants, have souls.

Life is only bearable when you believe in a higher power guiding your evolution.

Unfortunately, your ego won't like to hear that, and will initially sabotage your efforts to break free of its hold.

When Marco attended his first Kundalini yoga festival in New Mexico, he firmly believed that he'd encounter the perfect woman with whom to establish the ultimate spiritual connection.

He had just finished his teacher' training. That community of yogis was now his tribe.

What better place than Ram Das Puri, 160 acres of sacred land in the Jemez mountains of Northern New Mexico?

For over forty years, thousands of souls had commingled every summer Solstice in search of Divinity itself.

During the festival, he was parading like a peacock, showing the exquisite design and colors of his wheel.

He was indeed suffering from spiritual delusions. His separation from his wife lasted three years, and he still hadn't found peace with his issues.

No peahens showed up that summer, nor for many summers after that. He was full of heat, but his heart was cold as the Arctic ice.

Marco had a good understanding of the ego by then.

However, since he hadn't yet learned how to tame it, how could he merge with the light, with his head still buried in the sand?

A couple of years later, he had a numerology reading online, by one of his former teachers in New Mexico.

In her eighties, Sangeet Kaur, a remarkable teacher, fought death and paralysis because she believed she hadn't yet finished her work on this planet.

She conveyed to him that his duty involved perceiving and aiding in unveiling the Divine within a woman.

His choice was to find someone already moving on levels of higher learning.

That was Marco's conundrum.

He had standards and had set the bar high, maybe too high. This prediction will take a few more years to be fulfilled.

Careful here, I'm just projecting into the future. I figured that this would have no chance of happening until this book sat on your bookshelf.

Until then, Marco will only be intimate with the visualization of her grace.

As long as he didn't get entrapped in a fusional and neurotic relationship—a term coined by his sister, Arielle—he was game.

At one point, he wondered whether this would happen in a different lifetime.

Since then, Marco has become attuned to her wavelength. Their souls will need to cling to each other for the magic to happen.

I sometimes fancy that they might find each other through this book, although I wonder whether these thoughts aren't just the fruits of shameless self-promotion.

After reading this book, it remains to be seen whether she'd still want to meet him?

Sayed H. Fatimi said:

"Do you believe, as I do, that our souls spoke, long before our lips ever got a chance to?"

It was clear that Marco couldn't help himself in this process.

He needed to step aside from this false sense of identity and savor his own unimportance.

As long as he had things to prove to himself and especially to others, through the distorted lens of his upbringing, he wouldn't transcend his ego.

He would continue to drag it around like a ball and chain.

- Let's fast forward to 2025, shall we?

I'm sure you've noticed that this book isn't arranged chronologically.

Throughout this tale, Marco had been swimming against the current of linear time. No surprises here.

A year passed in India for him between his stay in Nepal and Thailand.

While riding his new Royal Enfield, he took a 10 day Vipassana course in Arunachal Pradesh.

Vipassana meditation focuses on the breath and the body sensations.

Ten days of silence with eight hours of meditation and two and a half hours of lectures daily. Quite an ordeal!

Marco preferred meditation while trekking in the Himalayas, as opposed to standing still.

He was up to the challenge, though. It added spices to his life and kept him forever young.

The restless mind is meditation's constant opponent. Marco, that free spirit, combined different techniques to escape his inescapable boredom throughout the course, contrary to the teacher's instructions.

He was practicing Ho' oponopono who had become his daily go-to.

Suddenly he thought of sending copies of his book to past girlfriends and a couple of male friends, those he kept in touch with or he could track down.

As an invitation of sorts to a calumet ceremony for peace and goodwill.

Until he caught himself picking and choosing whom in terms of merits or demerits. That technique proved ineffective for forgiveness.

Forgiveness needs to be watered, just like your pot plants in your home. Otherwise, they will wither.

Once you have forgiven someone or yourself, you have to keep nurturing that feeling of forgiveness.

When the course ended a couple of days later, Marco first contacted a Brazilian woman by the name of Sofia, who hailed from Salvador de Bahia, famous for its carnival.

He had felt a little guilty about not mentioning her in his book.

They had only known each other for two months, yet their drama-free relationship was intense. She had a warm place in his heart.

When he took her out to the Albuquerque airport for her flight back to Brazil, he locked himself in the bathroom as soon as they were separated and cried nonstop for ten minutes like a baby abandoned on a sidewalk.

They'd connected on Facebook, yet rarely interacted over the years.

Sofia had since remarried a Canadian and moved to Calgary, Alberta.

She soon mentioned that she still had the email he had sent her years ago, to which Marco replied:

" I would love to read it. "

Here's the email, unedited, word for word.

"Sofía meu amor,

I remember you asking me to be honest with you and I would not want it any other way, so here it is:

I don't quite know what I am about to write, so I decided to go with the flow and let my feelings and emotions take over my proverbial pen, so to speak.

You and I had a great adventure, full of passion and positive energy.

Do I feel love for you?

Absolutely.. for you sent inside of me vibes of joy and contentment and I am still feeling them resonating inside my core, like conga drums in a salsa song.

And my body would want to keep shaking to these exotic rhythms for ever, in order to get rid of the burden of solitude and worries of this world.

I would like nothing more right now than to hold you tight in my arms and feel your breath mingle with mine.

It would also be nice to take you along this evening to the Cine Capri to go and see "Interstellar" instead of going by myself.

After going back home, I would beat you in a game of Uno (I wish) and we would make love till the wee hours, at the despair of the neighbors below.

Then the sun would rise and life would carry on, uncomplicated and mellow.

The reality, dear Sofía is that we are from two different worlds; we like music, good food and dance, adventures, travels, laughter and we are both in dire needs of shelter from loneliness and pain but ultimately, we are two pods that grow in different fields, in opposite seasons and in uncompromising worlds.

I would love to tell you that I can't live without you and that my dreams have no reason to sustain me, without you being part of them but I would be deceiving you and that is the last thing that you deserve.

It is the full moon tonight; I feel compelled to shout out these words because I feel her pull and she is tearing me apart from my next flight to Brazil.

You are a gentle soul, Sofía and I love your energy, your insouciance and your kind heart.

Please do not wait for me to come and take you away on my magic carpet because the truth is that I am more pauper than prince and my only mode of transportation is an old Lexus that has seen better days and my two bare feet.

Sure, I dream of eternal, unconditional Love and I still have wet eyes and an aching heart when I take a sniff of your perfume on the lonely pillow next to mine, on my bed at night.

However, I don't want to hurt you and behave in an insensitive manner because you taught me something very profound the last two months and I am so thankful for that, to the point that it makes me want to reach out across the ocean and fill your smiling face with kisses.

You taught me that Love soothes the soul in the same way than fresh and pure water quenches the thirst.

From now on, I don't want to live without Love any longer , otherwise I would become a dried out flower in a book or a random rock in the desert.

I want passion and I so badly need the emotions emanating from a loving relationship, to fill my cup and enable me to celebrate my faith in a more divine power.

I am no longer satisfied with being an empty shell of a man, succumbing to the fears of a common mortal.

In a weird way, you woke me up from a passionless existence.

We got along great the two of us, we cried and moaned like we really belonged to each other.

We danced like we were mating on the dance floor and we laughed like two kids for whom tomorrow doesn't exist.

I would like to remain friend with you Sofía and I hope that you will forgive me for being so candid.

I don't have a girlfriend yet but you know darn well that I will.

In her, I will be looking for a lot of the things that attracted me to you in the first place and that is the biggest compliment I could ever pay you.

Please do not underestimate the effects you had on my

psyche or feel bad for yourself, or even worse feel guilty because it has nothing to do with you or eventually, your worth as a person.

What I know for sure is that I don't want to be tamed, I feel like a wild beast in the jungle and I am either still fighting for survival or rather more intent on the pleasures of the hunt. And I am pretty lost in the process.

That is the one thing that bothered me with us. I long to be swept off my feet and lose total control instead of being the one ultimately responsible for our two destinies.

Maybe I am being selfish?

Possibly so... but in truth, I feel like a little boy running about the streets and I don't want to go home yet.

We will see each other again, that I promise you.

Would you still want to be my friend and my confident?

I hope so because when I look at the sky at night, I will continue to search for the brightest star dancing the night away in the Southern Hemisphere galaxy. She is quite a sight..

I love you Sofía..

Your friend, Marco."

Folks, this email was written in Nov 2014, nearly eleven years ago.

"This couldn't be vintage Marco", I thought upon reading it.

It must have retrograded from latter years.

Once again, the present and the past were riding on the same wave of the time continuum.

This raised an elevated feeling of euphoria to my heart.

That instantly freed me from being the jerk I used to be.

Imagine that infinite potential to accelerate payments on your karma debt!

From now on, I shall reap the harvest of yesteryears by the seeds I plant today.

It was so blatantly clear.

FIFTY-ONE

"Life begins at the end of your comfort zone."

— NEALE DONALD WALSH.

When Marco lived in McLeod Ganj, he and a couple of friends went paragliding in tandem.

The paragliding capital of India, Bir, is just a short drive from Dharamshala.

It's also the location of the Bir Tibetan Colony, founded in the early sixties as a settlement for Tibetan refugees after the 1959 uprising.

The Dalai Lama escaped the Potala Palace in Lhasa and sought asylum in India after a two-week trek through the Himalayas with twenty family members and soldiers. Eventually, they settled in McLeod Ganj.

Marco knew nothing about paragliding.

A tandem flight seemed as if it would be enjoyable.

Who hasn't dreamed about flying like a bird? It must be every kid's fantasy.

The road from Bir to Billing, the takeoff site at 2,444 meters (8,018 feet), was scarier than the flight itself.

He had too much to eat at lunch, and he threw up twice before landing 1,100 meters down the valley in Bir Landing. It didn't help that the instructor was showing off and doing spirals before landing. He has a video of his flight and the subsequent throwing up that he posted on Facebook.

They all found the experience as exhilarating as expected. After doing a little research on the subject, Marco returned to the town to get his paragliding license.

Woody Allen joked:

"I am not afraid of death. I don't want to be there when it happens."

Paragliding is pretty safe. The first ten flights result in the majority of injuries — a thought-provoking fact.

The day before he arrived, a senior Frenchman from Marseille had crashed into the woods and died from his injuries.

From his perspective, Marco had wasted enough years paralyzed by fear. It was an insidious fear that prevented him from being his authentic self.

Michael Singer calls it the difference between your self and your personal self.

"Your self is the pure stream of consciousness that just keeps on flowing. Your personal self is the identity you form, based on how your inner voice perceives this stream of consciousness and the thought patterns that emerge from it."

As Marco tried to evolve within the confines of his personal self, he realized he needed to perceive this stream of consciousness differently in order to change his paradigms.

He felt a magnetic pull towards risky endeavors. If he could transcend his fears, he would become free in the process.

I considered 'The Alchemy of Fear as a book title, but someone had already used it.

Three intense days of ground training left him feeling on top of the world as he familiarized himself with the glider and mastered take-off techniques.

With just a harness and fabric wing, he prepared to leap off the mountain and soar.

He had a walkie-talkie attached to his gear. The instructor at the top of the mountain and the owner at the landing ground would be shouting instructions.

Marco remembered John Lennon's quote:

"Tame birds sing of freedom. Wild birds fly."

No other noise, just the flapping sail. It felt invigorating to defy death and feel so light and free.

They had two flights scheduled per day. The next morning, he had another glorious flight. After lunch, they returned to Billing and when it was his turn, he took off like thunder.

He immersed himself in the moment, becoming one with the elements. Nobody had directed him yet. There was an eerie silence during the entire flight.

He assumed that was part of the plan.

As he was getting closer to the landing zone, there were still no instructions.

Before landing, check the direction of the wind. There was a windsock on the top of a small house, but he couldn't figure out the direction the wind was blowing in.

To prevent missing the landing zone, ensure you land against the wind.

You have to make a series of figure-eight turns in order to lose altitude and position yourself for landing.

Marco observed the head instructor waving his arms on the ground.

He kept turning and prepared to approach at the same angle as earlier in the morning.

His excessive speed caused the problem.

Attempting the last turn, he overshot the landing zone and landed in a field on the opposite side of the road.

Sliding on his butt, he came to a stop in front of a boulder the size of a small backpack. His groin was two centimeters from the boulder. He considered it a drastic close call to calm down his libido.

He grabbed the glider and headed to the designated area for

landing. The instructor was sprinting hurriedly while yelling, visibly agitated.

"Why weren't you following my instructions?"

"I heard nothing," Marco responded, feeling a little lightheaded.

After checking the walkie-talkie, the school owner realized that the teacher on the top had forgotten to turn it on. It never occurred to Marco to check it out. 'Fly Like an Eagle' by The Steve Miller Band was still rocking in the background.

Welcome to India. People can be loving, but they may not meet their obligations according to Western norms.

The wind had changed since the morning.

Marco tried to land with the full force of the wind behind his sail. To his credit, he didn't panic and improvised a few extra turns before selecting a safe spot for a touchdown away from trouble.

Most crashes occur during takeoff or landing, making it a valuable learning experience.

A couple of days later, after he executed a perfect landing, the head instructor was teaching him how to pack the glider. At one point, he told him to be especially careful about the position of the parachute.

Marco stared at him, curious and concerned. *"Which parachute are you talking about?"*

You see, he'd flown seven times by then, and nobody had told him that paragliders had a reserve parachute. They keep it in a pouch under the seat.

It's hard to imagine what could have happened if he'd used his reserve chute, given that he did not know of its existence, location, or deployment procedure.

His first evening before the start of his course, they had a briefing. It was a casual affair where they discussed some technical terms, nothing more than that.

After ten or twelve flights, they grant you a license, but it doesn't mean you know what you're doing, far from it.

Marco wanted to learn more about thermals.

For that reason, he joined a competing team of two experienced brothers. Safety was the most important topic from the beginning, which he found reassuring. Thermals happen in zones where warm air is below the cool air.

Being lighter, they rise and help the glider gain altitude. Instead of the twenty or twenty-five minutes it takes to land, now you can stay way longer in the air. He was told it was a sensational experience.

The distance record for paragliding was broken by Sébastian Kayrouz in 2021. He flew 612 km (380 miles) in a straight-line flight in Texas. He spent eleven hours in the air at an altitude between 1,000 and 2,000 meters (3,280 and 6,560 feet).

He had four flights over four days, practicing all kinds of techniques to prepare for an advanced course. The season was coming to an end.

He would have to come back at a later date. The last scheduled flight was on New Year's Day.

Hundreds of tourists had come from Delhi or from Punjab to fly in tandem.

They waited until the afternoon for the wind to calm down before they made their way to Billing.

He stood at the front of the queue that day. He stayed there, on a flat spot above the precipice with the glider's lines in his hand, for the longest time. The wind's strength and constant shifts made it difficult for the instructor to read. They had a glorious New Year's party at the home of the two brothers, with some succulent food and lots of beers.

Marco ran into the New Year with a certain degree of uncertainty.

Either the wind shifted direction while he was catching it in his sail, or he released the lines a little too early. The glider's sail filled up and then collapsed like the cheeks of a starved man (thank you, Charles Dickens, for this amusing simile). He hopped in mid-air and crashed fifty meters (164 feet) below.

This wasn't his first rodeo, but that one hurt. He stood up, shaken but in one piece.

The instructor aborted the mission after that, deeming it too dangerous. They waited for the truck to arrive and take them away.

Over the next two hours, their group of six watched, amazed, as tandem pilots attempted to take off. It was New Year's Day, and tourists packed the mountain.

The wind scattered as darkness approached.

There were close to fifty pilots looking to earn a paycheck, and it was getting late.

It was the first flight for many since pilots rotated based on experience and tenure.

Earlier, Marco met the man with whom he'd completed his first tandem flight. It's crazy to think that it was his sixth flight that day, given that it took forty-five minutes to drive up to the top.

Well, he was also the owner's brother.

They witnessed a pilot and a young woman crash at the bottom of the hill. Two men aided her as she walked back to the parking lot, visibly hurt.

They watched in horror as other pilots hovered over the ground for a long time, because of the excess weight of two people. They then caught enough wind and took flight at the last moment, dangerously close to crashing on the rocky terrain.

Another couple of gliders crashed after take-off, but they were too far away to assess the damage. It was getting dark as every remaining glider flew off the mountaintop.

Our instructor told us that the pilots had no choice but to take off that day.

For one, if they decided it was too risky to fly, they wouldn't have received payment. The client would've also been entitled to a refund. It wasn't something that their boss would've tolerated. A few of them had old gliders they couldn't afford to replace, way too heavy for two bodies to take off in this wind. A straight recipe for disaster.

Being involved in dangerous activities – in a competitive environment where price is often the deciding factor – makes you wonder whether your life is worth risking to save a buck.

Marco will have to wait for his next opportunity to improve his gliding skills.

He was planning to go to Pokhara in Nepal to learn how to fly the thermals after his trek to Mt. Kailash. Then his passports got stolen.

As they say: *"The rest is history."*

FIFTY-TWO

"Human beings had polluted the seawater and mechanically destroyed the nearby coast; all life had paid this price. Often, in airports, on sidewalks, at restaurants, children and adults alike stop me to ask about barracuda and sharks; killer whales; the deadly sorcery of the Bermuda Triangle and the Loch Ness Monster. I believed that the sea's most monstrous force doesn't live in Loch Ness. It lives in us."

— JACQUES-YVES COUSTEAU.

This episode happened in Oman, right after Marco passed his open-water diving license.

He was back in Muscat for a few days and went diving in the Daymaniyat Islands, a beautiful nature preserve that comprises nine small islands.

They were a group of eight divers with an Egyptian instructor. Marco was the least experienced in the group. A few of them had over 500 dives. He was on his seventh.

It was a shallow dive, about twelve meters deep.

After about fifteen minutes, the instructor got Marco's attention and pointed to his oxygen bottle. He couldn't see anything but took a quick look at his gauge. It was in the red, close to zero. He talked afterward with many divers who had thousands of dives, and it never happened to them.

Running out of air is the biggest fear, after being eaten by a shark.

Of course, if that happened at forty meters or inside a shipwreck, that would be scarier than at twelve meters.

In this situation, which you practiced in your open water course, you'd face your partner and use his alternate air source called an octopus. You would then grab him by the harness, and then go back to the surface together, respecting the steps required, according to your depth.

Marco was feeling quite at ease. He assumed it would be an excellent learning experience.

He discarded his hose. By then the tank was completely empty, and he reached for the instructor's octopus.

He had learned never to hold his breath while underwater, so he was making a few casual bubbles.

As soon as the instructor tried to put the mouthpiece in Marco's mouth, the top plastic part fell off. Trying to put it back on was a struggle.

It took him thirty to forty seconds. Marco wasn't panicking yet. However, his name wasn't Herbert Nitsch.

The Austrian free diver champion holds the world record with a dive at 253.2 meters (831 feet) and once held his breath for nine minutes in a swimming pool.

On a side note, after his record-breaking dive, he suffered decompression sickness and arrived comatose at the hyperbaric chamber. He had a prognosis of remaining a wheelchair-bound, care-dependent patient. He took his healing into his own hands and was fit and diving again two years later.

His best advice for future free divers applies to pretty much anything else in life:

"Listen, learn, and innovate — Work on the weakest links — Visualize and believe you can do it — Never give up because there's no limit — Keep this motto at heart: every time I think I've reached a limit... there is a door... it opens... and the limit is gone."

Back to the story. Marco expected to resurface, but the instructor had him leap on his back. He started riding on him, like on a turtle's back. They kept diving for another forty minutes.

Other divers advised him that this was a no-no, a breach of protocol.

As for Marco, although it was a little unconventional, he found it amusing. The most important thing is that he learned from it.

Later, he spoke with the instructor's boss. Due to clear financial motives, he was glad they didn't all return to the surface. His instructor deserved a spiff (sales performance incentive fund) that day.

Apparently, the o-ring on the cylinder's valve was leaking. This wasn't a common occurrence in the diving world, but you need to be prepared for anything.

CHAPTER
FIFTY-THREE

"You were born with wings, why prefer to crawl through life?"

— RUMI.

Marco had always fantasized about jumping out of an airplane.

He couldn't think of anything more thrilling or more terrifying. For the last couple of years, he'd made a habit of looking at fear in the face, which had a liberating effect on his perception of the world.

How could you fear death when you hadn't even started to live?

After doing a little research, Dubai would be a good place to learn skydiving. You need at least twenty-five skydives to get your license. Time was on his side.

The World Expo extended because of COVID-19, creating a perfect opportunity to combine culture, entertainment, and high-adrenaline sporting activities.

He didn't want to dive in tandem. He thought that jumping by himself out of a plane at 3,810 meters (12,500 feet) with a parachute for the first time would be an even bigger challenge.

Leave behind the idea of static line jumping where you're attached to a cord, and the parachute deploys automatically.

The Accelerated Free Fall course enables you to experience free-falling straight away. You're in the air for sixty seconds at a speed of up to 200 kilometers per hour before deploying your parachute.

Flying like Superman across the sky? It's the closest you'll ever get.

People equate the sensation to floating on a cushion of air. Marco believed it would be much more Zen.

Two instructors accompany you for the first three jumps. The next four jumps, you jump with one instructor. After that, you're on your own.

The instructors use sign language to guide you during drills. They can also hold on to the sides of your beginner's jumping suit to prevent you from spinning out of control.

Marco had taken his scuba diving course a few weeks before, and he had the hand signals all mixed up.

On his third sky jump, he was so spaced out that he forgot to follow the instructions and deploy his parachute. Thankfully, one instructor was present for him.

He had no issues with the physicality of the course, but on the cognitive thinking side of it, he felt his age.
After successfully completing the required tests, you could jump solo after about fifteen jumps.

Once you've had ten solo jumps, you're now eligible to pass your license.

It had been windy all day long. Marco was sipping coffee and watching the experienced divers with at least 100 jumps land. He was getting bored. He wanted to soar among the clouds.

Some days, he drove all across the city to the desert site, but they didn't allow him to jump because of the high wind.

It was five o'clock, the last jump of the day, and the wind had calmed. This was his last required jump before he could get certified.

The speakerphone declared that there were no minimum jumps necessary for this last flight of the day.

He was so excited. Jumping into the sunset promised to be an out-of-this-world experience.

Everything went smoothly.

As soon as he deployed his parachute, the wind took him away from the landing zone. No matter how much he tried to steer back toward it, he was going in the direction of the sand dunes.

The desert surrounded the school. Occasionally, he'd missed the grass in the landing zone and landed in the sand, which wasn't a bad thing since it cushioned the fall. This time, it felt like he was heading towards Saudi Arabia. Judging by the parachutes soaring around him, he wasn't the only one.

Just like in paragliding, land across the wind. There was a big, inflated plastic arrow in one corner of the landing zone that showed the direction of the wind.

In the sand dunes, he couldn't figure it out. He made his

customary ninety-degree turns before landing. Then, he second-guessed himself and changed direction.

While aiming towards the top of one dune and pulling on the brake handles, his parachute suddenly caught speed. He crashed at the bottom of the next dune, his right shoulder absorbing the full impact.

This was the same shoulder he bruised when an overzealous student slammed him on the mat back in his days training in MMA.

He had landed with the wind behind him. So much for his last-minute intuition to change direction. Luckily, he had landed on the sand, although it felt like concrete.

Now he knew why the students couldn't jump in high winds.

That was his thirtieth and last jump. Until next time.
Marco had a knack for the dramatic. That was an allegory of his entire life.

Have you ever wondered what it would feel like to land your parachute without using the brakes to slow you down?

Well, Marco did just that. You're supposed to engage your brakes in order to reduce your descent rate, besides decreasing your forward speed. The technique is to use the brakes midway when you reach a specific distance from the ground and then engage the brake fully just before landing.

Maintain your focus ahead, concentrating on the horizon rather than looking downwards.

When you look straight down, the terrain appears closer, and you end up braking too early. Suspended in mid-air, you become susceptible to gusts of wind and speed up, potentially resulting in a hard landing.

Marco had both smooth and not-so-smooth landings. They taught you to execute a body roll to cushion the fall. Desert surrounded the grass landing area. If you missed the mark, you'd end up eating sand.

Marco had applied the brakes too early on several occasions. He told his instructor that wouldn't happen again. The next jump, he was true to his word.

The trainer was already on the ground, directing him from his walkie-talkie a good 200 meters from where Marco landed. He told him afterward that he heard an enormous thump in the grass area.

Marco was so intent on not applying his brakes too early that he didn't brake at all.

The impact still reverberates through his body.

He had to learn on his terms, even if it meant breaking codes or bones. He couldn't help it. That's just how he functioned.

CHAPTER
FIFTY-FOUR

"There is a garden in her face, where roses and white lilies grow."

— THOMAS CAMPION.

A couple of years after Bryce was born, his parents considered adopting a baby. They'd started late as a mother and father. The timing was right for a new addition to their family, and their son would benefit from having a sibling.

Marco recalled that having a younger sister had been a true blessing in his life.

He was adamant it should be a little girl. Her name would be Chloé.

Research suggested that Guatemala was a suitable place for Americans to adopt. The paperwork process was quick and easy, as opposed to traditional adoption programs, which could take years and cost up to $100,000.

The United States and Guatemala had had a well-established system in place for a long time. For just one tenth of the price, you could fly to Antigua, spend a couple of weeks there, and bring home a baby girl less than two months old.

The babies came from uneducated single mothers living in the countryside.

Women in rural areas didn't face the same drug and violence issues as those in cities.

They started filling out the paperwork. It was supposed to be a six-month process.

Marco had backpacked through South America and liked Latin people and their culture. Taking a baby from a dirt-poor family and providing love, protection, and education was a noble act.

They received a notification halfway through the waiting period that the U.S. government had severed its involvement with Guatemala regarding adoption. Their explanation was that young women were getting pregnant with the sole purpose of selling their babies. It had become a business, so they cracked down on the program.

That was a big disappointment, and the potential step-parents gave up their plans of adopting.

You can't rewrite the past or obsess about the consequences of certain events.

A profound sense of unfulfillment will forever burden Marco. It's hard to express in words. Sometimes, you lose something that you never had, yet it feels like it was already a part of you. It soon becomes your biggest regret.

Had Hazel's abortion in Sydney begun to seep into his consciousness?

Maybe it simply wasn't meant to be. But their family's destiny as a dysfunctional trio would've been altered.

FIFTY-FIVE

"I'm not afraid of storms, for I'm learning how to sail my ship."

— LOUISA MAY ALCOTT.

When riding in India, you have to be one 100% focused at all times.

Indians never acquired driving abilities. Purchasing a license for a few hundred rupees doesn't give them stewardship of the road.

They have no clue about rules or etiquette.

A motorbike is at the bottom of the ladder, as far as Indians are concerned.

You can't stay in the middle of your lane, even when you're closely following the traffic. The typical Indian driver wants to overtake you and will honk their horn repeatedly if you don't let them overtake.

The bigger the vehicle, the more reckless and inconsiderate they are.

Marco had purchased his bike in Dharamshala. He had only ridden on mountain roads in Himachal Pradesh, when the time came to explore the country.

Soon, he crossed into Punjab. His next destination was the Golden Temple in Amritsar.

Sikhs consider this site sacred. They gilded the temple's dome with 750 kilos of pure gold.

Upon entering the plains, the narrow and sinuous mountain road turned into a five-lane highway with little notice. It was complete pandemonium.

Marco soon realized that the slow lane was the most dangerous lane. Vehicles jostled for position, many unfit for the freeway.

The next lane wasn't much better.

Trucks in India remain in the fast lane unless passing a slower truck. The fast and erratic drivers must switch lanes while maneuvering through the traffic, resembling aimless torpedoes.

Riding in the third lane was a suitable compromise. Overtake slower vehicles from either side, while being mindful of the traffic behind you.

It was chaotic, but not devoid of exhilaration.

Suddenly, an SUV zoomed by, too close to his bike for comfort.

Marco, never afraid to speak his mind, flashed the driver his middle finger.

I'm aware this is an American thing and not the wisest choice.

The cult movie *'Easy Rider'* crossed my mind. When someone compromises your freedom or invades your privacy, 'flip them the bird' anyway.

The motorist slowed down and was furious. He let Marco pass him to the left. For good measure, Marco pretended to load his pump-action shotgun and deliver a couple of rounds at the vehicle. They played a game of tag for a while.

Five or ten minutes later, the vehicle reappeared in the fast lane. He let Marco come close, then abruptly came to a stop. Cars were coming fast behind and in the next lane, so Marco had to slam on his brakes.

Making his way to the side of the car, he spotted three Sikhs inside the SUV. Without hesitation, he fired a defiant *"Sat Sri Akal"* at them, a Sikh greeting that roughly signifies *'God is the truth'* or *'True is the name of God.'*

The driver went off on a wild rant in Punjabi for some time.

Seeing the immense size of the two passengers, Marco recalled Sikhs were known as fierce warriors. He expected one of them to jump out of the vehicle with his sword and separate his head, helmet and everything else from his torso.

His response was that Sikhs, being God's servants, should advocate for peace rather than engage in violence, as they did by targeting a motorcyclist on the highway.
They debated until the driver, fed up with this infidel, sped away.

The traffic on the two fast lanes had come to a standstill by then. What a way to start his Indian odyssey!

"*Welcome to Punjab!*" Marco thought. "*I should check my blood pressure, just in case.*"

After that, he resolved to use the two-finger peace sign in the future. While not condescending, it can still be sarcastically effective.

However, he repeatedly broke that promise in the year that followed.

He couldn't help it. His emotions short-circuited his brain.

Marco rode 20,000 kilometers around India. When the Indian government stopped extending visas for stranded foreigners, he had to halt his activities because of the increased difficulty in obtaining a visa extension. Otherwise, he'd still be there riding now.

He put his bike in storage in West Bengal and, like Arnold in '*The Terminator*,' promised: "*I'll be back.*"

His love-hate relationship with drivers from India didn't improve with the years or the miles completed.

He was lucky to still be alive. He had a few close calls, though.

In Ladakh, he was determined to pass a van. The driver was transporting Indian tourists. It slowed down at every curve but sped up when in range to overtake.

Indian drivers, especially the shuttle and the bus drivers, have no consideration for other road users. Once home with their families, they revert to the sweet, humble, and hospitable nature that characterizes many Indians. However, put a steering wheel in their hands, and they transform into egomaniacs and murderous lunatics.

The driver put his right blinker on. No intention to turn right indicates a clear opportunity to overtake.

Marco was halfway past the van when it accelerated, leaving him with no road. When he saw a massive collection of rocks in his path, he threw his bike to the right and hoped for the best.

Fortunately, he fell on a soft patch of road, then quickly rose and sprinted over to the van. He screamed at the coward to get out of his vehicle. The driver had locked his door and pretended not to understand.

An Indian biker who'd arrived on the scene refused to translate Marco's homicidal words into Hindi.

After a while, he calmed down and let the '*poor bugger*' return home to his family in one piece.

Despite his eighteen-month stay in India, Marco was still far from being able to control his emotions. He was short-tempered.

When life flashes before your eyes, what would you expect from a mere mortal?

Marco didn't like anybody invading his space or privacy. His young, frustrated inner child had acquired the ability to fight back.

In fact, he needed that interaction in order to feel worthy, as disruptive as it was to his peace of mind. Throughout his life, that would remain his Achilles' heel.

He often felt alone and abandoned, just him against creation.

Jean-Paul Sartre wrote: *"If you are lonely when alone, you're in bad company."*

Marco sometimes wondered if he could surrender to his beloved when the time came. He pondered whether he would allow her to intricately weave the threads of love into his heart and soul.

FIFTY-SIX

"The key to growth is the introduction of higher dimensions of consciousness into our awareness."

— LAO TZU.

Following his stay at an ashram near Rishikesh, he set off for Uttarakhand's Valley of Flowers. For a few hours, he faced a tough and narrow route.

While leaving a small village, he lowered his guard and passed an older man walking on the road without honking.

When he lived in the States, he rarely used his horn. In India, it was a condition *sine qua non* of survival. He had installed a more powerful klaxon on his bike to emphasize this point.

The old man crossed the road without looking. He must've been hard of hearing or inebriated.

When riding in India, you need to signal your passing to everything in your line of vision, including passersby, animals, vehicles, and especially grandmothers with baskets on their heads.

Lest they didn't see you, honk your horn, several times if need be. Always assume they're blind, intoxicated, or not paying attention.

As the old man made a sudden move to cross the road, Marco hit his right shoulder with the left rear-view mirror of his Royal Enfield. It had the effect of turning the front fork violently to the opposite side.

Marco crashed hard on the pavement, with no gliding at all.

If you don't ride a motorbike with full gear on, you're a complete fool, or you have no empathy for your own skin. Not if, but when will you crash?

Marco always rode fully equipped. He landed on his side, and the bike fell on his right shin and foot for good measure.

Lost in thought, considering your evening' meal and accommodation, suddenly you're on the ground in agony.

So intense was the pain, Marco assumed he'd broken his leg. He sat by the road, examining his limbs.

He removed his right shoe, not knowing whether he'd be able to put it back on again.

His toe and big finger were pretty beat up. He assumed his day was over.

The elderly man lay motionless.

People from the village started dashing towards them. They attended to the old man.

They spoke in Hindustani, the language in this state.

A few of them were in a lynching mood. Two villagers who spoke English accused him of running over the old man through negligence. Marco responded with a passionate tirade filled with incendiary words never uttered before in those parts.

As Marco prepared himself to die fighting for his life on one leg, they lost interest in him, and helped the elderly gentleman back to the village.

He refused any assistance. These people didn't make him feel too welcome.

He figured he would continue his journey the best way he could. That was nothing new to him.

The bike gear had done its job. Marco fell on the right side of his helmet. His right hand, elbow, shoulder, knee, and hip had taken all the impact.

Marco wore knee pads over his protective pants, but he'd left them at a hotel the week before. Although he had a pair of Royal Enfield boots, they provided more comfort than protection.

The bike fell on the small, unprotected part of his shin and toes.

Had he worn his usual knee pads and a solid pair of motocross boots, he would've suffered no injury. Here was a lesson to be learned.

Following the incident, he stayed by the road for an extra twenty minutes, grateful for his minor injuries and the old man's safe return to the village.

No worries there. His bike was built like a tractor. Just don't go to the gym and drop a 220-kilo barbell on your shin and foot. It hurts.

He experienced significant swelling in his right foot and severe soreness in his leg.

Seeking solace in his misery, he waited for the crowd to disperse.

He put his boot on without lacing it up. Then, he jumped on his bike like a distraught rodeo cowboy after being trampled by his horse, and rode off into the sunset.

Well, he could ride but wasn't able to use the brake pedal, which was sending too much pain through his leg.

He stopped at a pharmacy on the mountain road, thirty kilometers up, and had a medical professional examine his injuries.

He had bruising and possibly a broken bone in the long toe, the doctor said. He also had a big hematoma on his shin. The man massaged his foot with ointment before bandaging it. He was adamant that he should have an injection for the pain. Disliking needles, Marco chose pills and a beer as a suitable alternative.

It was getting dark. The woman in the guesthouse nearby prepared a room for him and cooked him an enjoyable meal.

Marco's bones seem to be made of rubber. He had never broken a bone in his life. However, he had torn his share of ligaments.

The next morning, he dragged himself out of bed after a long battle with his mind.

"What doesn't kill you makes you stronger," he thought in his pertinacious head.

He had planned to go hiking in the Valley of Flowers. Even if he had to hop on one leg, he wouldn't miss it. We're meant to surmount obstacles and learn from them, aren't we?

Two days later, he arrived at the end of the road. He spent an extra day recovering at a hotel, then he left his bike there and started walking the next morning.

It had been four days since his accident.

The Valley of Flowers National Park is unlike any other place in the world. Known for its meadows of endemic flowers that cover an area two kilometers long and eight kilometers wide, it also features a varied fauna.

Now that you're more familiar with Marco, you'll concur that he's a smart guy who occasionally acts like a total moron.

Is it a deliberate act of rebellion to reject sense and logic in favor of mindlessness and absurdity, or does he do it without being aware?

His head, torn between stupidity and stubbornness, makes which one prevail uncertain.

Maybe he'd suffered too many blows to the head? Remember, it was the time before they knew about concussions.

At around age eleven, he received a ten-speed bike as a gift. That was his pride and joy.

In those days, it was the equivalent of a high-performance bicycle.

The neighborhood was full of hills and gravel roads.

Every day after school, he'd go riding downhill as fast as he could until he crashed.

Then he would return home all bloodied until the next time. It felt like the natural thing to do.

Riders didn't wear helmets in those days. Then, at sixteen, he graduated to a moped.

Substance abuse didn't improve things. He kept his guardian angels busy throughout that period.

His grandmother's house sat at the bottom of a big hill. One afternoon, he was speeding down the road with his sister riding pillion. Right past his granny's gate, a light pole made out of wood stood guard in front of a drainage ditch.

His wheels slid on the gravel; he hit the post head-on with his forehead and ended up in the gully. His cranium was surely made out of titanium. But he was stuck to the concrete, unable to move his back.

Despite her bloody knee, Arielle sprinted to the house for help.

As soon as his mother and grandma arrived on the scene, he glanced at them, made a weird guttural sound, and lost consciousness.

They all thought he'd died right before their eyes.

When the ambulance arrived, he regained his wits.

However, he remained paralyzed, and the paramedics placed him on a gurney.

By the time he got to the hospital, he could move his limbs.

The doctors did all kinds of tests. He had broken his front tooth and got a burn from the muffler on his left shin. His back had recovered by then. Maybe it seized, or the blow short-circuited his nervous system? They will never know now.

A few hours later, he returned home joking as if nothing had happened.

FIFTY-SEVEN

"Out of suffering have emerged the strongest souls; the most massive characters are seared with scars."

— KAHLIL GIBRAN.

To those among you who enjoy dwelling in their own drama, let me introduce you to Durga.

Marco met her on the trail up to Hemkund Sahib in Uttarakhand (next to the Valley of Flowers National Park) as she sped past him like a lost soul. Hemkung Sahib is the highest gurdwara (place of assembly for Sikhs) in the world at 4,572 meters (15,000 feet).

As she passed him, he joked that she must be some kind of centaur: half-woman, half-pony. They ended up spending a few hours trekking together until she vanished into thin air as he had anticipated.

I will try to do justice to her story.

Durga was a thirty-four-year-old woman from Rajasthan.

Her parents died in a car accident when she was only ten-and-a-half months old.

She was raised by her maternal grandmother, a devoted and strict woman.

She passed when Durga was fifteen-and-a-half.

Left on her own, her uncle and the rest of the family pressured her to marry. Girls in Rajasthan, as in many other Indian states, traditionally marry young and have children. A life of duty, hard work, and total devotion to their husbands await them.

She wouldn't have any of it, so she ran away.

She was arrested by a policeman who struck a deal with her. She had to show him that she could take care of herself for at least six months. Otherwise, he'd turn her over to the authorities, on account of her still being a minor.

The generous officer gave her hospitality for six weeks with his relatives. Then, she moved into a homestay with another family who didn't charge her rent for eighteen months.

She successfully attended college, and then, at twenty-one, her existence was completely turned on its head.

Waiting at a red light with her motorcycle in Jodhpur, a bus hit her from behind.

The driver, probably too scared, didn't bother to stop, and ran her over.

She had twenty-seven fractures, including all her toes and ankles.

The doctors amputated three fingers from her right hand. She also needed many stitches on her forehead.

Her helmet saved her life, though.

She spent six months in a hospital bed, covered in a full body cast like an Egyptian mummy, incapable of feeding herself.

She was confined to a wheelchair for three years.

After being told by her doctor that she'd never walk again, she underwent endless rehabilitation.

Add to that years of addiction to painkillers and sleeping pills. Severe depression followed.

What gave this young woman the strength and incentive to keep fighting?

Influential people in her life, yoga, meditation, and physical activity in total communion with nature changed her paradigm.

She discovered a passion for traveling.

Already a bit of a tomboy as a kid, she indulged in sporting activities like mountain biking, paragliding, scuba diving, and trekking.

With an online women's clothing business and three employees, she frequently travels solo.

Every twenty days, she dedicates one week to her adventures.

Her plan is to buy another motorcycle and live in Europe by the time she turns forty.

Owning a motorcycle again? Had this woman no fear at all?

Marco found her inspiring and was in awe of her.

Jean-Paul Sartre wrote:

"Life begins on the other side of despair."

So, Durga, continue being the free bird you are, and I'll see you above the tree canopy, commingling with the angels, the elves, and the fairies.

After he found out they were staying in the same hotel, he invited this Goddess to his room in the evening, for a massage. What a slick gentleman!

He's still waiting for her to knock on his door.

A few months ago, he saw a post on Facebook.

There she was at the peak of Khardung La at 5,481 meters (17,982 feet), one of the three highest motorable passes in the world, on her new motorbike.

Marco had been there himself on his Royal Enfield a couple of years before. This is a rite of passage for motorcyclists riding in India, and he was full of admiration for her.

He has no doubts that this woman will accomplish all her dreams.

FIFTY-EIGHT

"Be alert as you watch a dog at play or at rest. Let the animal teach you to feel at home in the now, to celebrate life by being completely present. You just watch the tail... with some dogs you just look at them – just a brief look is enough – and their tail goes... 'Life is good!' And they are not telling themselves a story of why life is good. It's a direct realization."

— ELKHART TOLLE.

B ryce had long been asking for a puppy.

His parents thoughtfully debated about having a dog because of their passion for travel.

They gave in to his demands and got a beautiful red-haired bitch months after Bryce turned eight. Many people they met praised the qualities of the Golden Retriever.

When they went to choose her, there were four puppies (all females) remaining from the litter of eleven. They knew beforehand they wanted a bitch.

The family raised both parents as pure Golden since they were young.

The house lady worked with a local association for stray canines.

They had up to seven dogs that reigned supreme inside their house.

At once, Marco decided on the smallest of the four puppies. She had problems walking and was the tiniest among them. Apparently, a door had hit her back leg, but the veterinarian had assured them she would recover.

Hazel favored her as well. There was another contender that Bryce seemed to prefer, a bigger female with blond hair and full of energy.

People always choose the biggest, healthiest puppies in this case.

This red-head had something intangible that had captured their hearts, though.

They let Bryce decide between the two females. In the end, after a lot of hesitation, he made his choice. To his parents' relief, he picked the bitch of their fancy.

Marco had been manifesting a baby girl named Chloé for a long time. Since he wasn't fortunate enough to have a daughter, he decided to compensate by getting a cute puppy.

It comes from the Greek *Khlóe*, meaning young green shoot of a plant.

This bitch would be blooming in their home. She was the sweetest.

Marco doesn't recall her ever doing anything wrong, except chewing the occasional slipper when she was a puppy and digging holes in the yard.

Her affection for people was genuine, and she showed it with exuberance, and no hint of discrimination. She adored children and was drawn to them like a magnet.

In hindsight, Marco firmly believes that she was brought into their home with the purpose of teaching them how to love.

Did the lessons take too long to sink in? Time is always of the essence.

Bryce grew very attached to Chloé. He even mirrored his mother's overprotectiveness towards her. She was the younger sister he would never have.

Never before had Marco treasured something so much.

The overall mood inside their home had deteriorated, but Chloé was like that shining star on the top of the Christmas tree. Unlike his wife and son, she never judged Marco.

He contacted a volunteer organization called Buddy's Angels.

They worked with abused and disenfranchised kids. Marco trained Chloé as a therapy dog.

Golden Retrievers want to please their masters, so they're very obedient and easy to train. She was a natural.

It seemed unfathomable to him that an animal could be so overflowing with love.

To him, love always hinged on judgment, the only way he knew. Chloé showed him this wasn't the case. He truly loved her.

They worked different assignments together, but the most memorable was at a Boys & Girls Club in Albuquerque.

They visited every Wednesday, always at the same time. Kids waited outside, disregarding the summer heat, for her arrival.

Two dozen of them would yell "*Chloé, Chloéé, Chloééé*" as soon as they saw them in the parking lot.

Once inside, it would be mayhem.

About fifty children would go crazy, jumping, and taking turns rolling on the mat with her. Unfazed and buried in a pile of kids, she joyfully licked her way out of the chaos.

These moments were special for kids growing up in tough environments where violence often prevailed. This gorgeous red-haired dog embodied a love they never knew. Marco and the kids were in the same predicament.

When Bryce, Chloé, and Marco were together – whether playing soccer in the park or walking in the mountains not far from their home – they formed a joyful and fearless threesome. It was akin to a complete metaphorical triangle.

Once back home, the dynamic changed. It felt as though an invisible shield of animosity permeated the environment.

Years later, Marco learned that Chloé had contracted cancer out of the blue. She appeared youthful and fit. She barely had any white hair on her muzzle.

The veterinarian told Hazel that there were no available options.

She would die within the week, without too much suffering. In this case, dogs would usually drown in their own blood.

Bryce was at his university in Texas when he heard the heartbreaking news.

He flew home the next day.

Chloé died of visceral hemangiosarcoma cancer of the heart while he was on the plane from Houston to reunite with her. She was eleven-and-a-half.

I still believe she didn't want Bryce to witness her death. It'd have been too painful for him to see her during her passing.

She wanted to be remembered as full of light and full of love. This kind of love that touched even the most hardened souls was indeed immortal.

Even in death, she was noble and unselfish.

"She was one of the nicest souls you'll ever see," Bryce said afterwards.

Although Marco hadn't seen her in four years, he was longing for the day he would see her again.

"Perhaps in the afterlife, we will play throw and catch together, my sweet girl.

In the meantime, I'll keep thinking of you with a smile on my face and a joyful heart."

CHAPTER

FIFTY-NINE

"Without family, man alone in the world, trembles with the cold."

— ANDRÉ MAUROIS.

Marco had been planning his escape for a long time, but would he have the guts to do it?

Since Hazel was in control of the finances, she'd hidden a credit card in his name, with a full line of credit.

In the past, he'd made some purchases without consulting her.

Like the occasion in Portland, when he'd joined a network marketing company and purchased $5,000 of water filters and other worthless products from a company called Equinox.

That evening, she found the boxes stacked in a corner when she went to the garage.

This business opportunity, as usual, proved Hazel right:

"A fool and his money are easily parted."

He kept his promise to her of selling everything, although two-thirds of the items were sold at twenty cents to the dollar.

The company faced accusations of being a pyramid scheme, and it got busted.

Regardless, that wouldn't be the last time Marco tried his hand at network marketing.

He liked the idea of letting the others do the work. Only he seemed to attract less than desirable characters into his sphere.

Anyway, after a long search one morning, Marco got his hands on the credit card, buried under a bunch of inconspicuous documents. It was going to finance his freedom.

Although Marco thought he'd covered his tracks, Hazel was not your typical woman. Somehow, she discovered the missing card. Next day, she called him while he was driving, asking about the card. He had to tell her the truth.

After thirty years of communal life, she had to find out that her husband wanted a divorce over the phone.

In pure Marco style, it wasn't a very romantic way to end a relationship.

Women – and especially Hazel – are perceptive.

A couple of decades earlier, Marco was working as a photographer at a ski resort in Utah. Their apartment was twenty-five kilometers from the resort.

Late one evening, as soon as he opened the front door, Hazel said, as if it'd been a foregone conclusion: *"You got a speeding ticket, didn't you?"*

Marco had avoided getting ticketed for speeding for a long time. How did she even generate that thought?

Despite his five-year plan to divorce her, she still appeared surprised. Go figure. How she didn't see it coming was beyond him. It was written on Marco's forehead.

He told her they should speak to Bryce after school.

It's amazing how spouses could cheat for years while their lives remain undisturbed.

Perhaps they find solace in their blissful ignorance. Besides, why upset the status quo?

Imagine your spouse returning home after being with their lover. How could you fail to detect any signs of sex on their clothes or skin? What about the glimmer in their eyes or the deceit in their words?

Marco sometimes wished they had cheated on one another. Maybe their daily existence wouldn't have been so dreary?

It was time for them to sit down together and share the news with Bryce.

It came less than a week after his twelfth birthday. The timing was terrible, but Marco had already delayed his decision by six agonizing months for various reasons. He felt like an apnea diver having a syncope before reaching the surface.

He did all the talking. Hazel was probably engrossed in one of her Italian romance novels, when one of the characters announced his betrayal to the entire clan. Bryce acted really mature and stoic upon hearing that his dad was leaving.

Marco couldn't decide if he was relieved or lost in the truth of the moment.

Bryce must've known that their family was doomed. It had taken his father an excruciating amount of time to plot his escape. He's surely replayed that scenario a thousand times in his head over the last few years.

This was the hardest thing that Marco had ever done in his entire life, or the lives that preceded it.

There he was, enunciating his departure words with care.

He was acting in a rehearsed and methodical way. Meanwhile, it felt as if he was reaching deep into his chest with his bare hands and tearing a piece of his heart.

CHAPTER
SIXTY

"Those who are one with deprivation are deprived of deprivation."

— LAOZI.

Marco's sister Arielle had been studying psychology for a few years, and she was busy finishing her Master's thesis.

She had asked him whether he'd edit it for her. He was pretty happy to be of help.

He hadn't realized that he'd have to retype it word for word. The apostrophes, punctuation, typos, and grammar were out of whack.

He knew she'd based the characters on his ex-wife and son, along with her own relationship with her father.

"That promised to be enlightening," he thought.

It took him about forty hours to rework her masterpiece. Heck, he probably could've written his own research paper in that timeframe.

Little did he know, it was going to hit him like a brick wall.

His sister had always been there for him in his darkest moments, to restore his sanity. A professional opinion on his various predicaments would reveal much.

Marco read the passage where Arielle spoke about her first enormous loss when he left home to travel. She was thirteen.

It was impossible for him not to draw parallels with leaving his wife and his son at age twelve.

Their father was also thirteen when his sister was murdered by a serial killer.

At the time, he was too absorbed in his own thoughts to notice.

He felt like he finally got caught in the act, freezing him like a deer in headlights.

There was no denying it. Evolution is a tiresome journey, not a destination.

Cherish the brief moments of brilliance in your daily life to offset the inevitable challenges.

Her thesis was titled: '*Une société moderne où l'enfant se fait roi, l'incestuel se banalise et l'incestueux est à la mode*' – A modern society where the child is king, incestual is common-place, and incestuousness is fashionable.

A lot of water has passed under the bridge since then.

Incidentally, I recognized during the writing of this book that telling the story of my characters' past was the ultimate therapy.

Once expressed in words, the feelings and emotions take a form and substance of their own. First, they linger around, intent on teasing you.

For good measure, they sting you, just like wasps protecting their nest.

When pain and emotions vanish, like a genie out of a bottle, freedom awaits you.

To quote Anne Frank: *"I can shake off everything as I write."*

He had translated his sister's thesis summary, intending to share it with the readers.

While talking to Arielle, she felt the material was more suited to a psychiatric text in a hospital library than a travel and spirituality book.

It's best to leave some things unsaid, especially when they are beyond your level of expertise.

Let bygones be bygones.

CHAPTER

SIXTY-ONE

"Nietzsche was the one who did the job for me. At a certain moment in his life, the idea came to him of what he called 'the love of your fate.' Whatever your fate is, whatever the hell happens, you say, 'This is what I need.' It may look like a wreck, but go at it as though it were an opportunity, a challenge. If you bring love to that moment — not discouragement — you will find the strength is there. Any disaster you can survive is an improvement in your character, your stature, and your life. What a privilege! This is when the spontaneity of your own nature will have a chance to flow."

"Then, when looking back at your life, you will see that the moments which seemed to be great failures followed by wreckage were the incidents that shaped the life you have now. You'll see that this is really true. Nothing can happen to you that is not positive. Even though it looks and feels at the moment like a negative crisis, it is not. The crisis throws you back, and when you are required to exhibit strength, it comes."

— JOSEPH CAMPBELL (REFLECTIONS ON THE ART OF LIVING).

T hree years after separating from Hazel things fell apart.

In hindsight, an active and promiscuous sex life occurred every time Marco hit bottom. Multiple dates on Tinder, hookers, and even a few swinger parties.

He quit his job, and was blowing money left and right. The great American system encourages the use of credit cards. Why not take advantage of them?

With his good credit record, he'd collected as many as ten credit cards, with a $100,000 credit limit. When one card reached its limit, he'd switch to another card and make the minimum payments.

Similar to a pyramid scheme, there will eventually be no more cash flow. His divorce settlements, as his share of the two houses they owned, went up in smoke.

After a few months of promising his landlord that money was on its way, he got evicted.

He filed for bankruptcy; most of his debts were to banks and credit card companies.

Among the items he pawned were his Nikon camera and expensive lenses, Swiss watch, sound system, wedding ring, skis, golf clubs, and even his beloved Heckler & Koch 40 S&W gun.

He blew close to a $250,000 during that period.

Marco's deep fall was a twisted fate he chose, believing it would benefit him.

Stoically, he took responsibility, stored his belongings, and sought work.

The constant nagging in sales burnt him out, so he worked for a temporary agency at minimum wage.

He figured, wisely, that he deserved to be in this predicament. Embrace it like a man and wait for the dark skies to clear. He briefly shared a room in a suburban Albuquerque house, but grew tired of his roommate.

He began working door-to-door for a security company. Imagine knocking at doors all day long, with the sole purpose of selling an expensive security system?

You create your own reality. Here, he picked the job with the highest rejection rate, as if he unconsciously wanted to inflict more punishment on himself.

His company planned to open an office in Denver, so they sent a team to try out the market. It was a three-month experiment that didn't pan out well.

Upon returning to Albuquerque, he remained as broke as before. He slept in his Lexus; the front seat folded flat, and the windows had a dark tint. Nobody could see him from the outside. It was pretty comfortable.

Marco was in his redemption period. He didn't complain and made sure not to ask anybody for help.

He took full accountability for his past transgressions, like an injured animal licking its wounds in its den, far away from prying eyes.

Believe it or not, he was quite happy in his Lexus. He found some Latter-day Saints Temples where he could park his car in their lot and be undisturbed at night.

Joseph Smith made sure of that.

One of them, by a deliberate twist of irony, was less than two kilometers away from his old home in Albuquerque. He liked the neighborhood.

He missed his son, but he would not have traded the coziness of his car for Hazel's frigid bed under any circumstance: "*Quelle horreur!*"

At least he was free. Nobody was busting his balls.

His gym membership was in the local area. He went to the gym daily to shower and exercise. He joined a Kundalini yoga studio, and attended five or six classes a week.

Sevak Singh noticed Marco's unwavering dedication when he visited his Albuquerque studio for a weekend retreat. He approached him after class and suggested that he should enroll on his next teacher' training course, almost by Divine order.

Upon learning that Marco was working in an interim agency whenever there was work available and that he was broke, Sevak replied: "*You will pay when you have the money.*"

Marco alternated between his door-to-door job and the interim agency, depending on his mental state.

He worked whenever he wanted, went trekking in the mountains, did a lot of yoga, and used the gym as his second home. He would see Bryce twice a week.

Despite not being ideal, his son seemed satisfied to return to his mother's for the night, not questioning anything.

This little routine continued for thirteen months. Yes, you heard me right.

One morning when he woke up behind a Mormon temple, there was a police car parked twenty meters from his car. In front of his eyes, he caught a glimpse of his odyssey crashing all around him.

He drove with an old license plate he'd found in a yogi friend's garage. His friend was a little perplexed, but nice enough to let him have it.

A state trooper had confiscated his license plate a few months previously because his car insurance had expired. His vehicle, the sole barrier preventing him from being in the street, was bound to be impounded.

The officer, for some miraculous reason, remained in his vehicle and soon departed. Maybe he was having breakfast and didn't suspect a late model Lexus sedan was harboring a man on the fringes of the law.

Either way, Marco had a knack for testing the limits. It was as if someone had programmed him that way.

The fascinating insight is that this period proved liberating. Marco also realized that he was the only one responsible for his situation. No fingers to point, nobody to blame. Just himself against the rough topography of his destiny.

To shape our reality, we must wipe the blackboard clean and begin fresh on a white canvas. As simple as that.

Observing a man's predicament without judgment felt right for once, even if that man was staring at him in the mirror.

Before leaving the States, he had to empty the storage room that he'd been renting since being evicted from his condo.

Along the way, he pawned a few valuable items.

When spring cleaning, many things end up in the trash. There's no room for sentiment.

There was an apartment complex nearby.

Marco found a recessed corner of the building.

He dumped his mountain bike with a pair of cycling shoes sitting on the pedals, one pair of old skis, a set of dumbbells, a soccer ball with cleats, a tennis racket, and some boxing gloves.

He made a homemade sign and wrote with a magic marker in big letters: MERRY CHRISTMAS.

Ah, the glory of becoming a minimizer!

It's wonderful to give selflessly, without expecting anything in return.

In this particular case, Marco was also getting his freedom back.

SIXTY-TWO

"Once you sell your soul to the devil, you can't then ask for it back."

— TOM WOOD.

One evening, in the office of a Lexus' dealership in Albuquerque, Marco completed the sale of a brand-new sedan to a Turkish guy who worked in timeshare sales.

When his client filled out the credit application, Marco asked him to write his monthly income, not yearly income. The man responded with delighted pride. He had indeed written his monthly income, and he could show him his pay stubs.

Since the internet, the car business has become a grind. The minimum commission started at $100 (they didn't call them minis for nothing), with profit mostly in the back-end. The good old days were gone. He made the instant decision to embrace a new challenge and receive rewards for his efforts.

The next day, the unsatisfied salesman took the first steps to getting a real estate license.

Soon, he was working in a resort in the suburbs of Albuquerque, surrounded by a diverse cast of con artists and misfits.

What went on behind the scenes of that enterprise, which resembled a bad movie set, could fill an entire book.

Marco liked to say that he wasn't lying, just embellishing the truth. Then again, he thought he was a straight shooter compared to some of his co-workers, who were serious pathological liars.

It seemed the biggest fraudsters made the most money.

This wasn't an environment conducive to transparency and honesty.

Marco had sold cars for thirteen years, half of them before computers, so he knew his way around blatant dishonesty. He viewed himself as one of the good guys selling timeshares, albeit only partly true.

They assigned him a table and three chairs on the sales floor for two-and-a-half years. His colleague next to him was a tall, handsome Italian by the name of Luigi.

With his tight shirt showcasing his biceps, his Gucci sunglasses, and expensive loafers, he walked around the showroom like one of the *'Goodfellas.'*

He spoke perfect English with a thick Italian accent, and it never took him long to open a bottle of champagne with his clients to celebrate a sale.

Marco was a green pea (beginner), and his ninety-minute

presentation usually dragged on for three hours. He couldn't help it. He was a bona fide grinder and was also afraid to ask directly for the sale. This man's quick results perplexed him and made him a little envious.

He once asked Luigi his secret to success.

Luigi ensured their comfortable seating, as if ready to disclose universal secrets.

He said with complete control of his delivery:

"When I have a couple, regardless of their age, I have one sole aim in mind. The woman will soon have the urge to fuck me right here on the top of the table, while the man will desperately dream of being in my place."

Marco was expecting him to laugh as if he were cracking a joke. However, he believed every word he said. What a lesson in humility!

Now comes the ironic twist in this tale.

His American wife, who'd been taking care of their kids in Florida, came to work at the resort one year later as a manager. She was a heavyset, dirty blonde who bossed him around like a bully. It was a real sight to behold.

One table further down was 'Bubbles,' a nickname she picked up at another sales center. *"Come quickly, I am tasting the stars,"* Dom Perignon used to say.

She wore provocative outfits and worked her magic on the opposite sex. She was also a chameleon, changing her colors with an enticing smile and a calculating mind.

A forty-year-old man of Italian descent named Toni joined the team soon after. He called himself an expert on the Law of Attraction, to which he'd applied his own brand of Quantum physics.

All staff strived to master manifestation techniques post 'The Secret' movie release.

Toni was a maestro at it. A short, fat individual, he was unkempt with balding hair in the pure Italian style. Every con man seems to have the perfect story that makes him human and believable.

Toni had tasted death on his doctor's operating table. A brain tumor detected any later would've killed him, save for his surgeon's skills.

He proudly displayed a prominent scar on the back of his head as if it were a Divine testament to his survival. He painted that story with the masterful strokes of Michelangelo unveiling his work in the Sistine Chapel.

His lack of empathy towards others and his arrogance were only overshadowed by his ego.

He became the number one producer at the resort and shot into the top five for the entire company. There were several hundred salesmen across a few countries, but mainly in the U.S.

His numbers were disproportionally high, and the managers couldn't comprehend why. Due to the great commissions they earned from his sales, they tolerated his grumpiness.

The Law of Attraction made some kind of sense to most, yet implementing its basic rules remained a challenge.

Toni had the key to the puzzle. He acted as though he wished to reveal his secrets. In hindsight, he confused them on purpose.

He wanted all the pie for himself.

Later, Marco recognized that moral character, wealth, and success in business were not correlated.

Many controlling individuals who happen to be bad people exist on this planet for that very reason.

History has its share of evil people, and it also has the habit of repeating itself.

Quantum physics doesn't care about empathy or compassion, at least not in our respective incarnations. Regarding karma, this narrative differs.

Overall, Toni was a despicable character. Marco didn't like him because he mirrored the greedy aspects of his own character. There was a little jealousy as well. He fancied his paycheck.

Toni's presence led to his eventual departure from the company after two-and-a-half years.

Marco never applied for a sales manager (closer) position during the first two years, although there were some opportunities.

He probably suffered from a lack of confidence disguised as 'I prefer being my own man type of bravado.'

The second year, he became a million-dollar producer, which was no minor feat.

His performance was commendable. The managers seemed to admire his never-say-die attitude.

When the opportunity presented itself to apply for a closer position again, he was ready. Only Toni applied as well.

Management wasn't too keen on losing such a top producer, and they didn't care too much about his arrogant demeanor. So, on paper, Marco, who was higher on the popularity scale, had a chance.

In the end, they couldn't deny him, and he got the promotion. But Toni threatened to call the owner of the company if they rejected him.

The managers had no choice but to accept this bully in their ranks.
Marco took this rejection as a sign to look for greener pastures.

One of the long-time sales managers was a short, charismatic guy from Pittsburg, Pennsylvania.

He was an expert at building an instant connection with the customers based on his knowledge and interest in their hometown and state.

They liked each other from the start. Duke was skilled at making things up on the fly and getting clients engrossed in his imaginary tales.

It would be hard for you to find a more personable liar.

It never occurred to Marco until recently. Duke had access to all the client's information beforehand via his computer.

By doing research on their hometown and all the tourist activities in their state, he must have prepared for each individual. He feigned familiarity as if he and his wife had visited their cherished place of residence. He could then adjust his delivery based on their education and profession.

Americans are pretty gullible and proud of their roots. That was genius when you think about it.

Marco had a record summer following his application for a management position. It motivated him to show his worth.

Then he committed (proverbial) *harakiri* – ritual suicide by disembowelment with a sword, formerly practiced in Japan by samurai – and went from hero to zero in a couple of months. Despite Duke's support, he left the company to work for the Marriott Vacation Club.

Mistakenly, he believed that it would be easier to part with wealthier people from their money.

Rejecting the people who believed in him was a recurring pattern.

The grass was always greener in the neighbor's yard.

Another entire book could detail the sales floor and behind-the-scenes action at this resort.

Amidst backstabbing and enough big egos and deception to fill a football stadium, there were sexual intrigues and betrayals worthy of the most decadent soap operas.

Sometimes, Marco felt in his element, especially when the champagne was flowing.

Deep inside, his better conscience knew he didn't belong there. This whole place was a wrecking yard for damaged souls.

At home, he was becoming more unhappy. Something had to give.

Ironically, after a series of professional mishaps, Marco returned to that resort to work in Toni's team. The honeymoon was short-lived.

If he hadn't been on a suicidal mission, he could've been part of Duke's team again.

He had one last stint at that company just before he broke up with Hazel. By then, he worked on an '*exit team*' under a buffoon named Huckleberry.

Marco had a knack for picking his poison. Huckleberry had been a below-average performer but was the director of sales' golf and drinking buddy, in case you wondered how he earned his promotion.

Unlike Mark Twain's main character in '*The Adventures of Huckleberry Finn,*' rafting down the Mississippi River wasn't on his to-do list.

He was happier sitting on his butt with his protruding belly and delivering instructions like a schoolyard bully.

When Marco was intent on doing himself more harm, there wasn't any stopping him.

One evening past midnight, he was the last person left on the sales floor. He had run out of toilet paper in his condo and was too tired to consider stopping at a convenience store on his way home.

The lady in charge of the cleaning noticed that he took a couple of toilet rolls with him, and reported it to the big boss the next morning.

When confronted by his manager, Marco didn't deny it. To his mind, it was such an inconsequential thing.

A few days later, he was fired. Three weeks before, he'd been the salesman of the month.

By then, it was a different director of sales, a bodybuilder with an ego the size of a firehouse, and they didn't care much for each other.

It was reminiscent of the story of Jean Valjean in Victor Hugo's *'Les Misérables,'* who was condemned to hard labor in the *bagne* of Toulon (Marco's hometown) for stealing a loaf of bread.

The punishment didn't fit the crime, but Marco saw it as a sign of redemption.

That would be the end of his timeshare sales career.

Truth be told, he had it coming. By then, his bad attitude had sapped him of all goodness.

Years later, while reminiscing, Arielle remembered that, in those days he was gloomy and fiercely stubborn.

After that incident, he didn't work for eighteen months. Like a Buddhist protester in the most extreme circumstances, he self-immolated.

When you're on your way down, you might as well go down in flames, right?

CHAPTER

SIXTY-THREE

"Death is close enough at hand that we don't need to be afraid of life."

— FRIEDRICH NIETZSCHE.

At the present time, Marco is renting a cottage overlooking the sea near Coti-Chiavari, fifty kilometers south of Ajaccio, on the island of Corsica.

This morning, the owner of a local mini-mart told him that a two-year-old girl had been run-over by her grandfather while he was reversing his car.

She was in his store two weeks ago eating candy. He had known the family for a long time, and appeared visibly shaken.

How are we supposed to process a tragedy of this magnitude? If death is certain, what about the demise of a beautiful, innocent girl in this situation?

Some skeptics would argue that if God existed, he wouldn't allow such things to happen.

Now, we enter the complex and often misunderstood territory of karma.

Before Marco went to India, he didn't understand what karma was, besides the mere concepts of action, reaction, rewards, and punishments.

Sadghuru, in his book '*Karma*', challenges the reader to look well beyond standard definitions.

"Every moment of your life, you perform action — physically, mentally, emotionally and energy-wise. Each action creates a certain memory. That is karma."

This would make sense if you believed in reincarnation. It's also not too distant from the concept of Ho'oponopono.

It would appear that you could create your own reality and influence the wheel of karma, and in the process, you could alter your destiny.

"Karma functions through certain tendencies. But with some awareness and focus, you can push it in the direction that you wish."

My favorite quote:

"Old layers of karma can stick to you only if you keep adding new layers to it."

It's up to you to interpret what these statements mean for a girl who died at her grandpa's hands.

When Sadghuru elaborates: "*Devotion demolishes karma and*

leads to liberation," it reminds us that faith which precedes devotion can make us free.

Faith doesn't imply a firm belief in the doctrines of a religion.

Frank Lloyd Wright, the famous American architect said:

"I believe in God, only I spell it Nature."

CHAPTER
SIXTY-FOUR

"This pandemic has magnified every existing inequality in our society — like systematic racism, gender inequality, and poverty."

— MELINDA GATES.

With respect for all of COVID-19's victims, including Marco's father, it was a great time to travel during those times. It was reminiscent of traveling back in the seventies. Only a handful of dedicated travelers weren't confined to their home countries.

Marco was lucky to be in India during the lockdown. He had nowhere to go afterward, so he continued traveling as the frontiers reopened.

He rode around India on his motorbike. Many people didn't wear masks, and those who did had them below their chin.
Marco expected to contract COVID-19.

He wasn't any more afraid of it than catching a cold. The politicizing of COVID-19 transformed it into a tool for control and profit for a chosen few.

As always, the most affected were the little people and small businesses.

Data compiled by Forbes shows that 573 individuals have joined the billionaire ranks since 2020.

And that existing billionaires saw their total net worth soar by 42% percent.

The head of inequality policy at Oxfam commented: "*I had never seen such a dramatic growth in property and growth in wealth at the same moment in history. It's going to hurt many people.*"

Marco caught COVID-19 and didn't even know it.

He had a persistent cough, which he ignored prior to crossing into Ladakh. Testing positively, he extended his stay in Kashmir for ten days. They call it the mini Switzerland of India, and also 'Paradise on Earth'. What a sweet punishment!

He went trekking in Nepal as soon as they reopened the border.

He couldn't have chosen a better time to trek to Everest base camp and later to Annapurna base camp.

Tour groups had resumed by then, but the number of tourists was still low.

Around 500 individuals daily reach EBC. When Marco was there, there were only around thirty or forty people that day.
If you ever watched the Worldometer online, it shows you the figures of our planet's life.

There were 8,075,650,483 people on this planet when I started this sentence. The world's population increases by about 150 every minute, so do your math. Many scientists think the Earth has a maximum capacity of nine to ten billion.

Marco deemed COVID-19 as a test, anticipating a future pandemic decimating half of the world's population.

The Spanish flu, caused by a bird-originated virus, infected 400 million people worldwide. This accounted for a quarter of the world's population then.

Experts estimate that between 20 and 40 million individuals died between 1918 and 1919.

Then again, when Marco was a teenager, everybody lived under the (imminent) threat of nuclear holocaust.

Death only poses problems for your loved ones when scrutinized. In the worst of cases, a few hundred years of peace sounded good to Marco.

"Carpe diem, quam minimum credula postero," wrote Horace in the Odes. Seize the day, put very little trust in tomorrow.

Envisioning a better world was required to keep an undying optimism, but the present moment held ultimate power.

CHAPTER

SIXTY-FIVE

"Let no man in the world live in delusion. Without a guru, none can cross over to the shore."

— GURU NANAK.

In August 2020, an Olive Branch report was published about the many allegations that had surfaced since the death of Yogi Bhajan in 2004.

Marco forced himself to read through the seventy-two pages of the report.

It was gruesome and disgusting. He couldn't imagine how a woman would feel.

He had grown up in a very disrespectful environment for women, starting with his own mother.

Those teachings always revered women.

He viewed it as a means to rectify the situation.

The scenes depicted in the report were so degrading to females, that it still gives him chills to this day.

For three years, he refused to say Yogi Bhajan's name. He blocked any of his contacts on social media who were in denial or posted positive comments about the accused.

He gave up his yoga practice and stopped teaching.

I would bet that most teachers and students never read the report. Sometimes, it's better not to know.

Insane amounts of money, control, and power were at stake.

Individuals had to assert themselves, aligning with their interests.

Yoga is an oral tradition that's been passed from mentors to students for many ages.

The saints and yogis used yoga to spread the spiritual message of well-being.

Teachers possess special powers and are perceived as godly figures. Unfortunately, reality tells us otherwise.

Several yoga masters have been involved in controversy and accused of sexual abuse.

Look no further than the founders of Ashtanga yoga, and Bikram yoga: Krishna Pattabhi and Bikram Choudhury.

Allegations against Vishnudevananda who founded Sivananda yoga, have never been fully investigated.

During the COVID-19 lockdown, Marco spent three months at one of the major Sivananda ashrams in Tamil Nadu, where the people revere Vishnudevananda as a God.

In America, John Friend, the creator of Anusara yoga, and Amrit Desai, the originator of Kripalu Center for Yoga and Health, faced forced resignation from their positions.

What about Bhagwan Shree Rajneesh, known as '*Osho*', with his fleet of ninety-three Rolls Royces and his army of Rajneeshees or orange people?

By all accounts, he was a brilliant man; his talks have been transcribed into over 300 books.

The U.S. deported him in 1985 after authorities arrested members of his staff for an attempted assassination plot and even a bioterror attack.

Following his wife's death, Gandhi often shared his bed with naked young women, This included his personal doctor, Sushila Nayar, as well as his grandnieces Abha and Manu, who were in their late teens, and approximately 60 years younger than him.

This was his method of attaining the nirvana state of perfect *Brahmacharya*, to maintain abstinence while sleeping next to attractive young women.

Marco hadn't tried this yet, but I doubt he would succeed.

Sadghuru, the founder of the Isha Foundation, has the unique ability to make the ancient yogic sciences relevant to contemporary minds.

His foundation carries in his work towards education, empowerment, and enrichment in rural India, free of cost. He has over 17 million volunteers around the world.

Marco volunteered at his ashram in Coimbatore, Tamil Nadu, prior to the COVID-19 lockdown.

It has over 3,000 full-time volunteers and is beyond description.

Upon learning of his arrival from Bali five weeks earlier, he was unceremoniously expelled from his ashram. It made no sense from a medical point of view.

It turned out that Sadhguru had strong ties to Narendra Modi, the Prime Minister of India. Who thought that spirituality and politics couldn't lay in the same bed?

He foresaw a full lockdown in the country three weeks prior. I suspect his wish was for the foreigners to depart from the ashram.

Marco had firsthand accounts of people who knew members of his family. His tales of enlightenment might not align with what really happened.

Sadguru's controversies aside, his impact on millions of people around the planet is undeniable.

Haters and naysayers will always exist.

Had you been to his ashram in Tamil Nadu, you'd realize this isn't the work of a mere mortal.

Marco was lucky to be part of Mahashivatri at the ashram, volunteering and observing. It is a festival celebrating Lord Shiva that lasts through the night and the following day.

It was an exuberant show with meditations by Sadghuru, martial arts, and musical performances. The icing on the cake was a powerful imaging show on the statue of Adiyogi next to the stage.

They had constructed a wooden path, similar to what Mick Jagger would use during one of the Stones' performances. Over 1 million people attended. The ashram was buzzing like a bee's hive.

The runway seemed to stretch all the way to the Velliangiri mountains, and Sadghuru was making his best Shiva's imitation along the runway, to whip the crowd into a frenzy.

Without visiting India, it's difficult to imagine 1 million people in a crowded place, embracing chaos and insanity peacefully.

Mahashivratri is the night when Lord Shiva danced, creating and destroying the universe.

Shiva gains recognition as the destroyer and holds a significant position among the deities of the Hindu trinity, along with Vishnu, the preserver, and Brahma, the creator.

Shiva has many aspects, benevolent as well as fearsome. In his benevolent aspects, he is an omniscient Yogi who lives an ascetic life on Mt. Kailash.

Or he could slay demons.

SIXTY-SIX

"Forgiveness is the fragrance that the violet sheds on the heel that had crushed it."

— MARK TWAIN.

Six years later, Marco was returning to a Kundalini yoga festival. He wanted primarily to see whether he had forgiven Yogi Bhajan for his wrongdoings.

He intended to be an observer and not make too many judgments.

It was a challenge. Europeans don't have the amiable nature and approachability of Americans. Kundalini yoga had become too mainstream for his taste.

Spiritual ego permeated the grounds. Consciousness? What a pipe dream!

When you observe the impact that these gurus and yoga masters have on humanity, you should forget past offenses and reconcile.

It doesn't mean that you should be in denial. Unfortunately, for the spiritual followers of any guru or religious organization, brainwashing and denial often go hand in hand.

Many times, students have invested a lifetime studying with their respective gurus.

Exposing their imperfections can be overwhelming.

The graphic details of the olive branch report were appalling. Marco felt cheated. The man's pedestal shattered as his teachings plunged into the sewer.

He was more a monster than a saint. Given his absence of integrity, how could you regain faith in this man and believe his words?

The problem was that Kundalini yoga was Yogi Bhajan-centric. Everything revolved around him, like the sun and the Earth.

The stakes were too high for controversy to overshadow the glow of the sun.

COVID-19's arrival provided the powers that be and their attorneys with abundant time to devise a strategic plan. In the end, under the appearance of righting a wrong, nothing had changed. Politics had taken control of the situation.

Yes, Marco had forgiven Yogi Bhajan.

It didn't mean that he should keep his blinkers on and live in delusion like nothing wrong had happened.

CHAPTER
SIXTY-SEVEN

"I don't believe there's anything in life you can't go back and fix. The ancient Vedas – the oldest Hindu philosophy – and modern science agree that time is an illusion. If that's true, there's no such thing as a past or a future – it's all one huge now. So what you fix now affects the past and the future."

— ALAN ARKIN.

In 'The Untethered Soul', Michael Singer reminds us we aren't the image we see, we're the ones doing the seeing.

We are re-creating the outside world inside ourselves and then living in our minds.

Once on the spiritual path, the danger often lies in developing a sense of entitlement.

Michael Singer emphasized prizing humility, gratitude, and remaining open to continuous growth and learning. Pain is the price to pay for freedom.

The potential of our souls is infinite, as long as we don't let fear, and being in our comfort zone, interfere with it.

Surrendering to the flow of life allows for greater alignment with the universe and the unfolding of your true purpose.

"Enlightenment is not a 10,000 hours thing that only happens to Buddhist monks who spend decades meditating in the Tibetan mountains."

Dr. Jeffery Martin's research suggests that enlightenment is a learnable skill. As per his findings, 65% of motivated individuals can attain it within forty-five days.

"A common myth is that enlightened people experience only positive emotions; they live in a state of perpetual calm."

"Only those who dedicate extensive time to prayer or meditation can access it."

"It's important to realize that enlightened people are accessible in our daily lives. We can commonly find them in everyday settings, such as shopping, working, and driving."

"The reason we miss this is our lack of understanding of enlightenment. Let's examine it."

Dr. Jeffery Martin, an entrepreneur and social scientist, has spent over a decade studying thousands of enlightened people through in-depth interviews. His technical term for enlightenment is a persistent non-symbolic experience (PNSE).

"Let me explain what it means."

"Persistent – Instead of being fleeting, it persists for months and years."

"Non-symbolic – This is the most difficult aspect to grasp unless you've experienced it (which you should have as a young baby). Another word for this is 'unmediated'. Rather than putting mental labels onto everything, such as 'cat' or 'book', you just see colors and shapes. You don't filter the world through symbols or words, you're just right there in your sensory experience, fully present."

"Experience – it's not a eureka moment or a new way of thinking. Rather, it's a way that you experience and sense the world."

CHAPTER
SIXTY-EIGHT

"The sea: I didn't lose myself in it. I found myself in it."

— ALBERT CAMUS.

Marco loved the sea. He probably had saltwater in his veins.

He never passed his scuba diving license though, despite having been in some incredible diving spots throughout his travels.

Being in the South of Oman, he finally explored the ocean's wonders and successfully obtained his open-water certification right after the New Year.

Over the next 123 days, he would take 120 dives in Oman, the Arab Emirates, the Philippines, and Indonesia. It wasn't a bad way to catch up with the past.

When you already like everything about the sea and you start scuba diving, your appreciation for the miracles of the underwater world grows exponentially.

As soon as you enter this eerie and fascinating world, you're forever hooked.

Travel worldwide, seeking incredible diving spots. You meet people who share your newfound passion. It's exhilarating.

Marco met a Frenchman in an isolated resort in Indonesia. He lived with his wife in Switzerland but traveled around the globe on his own with camera equipment. For the entire week, they dove in close proximity to each other. He was eighty-three years old.

Unsure about diving in his eighties, Marco found this man captivating. He had uncovered his fountain of youth by doing something he had a genuine passion for.

Marco longed to follow his true calling for a living. Now that he's retired, traveling was his new purpose.

With good health and a positive outlook, who knows how far he could go?

Nothing in the world is more exciting than diving with sharks.

They have a terrible reputation, which isn't warranted. Movies like 'Jaws' made many people suffer from Galeophobia (from Galeo, which means shark in Greek).

The International Fund for Animal Welfare estimates that humans kill around 100 million sharks every year. It's a devastating figure, given that sharks are a vital part of a healthy ocean ecosystem.

In contrast, shark attacks in the most recent five-year global average are seventy-two, with a death count average of five swimmers every year.

Within a short time of scuba diving, Marco realized the extensive destruction caused underwater in the last twenty years, as reported by other divers. The magnification is disproportionate compared to the damage caused to the Earth.

Being older nowadays is not a drawback. Marco's generation won't be here much longer to worry about it.

Scientists forecast that there will be no sharks in the ocean by 2040 if trends continue. That's pretty scary.

Two weeks after the Philippines reopened its borders after COVID-19, Marco was on Malapascua Island, a few hours' drive from Cebu. This island is the sole location worldwide for daily dives with magnificent thresher sharks (fox sharks).

The elongated upper lobe of their caudal fin, which they use like a whip to strike their prey, characterizes these predatory creatures.

While walking around the small island, it was easy to see that COVID-19 caused significant damage to the economy, particularly affecting tourism.

Almost all the diving shops on the island had closed.

Marco found a shop that hadn't seen tourists in a couple of years. He passed his advanced diving license and could now dive as low as forty meters.

A couple of days later, he found a genial Flemish man with a renovated fast boat who agreed to take him to Monad Shad. The sharks' cleaning stations are located there, half an hour by fast boat.

Sergei needed at least four divers to make it cost-efficient. Gasoline is expensive in the Philippines, and Marco was the only client. Sergie was so eager to go diving again and so excited to see a paying customer that they left at dawn the next day with his dive master.

Thresher sharks are nocturnal. They come to shallow waters early in the day to let fish on the reef clean the parasites from their bodies. After that, they descend to depths between 200 and 500 meters.

The cleaning stations cover an extensive area of several kilometers.

There was only one boat that day. Someone told Marco that the usual number of boats anchored there before COVID-19 exceeded forty.

It felt great to be a V.I.P. They saw groups consisting of half a dozen sharks swimming in a circle, at a depth as low as fifteen meters.

They came back the next two mornings. You could never tire of such a spectacular sight.

SIXTY-NINE

"And so rock bottom became the solid foundation on which I rebuilt my life."

— J.K. ROWLING.

Right after Marco and Hazel filed for divorce, the state of New Mexico requested them to meet a psychologist in the mayor's office of Albuquerque.

They each spent about one hour talking with the female therapist in private, and then they met together at the end.

Marco was his belligerent self and mounted an all-out attack on his spouse.

When it was the turn of the mediator to render her verdict, she didn't even try to offer these two unhappy souls a hint of hope for their predicament.

Marco saw in her body language that she'd given up.

Hazel emerged from the meeting room in tears. The only sensible (albeit selfish) comment that Marco could come up with at this moment was: "*You never loved me anyway!*"

Hazel responded: "*I loved you in my own way.*"

These comments could've been reversed. There was no good or evil at play, just a communication gap that turned into an insurmountable obstacle.

Truthfully, Hazel was always there for Marco in happy times and sad. Throughout their time together, she'd been more mother than spouse.

Marco had thought, in better moments, that she was saintlike.

Arielle commented recently that you couldn't blame Hazel for not being a loving mother, quite the opposite. Bryce was always her priority. No matter how obsessively she loved him, there's no denying that she loved him.

In contrast, Marco's mother lacked any emotional connection and focused on ensuring his safety and providing meals. He unconsciously looked for the same qualities in his spouse.

Hazel had learned to ignore the ramblings of such a wild kid, just like his mother had done when he was growing up.

SEVENTY

"The only devils in the world are those running around in our hearts. That is where the battle should be fought."

— GANDHI.

After years of unhappy marriage, Marco returned to dating with eagerness. He was a pretty healthy man with the libido to match his ego.

In order to make up for lost time, he thought he'd soon meet a suitable woman.

He met Lea online, and had scheduled their first meeting in a chic eatery in Albuquerque. When he arrived at the restaurant five minutes before the agreed time, she was already sitting at the bar sipping a glass of sparkling wine.

Upon glimpsing the stunning brunette with green eyes, his heart sank like a rock thrown into a pond.

She had a delicate figure behind elegant clothes, and he became infatuated with her straight away. She emitted the fragrance of orange blossoms in the spring.

They sat on the outside patio. After the appetizer, they kissed passionately, just like a couple of teenagers, and before dessert, they were dancing in between tables.

As the sparkling wine flowed, this woman had already cast her spell on him.

She lived in a small two-bedroom apartment with a girlfriend. Her kisses were ferocious, akin to a wild tigress, but she transformed into a frightened cub when it came to more intimate acts.

Since she had expensive taste and liked the art of seduction, it took Marco a lot of time, effort, and cash to catch her in his net.

Lea was addicted to pot. He hadn't done drugs in decades but believed it would be therapeutic for him at this stage of his life. Even in the worst case, sex and cannabis made for a fun combination.

One day, during lunch at a bistro, she was probing him with questions and found out that he'd just separated from his wife. She fled the table as though the restaurant were ablaze.

After an entire week of not answering his calls, he went to knock on her door with concert tickets and a bouquet of roses. She was playing him like a yoyo, but he was smitten with her by then.

He wrote her this piece a couple of days before the incident.

It reveals his naivety and hopelessness.

"Lea, I already love you, even without experiencing the taste of your thighs, the cadence of your moans, or the surrender of your body in my

arms. My longing for emotional control is futile as thoughts of you refuse to disappear.

Your destiny has me captivated, your every wish has me bound, and it makes me a little afraid. I long to be a noble horseman on a white steed, not a useless scarecrow in your yard.

I wish for the monsoon rain to flow down my desert wash and turn it into a permanent river without any debris.

My soul yearns for a sweet love blanket to envelop me, lifting my physical being toward heavenly realms.

I desire an unforgettable adventure, like an eagle soaring through the wind and the canyon walls, free from worldly worries.

In my vision, that journey has no limits, no schedule, and no fixed destination.

My heart is a sanctuary for conflicting feelings of desperation, dependence, cherishment, and dread. Could your sweet embrace liberate me, once and for all?

Please love me, and I will reciprocate tenfold with every sweet caress. I will shout my love for you to all the neighbors from my rooftop.

The kind of love that doesn't tolerate fools and transcends time and space."

By now, you know who the fool was.

Writing poems for potential conquests became a recurring activity for him. The exuberance of his style often caused it to have the opposite effect.

Lea would come to Marco's condo whenever she felt like it, two or three times a week.

One particular evening, she seemed agitated when she arrived at his place.

He assumed she had a tough day or was experiencing her cycle. She had run out of pot and couldn't get hold of her dealer after work.

She used to bring her dirty clothes over and promptly placed them in the washing machine as soon as she entered his condo.

Meanwhile, Marco had a chilled bottle of rosé and appetizers ready as he was relaxing on the sofa.

While living with Hazel all those years, he'd forgotten that he was a decent cook after all. Now that he was single, he enjoyed preparing a great meal for his girl.

He discovered that women love romantic treatment. It was always a nice prelude to an evening of passion and intimacy.

One of his regular 'ladies of the night' was fond of his chivalrous ways. She often teased him about whether he would consent to marry her.

Back on the sofa with Lea, the conversation soured when she suddenly stated she wasn't in the mood to give him a blowjob. That was an odd statement since Marco had never received a *'bona fide'* blow job from her yet.

He replied with a certain detachment: *"You are free to go home if you aren't happy!"*

He always suffered from an inability to dissociate his body language from his feelings, though.

She ran to the door and slammed it behind her without saying a word.

He had now leftovers for the next day.

He put her clothes in the dryer and, afterward, folded them neatly. Lea had pricey clothes, and she knew how to entice a man with her Victoria's Secret outfits and elegant attire.

Her perfume, a Giorgio Armani *'fleur d'oranger'* (orange blossom), drove him as crazy as a barrel of monkeys.

He expected her to return soon, acting like nothing had happened.

At a tipping point, he resolved she would take the first step this time. He wasn't expecting flowers or apologies, just maybe fewer games.

Meanwhile, imagining her sexy outfits folded neatly in his closet got his hormones into a frenzy. When would she surprise him and come knocking at his door? It was eating him alive not to spend time with her.

Lea didn't contact him in over two weeks, but he remained pig-headed.

He felt powerless and dependent on her every whim. It had to stop.

One morning, he impulsively drove to the Salvation Army to donate her clothes to charity.

Three weeks passed, and an email arrived from Lea. She expressed her desire to retrieve her belongings and rekindle their friendship, possibly even more.

Marco doesn't remember how he replied to her, but his response must've carried the sweet scent of revenge.

Despite the painful separation, he took pride in his display of willpower.

Believe it or not, it required thirteen dates before Marco tasted the forbidden fruit with Lea.

Yes, he'd counted them. It makes you wonder who was the sicker of the two.

He was telling this story to his friend Danny one evening over a few drinks.

Danny's jaw dropped in disbelief at someone's utter detachment from the dating world.

He explained the rule of three. He was pretty cheap, so that fitted him like a glove.

"You should never have over three dates with a woman before you hit the sack," he offered as the ultimate wisdom.

"The first date is always at Starbucks. I arrive early so she can get her own drink."

"If I don't feel it after a while, I pretend I have an emergency and sneak out."

"Let's have wine and kissing on our second date."

"I invite her to my place for dinner on the third date. If she comes, she knows what's expected of her. If she's reluctant, she's out."

That sounded really macho, even for a stray cat like Marco. He enjoyed being a romantic seducer, treating his partners to delightful dinners and concerts (sometimes both in one evening). Judging by Marco's less-than-stellar results, Danny had a valid point.

Within the next three years, Marco estimated a 15% conversion rate of 100 dates on the internet. No numbers to brag about.

Lois Greiam said: *"The theory of relativity doesn't amount to a hill of beans when you have a bonfire in your shorts."*

He also enjoyed the services of prostitutes. In that respect, his conversion rate was off the charts.

With the money he blew on Lea, he could've had a dozen hookers on multiple nights. Undoubtedly, the sex would've been better.

They consummated their relationship after an outing on a hot-air balloon overlooking the Rio Grande at sunrise. They were stoned out of their heads. Getting this woman's affection required a certain amount of creativity.

But let's return to the dynamics of his marriage.

Marco's sex life with Hazel had been pretty non-existent in the last five years of their relationship.

Both of their consciousnesses were also constipated.

Apart from an occasional 'happy ending' message, Marco hadn't cheated at all during their relationship. It would've resolved many problems, now that I think about it.

He was pretty old-fashioned that way. Besides, his mother's infidelities weren't the model he was aspiring to follow.

After his separation, he realized he had a healthy libido and that he loved sex.

That would help him make amends with the past and, more importantly, validate his ego.

His mid-life crisis was behind him. It was time to let go.

He had been a slow learner but started to apply Danny's rule of three.

The rule of one was even more satisfying. You met a girl and engaged in sexual activity on the first encounter. It tilted the stats in your favor.

Deep inside, he wanted to be in a committed relationship but was incapable of opening his bruised heart.

He would magnify minor flaws in the woman and use them as a reason to end things. More often than not, it was quick. Sometimes, he didn't even bother to do it in person. What a coward!

That was his way of admonishing himself for the past. By hurting others, you end up releasing some of the pain that's bottled up inside. You can't help it.

Marco read an article about French actress Brigitte Bardot. Famous for portraying emancipated characters, she'd slept with over 100 men in her life.

He felt like the B.B. of his time. He stopped counting after he reached 100 conquests.

It must be noted that half of them were prostitutes. That's an awful lot of destructive energy.

You should be careful with whom you compare yourself to. Wilt Chamberlain (one of basketball's greatest-ever players) claimed in his autobiography that he had slept with 20,000 women. I hope for his sake that he used condoms, unlike Marco, who preferred to leave it in the hands of God as far as protection was concerned.

For the record, he never caught a sexually transmitted disease. I know, you should have your head examined for having intimate relations with sex workers in third-world countries without condoms.

When he went to Peru for his first diet, Marco had a nasty bladder infection, and he sensed that his sacral (sexual) chakra was congested. Bobinsana, with all of its antibacterial properties, took good care of that.

In his new incarnation as a yogi, he was ready to find his soulmate at last.

It had been a long time in the making. At his first Kundalini yoga festival in the mountains of New Mexico, he was in awe of all those graceful ladies dressed in white.

One evening, sitting with a group of men of all ages, he asked: "*Where were all these beautiful women when I grew up?*" An old timer deadpan: "*They were here, you were not!*"

Everything felt out of sync for Marco. His body had aged, but his mind didn't want to believe it.

His ego was telling him he was ready for love and true happiness. He hadn't, however, made peace with the past, nor got rid of his inner demons.

Without it, no rapture would occur. It was as simple as that.

SEVENTY-ONE

"If you want to find the secrets of the universe, think in terms of energy, frequency, and vibration."

— NIKOLA TESLA.

E ven as an atheist, Marco believed in many advanced civilizations beyond our world.

Astronomers know the Milky Way's brightest region is a star-filled disk, 120,000 light-years wide.

Outside this disk is a vast halo of dark matter, but because it emits no light, it's impossible to measure. Alis Deason, an English astrophysicist, and her colleagues have used nearby galaxies to locate the edge of the Milky Way. The precise diameter is 1.9 million light years, give or take 0.4 million light years, according to their report.

One light year is 9,461 trillion kilometers or close to 6 trillion miles. That's 18 quintillion kilometers in diameter, 1 followed by 18 zeros.

Scientists have multiplied the number of stars in a typical galaxy (100 billion) by the number of galaxies in the universe (2 trillion), using the Milky Way as their model.

The number is massive, to put it mildly. There are 200 billion trillion stars in the universe or 200 sextillions, 200 followed by 21 zeros.

Researchers now believe there are 60 billion planets in our galaxy alone that could support life. Would it be safe and reasonable to suggest that we have company?

Elon Musk envisions having 1 million people living on Mars in twenty years. You could exclude me from the count.

I reckon he should use his considerable wealth (over $250 billion) to eliminate hunger and make our own planet sustainable.

A few months after his diet, Marco was calmer and more laid back. Throughout the day, he remembered to enjoy the moment.

Trusting what lay ahead, he embraced the flow.

He always loved kids, nature, and animals before other people. He often forced himself to find good in human beings. But it was difficult while constantly traveling.

He kept seeing the same patterns and traits. It was disconcerting to see individuals not evolving as he wished. Then again, he was cognizant of spiritual bypassing.

He practiced ho'oponopono every time he caught himself being judgmental.

Use affirmations to shift your inner dialogue and lay the groundwork for desired improvements in your life.

Marco had developed several over the past few years. They kept him centered and focused on the right thoughts he deemed essential for his well-being.

I'll share his little routine with you. You can create your own reality by making your own stuff.

It requires intention and consistency. If he forgets his affirmations one day, he'll do them twice the next day.

"Thank you 'Supreme Being' for healing me physically, mentally, emotionally, and ethereally; with thanks and in full trust."

Repeat two more times.

"Thank you, masters Hardesh and Supriti (his Pranic Healing teachers), for being great ambassadors of the Divine; with thanks and in full faith."

Repeat two more times.

"Thank you 'Divine Creator' for allowing me to be healthy and safe with all my travels on all continents. On all modes of transportation, including on foot, and all sporting activities. Thank you for making me vibrant, eager to learn, enthusiastic, curious, and abundant."

Repeat two more times.

"I am beautiful – body, mind, and soul."

"I am bountiful – I create my own reality. I have a white canvas. The sky is the limit."

"I am an expert manifestor. Everything I manifest comes true."

"I am the master of my fate and the captain of my soul."

*"I am blissful – I am full of love, light, and grace, thanks to
Ayahuasca, Bobinsana, and Noya Rao. Thanks to my shamans, my
relationships, my friends, my family, my experiences, my travels, and
my insights."*

Repeat two more times.

On the third repetition, he adds: *"My book, my son."*

For good measure, Marco reviews his thirteen maxims for a happy
and peaceful life.

When he has a relapse in judgment or excessive sexual thoughts, he
recites the cleansing prayer of forgiveness from the book *'Zero Limits'*.
Forgiveness and cleansing are endless.

*"If I, my family, relatives, or ancestors ever offended you, your family,
relatives, or ancestors, we ask for forgiveness. Clean and purify, cut,
and release all these negative energies, these programs, these memories,
these vibrations, so that all these unwanted energies be transmuted into
pure light. And it is done."*

Repeat two more times.

On the third repetition, Marco adds for his own glorification:

*"Cut, and release...these psychic impressions and be transmuted...and
into pure love."*

"And it is done. It is done. It is done."

SEVENTY-TWO

"We are not human beings having a spiritual experience, we are spiritual beings having a human experience."

— PIERRE TEILHARD DE CHARDIN.

Spirituality has become big business.

On one hand, it serves the purpose of awakening the Earth's inhabitants.

A rise in consciousness is what our planet needs.

Marco watched the documentary '*The Reality of Truth*'. The message was straightforward enough, eulogizing the merits and benefits of medicinal plants.

Overall, it was a blatant effort to sell their one-week programs at Rythmia, billed as a '*Life Advancement Center*' on the Guanacaste coast in Costa Rica.

To get closer to enlightenment, you just need to shell out $6,000 for a full week of pampering.

It didn't cost Marco that much to spend three months with his shamans in Peru, although it was less Hollywood-esque without Michelle Rodriguez and Adam Sandler.

It's not a bad thing for medicinal plants to go mainstream, like yoga and meditation. Just be sure to see the forest for the trees. No pun intended.

Marco had always connected with others.

As he traveled around the world, he learned to have empathy for the plight of the locals. The rest of us who had the fortune of an excellent education and free will should consider themselves blessed.

In order to compensate for past wrongdoings, Marco became benevolent towards those in need. He liked the idea of buying meals for strangers and giving coins to the homeless, besides donating to worthy causes.

The richest individuals are often the most generous philanthropists. Once you understand that money isn't evil and if your intentions are pure, you'll no longer be in scarcity.

SEVENTY-THREE

"Suffering has a noble purpose: the evolution of consciousness and the burning up of the ego."

— ELKHART TOLLE.

This was his last adventure before he left Bali.

He visited Amed, a town known for its long, black, sandy beach and scuba diving.

From Amed, the Mt. Agung volcano towered like a Gothic cathedral. It seemed to rise straight from the Indian ocean.

After a few days of great diving, he climbed Mt. Agung, an active volcano at 3,031 meters (9,944 feet).

He didn't organize a tour, he believed he could navigate solo. But it turned out that a guided tour was mandatory.

The park's office assigned him a guide. They departed Padar

Agung temple at 1 a.m. during the full eclipse of the moon (not visible in Bali).

Long story short, he busted his little toe while in the shower that morning, hitting his foot against a hard object.

His toe swelled up to the size of a big radish. No doubt, he'd have to forgo the trek up the volcano.

But he couldn't miss this cosmic event. His zodiac sign is cancer. During the full moon, he turns into a lunatic.

The voice inside Marco's head called him a quitter.

"Show some guts for once. What kind of free man are you, have you already given up?"

She was correct – that tiny voice. He had thrown away everything in his life in order to chase that illusionary freedom.

He owned a pair of trekking shoes, but his swollen foot prevented him from putting them on.

His other footwear was a pair of cheap imitation crocs that he'd purchased in the Philippines.

He remembered that his grandmother used to climb to a church on a hill with chickpeas inside her shoes, for penitence.

Since he'd been a sinner, what a glorious opportunity to make amends for his sins! There was no alternative – the Crocs would have to bail him out.

Nobody in his right mind would ascend Mt. Agung in imitation of crocs.

Salvatore Dali said: *"There is only one difference between a madman and me. The madman thinks he is sane. I know I am mad."*

Prior to the climb, the guide examined his plastic footwear and inquired about another more suitable pair of shoes. When he explained his situation, the Balinese man looked a little bemused.

Balinese culture recognizes a philosophy called 'Tri Hita Karana' or 'Three Causes of Goodness'. Harmony is achieved through living in unity with people, nature, and spirits. He smiled back, aware that Mt. Agung was the abode of God.

Four and a half hours later, after a hard and strenuous climb, they were watching the sunrise from the peak of the mountain.

Going down was the hardest part; it was steep and rocky. He had no traction and came down the mountain half-sliding on his butt. The sharp rocks were murdering his feet through the soft soles of the crocs. He would've gladly traded them for his trekking shoes and 200 grams of chickpeas.

SEVENTY-FOUR

"You can't save people, you only can like them."

— ANAIS NIN.

Marco studied Pranic healing for three months when he lived in Dharamkot, Himachal Pradesh.

It has been a life-altering experience for him.

He feels a deep sense of gratitude towards his teachers, Hardesh and Supriti Sood, for warmly inviting him into their home, and imparting their knowledge of the healing arts and sciences.

They took turns cooking for lunch and prepared the meals with genuine love. Without a doubt, the best and healthiest food he had in India.

A Pranic healer serves as a conduit between Divine energy and a patient's energy centers.

In short, the chakras are like wireless connectors between the organs and the Cosmic energy.

Any disease, physical or psychological, first manifests in the chakras, where energy depletes or congests.

This is a no-touch therapy. The healer can perform basic or color healing, whether in person or over distance.

Similar to Reiki, but without symbols. Just be willing and open-minded.

Efficient and grounded in authentic experiences, it's easy to grasp and become a believer.

Marco never had the ambition to turn into a healer.

He believed that he lacked the required empathy and the natural abilities. During the course, he understood energy and how to manipulate it. He learned how to measure auras, even over the phone.

Supriti kept telling him he would be a great healer.

He experimented on a few strangers and friends. He didn't realize he was sensitive to other people's energy. Empaths must develop coping mechanisms to avoid drowning in the negativity of others. His purpose on Earth wasn't to be a Pranic healer, that's the way he processed the experience.

He had to deal with his own demons before attempting to heal others.

Surely, he must have some other aptitudes in this world.

SEVENTY-FIVE

"There was a man who wanted to transcend his suffering, so he went to a Buddhist temple to find a Master to help him. He went to the Master and asked: "Master, if I meditate four hours a day, how long will it take me to transcend?"

The master looked at him and said: "If you meditate four hours a day, perhaps you will transcend in ten years."

Thinking he could do better, the man then said: "Oh, Master, what if I meditated eight hours a day, how long would it take me to transcend?

The Master looked at him and said: "If you meditate eight hours a day, perhaps you will transcend in twenty years."

"But why will it take me longer if I meditate more?" the man asked.

The Master replied, "You are not here to sacrifice your joy

or your life. You are here to live, to be happy, and to love. If you can do your best in two hours of meditation, but you spend eight hours instead, you will only grow tired, miss the point, and you won't enjoy your life.

"Do your best, and perhaps you will learn that no matter how long you meditate, you can live, love, and be happy."

— DON MIGUEL RUIZ, THE FOUR
AGREEMENTS.

CHAPTER
SEVENTY-SIX

"None are more hopelessly enslaved than those who falsely believe they are free."

— GOETHE.

The Dalai Lama, when asked what surprised him the most about humanity, answered:

"Man. Because he sacrifices his health in order to make money. Then, he sacrifices money in order to recuperate his health. And then he is so anxious about the future that he doesn't enjoy the present. The result being that he doesn't live in the present or the future. He lives as if he's never going to die, and then he dies, having never really lived."

The Global Burden of Disease (GBD) project, a massive database of what kills and sickens people around the world, published its latest figures for 2019:

Life without disability in the U.S. is 65.5 years, over 20 years less than in Japan.

403

Overall life expectancy in the U.S. hasn't risen since 2010, in part because of a 16.7% increase in the number of deaths due to cardiovascular disease since that year.

In 2019, 65,700 Americans died of drug overdoses, more than double the number in 2010. Those deaths account for more than half of all drug overdose fatalities worldwide.

Life expectancy for men has fallen to 73 years, six years less than women.

High blood pressure, obesity, and metabolic disorders are all on the rise.

Obesity prevalence was 42% in the U.S. in 2020, an 11% increase since 2000.

Almost one in five Americans use prescription or over-the-counter medicine to help them sleep, according to a new government report.

It is not far-fetched to imagine that the whole capitalist system will collapse in the distant future.

If that happened, Marco wouldn't want to be outside on the streets. There are over 393 million civilian-owned firearms in the United States, according to the Graduate Institute of International and Development Studies in Geneva.

SEVENTY-SEVEN

"I never got a chance you know
You had me at hello
Your chrome heart shining in the sun
Had me in its web spun

I never that the strength you know
To resist your odd glow
That tore my pain apart
And painted a rainbow in my heart

I never had the drive you know
I was stuck in slo-mo
And in my shopping cart
Had nothing but a broken heart

I never had the hope you know
To mend my heart with thou
Thou who with threads of love and fun
Sowed it for the long run."

— MARCO, 2014.

Why was it so difficult to be romantically involved with a woman?

Marco met a lot of women on his travels. With sex no longer being his primary motivation, he was now in search of a deep connection, something more transcending.

There were challenges to his predicament.

Since he was acting younger than his age in his everyday activities, the women in his age bracket never showed up to his party. Assuming it was just a material shortage, he decided to look elsewhere. He would often hear women complaining about the lack of good men. Maybe they weren't trying hard enough?

Just as a reformed alcoholic must surely fight the urge to have a drink, Marco will never escape his crazy libido.

It's surreal to think that Marco hasn't had a girlfriend since he lived in Mexico.

She was a divorce lawyer from Puerto Vallarta. Imagine that!

He was working in a timeshare resort in Cabo San Lucas. During a lunchtime break at work, he created a Tinder account. She was on vacation at the hotel nearby. They connected and met for a drink the same afternoon.

A natural bond formed between them as they conversed about

travel, the magic of life, and even the taboo subject of anal sex (which they never pursued).

After a couple of drinks, they went to her room.

Who knew Tinder was so efficient?

He liked her. She had good energy and an easy-going demeanor.

They fucked like teenagers. During the Christmas holidays, she returned to Cabo.

He meant a lot to her. She repeatedly claimed she had never encountered a man like him before.

It appeared she was sincere. At best, Marco figured he was one-of-a-(strange)-kind.

Over the next few months, they met in various cities and always enjoyed each other's company.

Eventually, he accepted a job offer at a resort in Malta and left Mexico. Her daughter was still at home, attending high school which was a major hurdle.

Moreover, his lifestyle was not suitable for maintaining a relationship.

The shocking part of this story is that when she told him she loved him, you know how he responded? *"I know, but I don't love you."*

Emulating Descartes, who believed that: *"In my opinion, everything happens in nature in a mathematical way,"* Marco had devised a scale of five categories pertaining to match-making.

With a maximum score of 4 in each category, that would make it a perfect 20.

The various elements were physical, intellectual, emotional, sexual, and spiritual.

He was striving for a minimum score of sixteen.

She wasn't meeting the required standards on his evaluation. What do you expect?

In hindsight, he would enjoy slapping that insolent and immature scoundrel.

He could have answered, for example: "*Thank you, I love you too. Let me massage your feet.*"

Or something more in the vein of Edgar Allan Poe: "*We loved with a love that was more than love.*"

That would have sounded really good in Spanish: "*Amamos con un amor que era más que amor.*"

For good measure, he would've repeated it in Italian: "*Abbiamo amato con un amore che era più dell'amore.*" By then, her heart would've melted like cheese in a *croque monsieur*.

Finishing with the French version, literally *le coup de grâce*: "*Nous avons aimé d'un amour qui était plus que de l'amour.*"

Marco could've become immortalized in Eros, the Greek God of carnal love, who made people fall in love by shooting an arrow into their hearts.

No chance. He was way too vain for that.

You can't erase the mistakes of the past, nor can you fantasize about the distinct ramifications of your actions either.

Life flows similar to a creek. The impediments and obstacles along its course are an intrinsic part of the dance of creation. Eventually, we go back to Stardust, our origin.

Marco realized he was blind as a bat.

He had an abundance of love to give and required little in return. So why search for perfection in a partner? To project his defects onto the poor soul in the first place?

What about his ability to love without conditions in the future?

Whatever love she would give him would still be an enormous improvement in his condition as a hermit hiding in his imaginary cave.

It was like being in a lucid dream at the exact moment when you realized you were dreaming. You're now in a sphere full of possibilities.

Vincent Van Gogh, who was reportedly color blind and suffered from epilepsy, accompanied by acute insanity and hallucinations, wrote: "*I dream of painting, and I paint my dream.*"

A few months after his diet, Marco saw a big transformation inside of himself.

He wasn't the crying type, although he'd shed his share of tears at certain heartbreaks during his life. Now he couldn't watch 'Downton Abbey' on Netflix without a box of tissues at hand.

He was riding on the crest of his noblest emotions with his proverbial board, blasting in the surf and soaking up the sun's rays.

His heart felt like a hummingbird hovering over a garden full of colorful flowers.

Was this love that he was feeling? Regardless of the answer, he wanted more of those etheric perceptions.

CHAPTER
SEVENTY-EIGHT

"Writing the story of your own life is a bit like drilling your own teeth."

— GLORIA SWANSON.

The most perplexing challenge for him was to rewrite his book. Even though he'd come to terms with starting over, his inspiration wasn't flowing like a mountain spring.

Since he'd written it in different circumstances, it was unrealistic to expect it to have the same patterns or tone of voice. Although he knew what he wanted to write about, he found out that his words had a will of their own and didn't follow his instructions.

A friend mentioned his altered state of consciousness.

Looking back at the history of famous writers and their substance abuse, it makes you wonder if taking drugs is a prerequisite for great writing.

Marco would pay a decent amount of money to recover the 40,000 words that he penned during his diet under the influence of medicinal plants.

Perhaps, like a bubble of genius from another realm, it was too avant-garde for its time, on the brink of bursting at any moment.

Honoré de Balzac supposedly drank fifty cups of coffee a day. He would wake up at 1 a.m. and write until 9 a.m., then take a nap, and write again in the afternoon. Voltaire only drank forty cups a day.

While writing his book, Marco enjoyed two cups of decaffeinated coffee each day and a cold beer in the evening. No wonder his inspiration was as flat as a gravestone.

Jean Cocteau depended on opium, Baudelaire was addicted to hashish, and Hemingway battled with alcoholism until he committed suicide in 1961.

Jack Kerouac, hooked on Benzedrine, took three weeks to pen 'On The Road.'

Robert Louis Stevenson's wife said: *"That an invalid in my husband's condition of health should have been able to perform the manual labor alone of putting 60,000 words on paper in six days seems almost incredible."*

The author wrote 'The Strange Case of Dr Jekyll and Mr Hyde' (1886) during a six-day cocaine binge.

One of the most prolific writers of all time, Stephen King, was also addicted to cocaine for ten years.

As for Marco, he could've drawn parallels with Aldous Huxley's book '*The Doors of Perception*' which inspired Jim Morrison's choice of band name.

Huxley recounts at length his experience with the drug mescaline. Found in the Peyote cactus and in the San Pedro cactus, mescaline induced hallucinations and ignited his creativity, inspiring him to write his book.

Marco drew inspiration from both mundane activities, like smoking *mapacho* in a hammock, and profound insights since the Big Bang, during his three-month diet.

Regardless of your stance on medicinal plants, René Descartes's famous quote: "*Cogito, ergo sum*" (I think, therefore I am), loses its meaning when you float in other dimensions.

When Einstein said: "*Reality is merely an illusion, albeit a persistent one,*" he was probably implying that it was impossible to prove that anything existed other than what was in your mind.

Descartes also said that everything that entered his thoughts was no more true than the illusions of his dreams, yet he believed the mere process of thinking proved a person's existence.

That lacked congruence when Marco sat in the *maloca* with his shamans.

His entire life he was guilty of excessive Cartesianism. Dualistic thinking is a condition of the '*egoic operating system*'. It's our way of reading reality from the position of our private and small selves.

Marco had already given up on the fountain of youth and immortality.

He was in Peru searching for the '*philosopher's stone*', primarily for spiritual revitalization.

This wasn't an item you could find on the shelves at Barnes & Noble.

CHAPTER
SEVENTY-NINE

"I picture you in my mind
Like a spring bursting
Out of the fusion of the earth
Your fluid and steady motion
Irrigating my soul
Like a beacon of light
Shining through a stormy sea.

Darling, I dream of you
Wispy butterfly
Wrapped in morning dew
Your free and fragile wings
Floating in the crimson sky.

When in your arms
My fears become ribbons of silk
Hanging from the clouds.
I suddenly feel warm
Sheltered in a blanket of flowers
That color the harsh desert floor.

Your lips cling to mine
    My breath lost in yours
    My will surrenders
    To the cadence of your moans.
    I am yours to keep
    Or to throw away
    But I don't care.

I sense your fingers
    Up and down my spine
    Awaken my root chakra
    And behold the gravitational
    Pull of your heart
    Turn the lead in my life
    Into pure gold."

— MARCO, 2014.

In her book '*Thrive*', Arianna Huffington makes some insightful comments about the little voice in our heads:

"Even our worst enemies don't talk about us the way we talk to ourselves. I call this voice the obnoxious roommate living in our head. It feeds on putting us down and strengthening our insecurities and doubts. I wish someone would invent a tape recorder that we could attach to our brains to record everything we tell ourselves. We would realize how important it is to stop this negative self-talk. It means pushing back against our obnoxious roommate with a dose of wisdom."

"Educating our obnoxious roommate requires redefining success and what it means to live a life that matters, which will be different for each of us, according to our own values and goals (and not those imposed upon us by society)."

"Humor helps in dealing with that constant inner critic. "Angels fly because they take themselves lightly," my mother used to tell my sister

and me, quoting G. K. Chesterton. What also worked was sending me a consistent and coherent alternative message. Since my roommate fed on my fears and negative fantasies, the message that resonated with me the most was the message with which John-Roger ends all his seminars: "The blessings already are."

"Or, as Julian of Norwich, the 15th century English mystic, put it: "And all shall be well, and all manner of things shall be well." Or, as Sophocles' Oedipus cried out: "Despite so many ordeals, my advanced age and the nobility of my soul make me conclude that all is well."

"I keep repeating it to myself until I am bathed in this calm and reassuring message — which has the added advantage of being true. So, find your own message. Don't let your constant critic filibuster your dreams."

Marco didn't want to filibuster his own dreams any longer and certainly didn't want somebody else to do it for him.

Despite being closer to the finish line, he realized there was still a long way ahead. He sure wasn't getting any younger, but he'd worked hard on the nobility of his soul. Such a refreshing view of life's essence. He was excited about the future, but detached from the meandering thoughts that prevented him from enjoying the present moment.

Eventually, the river will reach the ocean.

CHAPTER
EIGHTY

"There is a candle in your heart, ready to be kindled. There is a void in your soul, ready to be filled. You feel it, don't you?"

— RUMI.

An analysis of mummified heads and cadavers discovered on the southern coast of Peru has pushed back the earliest known date of psychedelic cactus use and other psychoactive plants. Toxicology reports on five individuals who were ritually executed 500 to 2,100 years ago revealed the use of coca leaves, hallucinogenic San Pedro cactus, and Banisteriopsis caapi, a plant often used in the psychedelic brew Ayahuasca.

The study, recently published in the Journal of Archaeological Science, sheds new light on religious practices, ancient trade routes, and plant-based medicine in the pre-Columbian Andes.

But archaeological evidence suggests some indigenous peoples were familiar with this drug for around 5,000 years before, at least through peyote. This analysis is the oldest evidence specifically of mescaline use, but potentially other psychoactive substances as well.

Before going back to Puccalpa to facilitate a retreat with his shamans, Marco went to Pisac, in the Sacred Valley, one hour drive from Cusco.

He booked a one-week stay with a third-generation shaman with twenty-five years of experience. He stayed in his small hotel with his lovely family, with the intention of doing three walking San Pedro ceremonies in the space of one week.

The first ceremony coincided with the full eclipse of the moon.

People have always seen lunar eclipses as powerful symbols of inner transformation and renewal throughout history. Many spiritual traditions consider these celestial events as powerful times for meditation, reflection, and setting intentions.

Believed to open a gateway to higher consciousness, a lunar eclipse is thought to offer an opportunity to release old, limiting beliefs and connect with the deeper, more intuitive aspects of oneself. This period, while aligning your purpose with universal energies, allows for personal growth.

Lunar eclipses, when they occur, serve as reminders of impermanence and new beginnings. It's a time when the veil between the physical and spiritual worlds is considered thinner, making it easier to receive messages and guidance from the universe or the Divine.

By embracing the energy of a lunar eclipse, deep insights and heightened awareness can be cultivated, fostering a sense of unity with all creation and a deeper understanding of one's place within it.

Marco, despite being warned about the tremendous intensity of such an event, remained skeptical about the eclipse's unsuitability for a ceremony.

Hernan assured him it would be a memorable experience. He planned to take him to pre-Inca ruins atop a mountain at 4,000 meters (13,123 feet).

He was growing his cacti in a secret spot up the mountains. He had been cooking his magic potion for four days, awaiting Marco's arrival.

At dawn, they hailed a taxi to the entrance of the Archaeological Park and began walking towards the ruins.

They stopped halfway up the mountain top.

After some rituals, which included blowing over the secret potion with *mapacho* and performing prayers, Hernan gave Marco a large goblet made of clay.

San Pedro is bitter but it doesn't have the foul taste of Ayahuasca.

Still, that container was several times bigger than a normal cup.

It felt like drinking milk from the bottle when he was a kid. Your belly is full, but you force yourself to continue drinking for the sake of it.

Marco's life flashed before his eyes. All his pain had turned into ecstasy.

Once inside one of the ruins, Hernan built an altar and started singing and banging his drum, and alternated by playing a couple of different flutes.

He instructed Marco to find himself a spot away from the altar and pay tributes to *Pachamama*.

Marco was free to roam among the Inca spirits in this sacred place.

He found himself a vantage point that offered a panoramic view of the surrounding mountains and valleys.

The medicine was strong. He stayed there for a long time in perfect harmony with the cosmic dance. With the wind blowing hard, the landscape morphed into colored dominoes cascading down the mountaintop.

Zeus, the God of the sky and thunder, kept a watchful eye, while the clouds billowed like whips of smoke.

In an instant, he understood that witnessing such elemental power would forever banish doubt and fear, as he himself embodied a part of that limitless energy force.

The only thing he needed was to believe and to act on it.

He was not only composed of flesh and bones. One day, he'll disappear into the immensity of existence.

His energy will disperse throughout the whole fullness of the cosmos.

In the following days, they scrambled up and down the mountains like a herd of mountain goats.

They made their way up to 4,200 meters (13,779 feet) and explored various volcanic lagoons, the magnificence of which I won't dare to describe.

Hernan had concocted a potion with Peruvian, Bolivian, and Chilean cacti.

This man was the personification of a creative spirit devoted to the sanctity of his art.

Marco was blessed to behold and partake in such authenticity. Around the ten-kilometer mark for the day, he told Hernan that he felt like a mythical beast: half-goat, half-bull.

Did such a creature ever exist?

It could well be a hybrid between a satyr and a minotaur from Greek mythology.

The minotaur, a man with a bull's head, serves as a symbol for our hidden fears and desires in our unconscious labyrinth.

The satyr, a God with the legs and horns of a goat, and an erect phallus, drank wine and played flute in the forest. Additionally, he was known for his highly sexual nature, leading him to chase after nymphs and mortal women alike.

Marco's imagination never strayed too far from reality warping.

He thought he heard Lou Reed's song *"Perfect Day"* echoing down in the valley.

"You're going to reap just what you sow..."

CHAPTER
EIGHTY-ONE

"And now here is my secret, a very simple secret; it is only with the heart that one can see rightly; what is essential is invisible to the eye."

— ANTOINE DE SAINT-EXUPÉRY.

Marco's godfather had given Marco '*Le Petit Prince*' for Christmas when he was a child.

That book stirred his imagination and became his most valued possession.

He recalls a child's journey through the universe, gaining wisdom.

He could empathize with le petit prince's quest for companionship on planet Earth. In a twist of irony, Marco was still on his own search decades later.

He had completed a full circle that resembled a set of spirals. The last time he was riding his Royal Enfield in India, he was spiraling downwards towards judgment and prejudice, not a comfortable place to be.

Marco had been gravitating towards a spiral of entropy.

Entropy is the tendency towards death, whereas syntropy is the tendency towards life. In order to sustain themselves, living systems need to minimize entropy and maximize syntropy.

Choosing life over death and love instead of anger, Marco had flown to Peru to meet his friends, Montserrat and Aum. He came to cherish that decision because it transformed his entire perspective on life and started the process of opening his closed heart.

They were evolved souls. He felt privileged to count on them as friends.

Meanwhile, this book was not ready to be published. Montserrat and Aum resurfaced as if by godly decree.

The Swiss owners of the retreat in Peru, where they were involved for over a year with their permaculture project, owned another property in Costa Rica.

The eco-lodge sits on the banks of the *Golfo Dulce,* a small tropical gulf on the southern coast of the country. Accessible by a small boat, the Pacific Ocean's blue waters encircle it.

Marco's friends had been working at the resort for over a year, wearing multiple hats.

They served as Ayahuasca ceremony facilitators for half of the year. During the other half, they catered to an older clientele who came to experience the wildlife and tropical forest surrounding the property. The lodge sits inside a National Park, spanning over thousands of hectares of lush tropical forest and is among the last remaining homes of the jaguar in Costa Rica.

Besides their other tasks, they've been busy tending to a food forest. Following agro-forestry norms, they've planted 200 trees, ensuring a plentiful harvest of fruit for future generations. Prior to departing the Peru jungle retreat, they cultivated over 500 trees and transformed the once barren land into a lush oasis.

Marco admired such vision and fortitude. Their goal was to build an eco-village with hundreds of residents seeking sustainable living. Aum was also an expert at building tree houses made with bamboo and ropes and without the use of nails.

To dream of a better world is one thing. To have the vision, the know-how, and the empathy to make it a reality is something else.

In comparison, Marco considered himself a young soul, although he had started to exhibit signs of a more advanced soul.

After trekking with him the entire day along the shore of Lake Titicaca in Bolivia, one of his acquaintances remarked: '*You know how I can tell you're a young soul? – You talk too much!*"

Marco felt out of his depth when discussing Montserrat's experience with the medicine, her visions, and her interaction with the spirits. He was like a kindergartener comparing his scribbles to the PhD dissertation of a college professor.

There's nothing wrong with that. We all evolve according to our own karma and other unfathomable factors. Time, as we conceptualize it as human beings, isn't part of the equation.

For instance, Marco thinks that Artificial Intelligence is the biggest threat facing humanity. A plutocratic system could emerge with exclusive access to advanced weaponry.

Montserrat and Aum, on the other hand, envision new consciousness emerging from this technology. Time will tell.

They invited Marco to the lodge for a few days, along with his ghost-writer. They never expected to return to Costa Rica, mirroring their respective destinies.

It was as close to paradise as you could hope to find. Letting things unfold was warranted.

Continuing this twist of fate, Montserrat and Aum had referred a few friends for a retreat in April, where Marco had done his three-month diet.

They asked him whether he would help facilitate. Marco, who wasn't even supposed to be on the American continent, said he'd consider it. He exploited the fact that everything had been synchronized. His unfinished business was located on the outskirts of the Peruvian Amazon.

He would assist his shamans and pursue an education with sacred plants.

In Star Wars, Darth Vader said: *"I've been waiting for you, Obi-Wan. We meet again at last. The circle is now complete. When I left you, I was but the learner. Now, I am the master."*

Marco could relate to this scenario, but he was far from achieving mastery. He had been yearning for peace, not for the glorification of his ego.

It still suffered a blow when he realized that the Shipibo family he'd bonded with behaved greedily towards the guests, even in his presence.

The era of European conquest saw the extraction of natural

resources in the Amazon, accompanied by the subjugation and exploitation of the workforce.

That resulted in the development of multiple forms of domination and extermination, especially targeting Indigenous peoples.

Being cognizant of history kept things in perspective.

High expectations tend to lead to great disappointment.

His sense of idealism often got in the way of his wits.

That was an important lesson to learn: to stay authentic and speak his mind without ruffling feathers. The story of his life, ladies and gentlemen!

His journey had brought him back to where he started. With renewed enthusiasm, he wanted to delve into uncharted territories.

Moreover, it dawned on him that he was still a work in progress.

This book may be close to completion, but that doesn't necessarily make him a more evolved human being than when he started it twenty-two months ago.

In some uncanny way, he felt unfulfilled by this whole process.

Spiritual bypassing had no reason to exist of its own volition. It was a by-product of fear and a lack of confidence.

By now, Marco knew better. All he had to do was to keep his compulsions in check.

Only the two maxims regarding addictions demanded work and

discipline, along with his long-time nemeses: keeping his emotions in check and not taking anything personally.

The key would be to turn the compulsive into the conscious.

What about eliminating sugar from his diet altogether?

He came to realize recently that sugar was often the trigger for his compulsions.

Consuming coffee, sweets, and alcohol goes against being a *brahmachari* (celibate — one in the stage of *brahmacharya*).

To avoid wasting his *jing* through masturbation, he should also consider eliminating garlic, onions, milk, and cheese (tough things to do for a Mediterranean man) from his diet.

The Taoists equate *jing* with life essence. It's considered the root of our vitality, akin to the roots of a tree. Once your allocated *jing*, primarily located in semen but also present in bodily fluids and saliva, has been depleted, your life will cease.

You need a more holistic diet to keep at bay those delusive passions and thoughts that rise endlessly.

According to Buddhists, when you have too many sexual thoughts, you should meditate on the decay of corpses. It would be a sure way to halt your libido.

Marco was anything but a buzzard. This certainly provided food for thought.

It was as clear as roses newly covered with dew drops. In typical Shakespearean fashion, the intrigues in Marco's life were still in bloom. He had yet to be true to his real purpose. What a noble endeavor indeed!

His plans for the future were nothing but grandiose, yet the present moment reigned supreme.

When all the smoke had cleared, his heart danced with joy, finally unburdened. The journey had been long and precarious.

He wouldn't have it any other way.

EIGHTY-TWO

"Dreams are not negotiable."

— PAULO COELHO.

Artur Mena wrote a beautiful song called *'Sirenita Bobinsana'*. It described how Bobinsana had earned the moniker "little mermaid."

Sirens and mermaids are different creatures. Sirens first appeared in Greek mythology, half-bird and half-woman who lured sailors to their death with their enchanting voices.

In Homer's *'The Odyssey'*, Odysseus instructed his sailors to plug their ears with wax to prevent them from hearing the songs of the sirens. He wanted to hear their voices and had himself tied to the mast so that he wouldn't steer the ship off its course and crash on the rocks or on land.

In comparison, the body of a mermaid consisted of a woman's face, torso, and a fishtail.

Emerging from the depths of Brazilian folklore is Lara, a mesmerizing water spirit whose beauty is as enchanting as the Amazonian waters she inhabits. Lara, often portrayed as a seductive mermaid with long, flowing hair and captivating eyes, lures unsuspecting travelers with her alluring song.

Legend has it that Lara bewitches those who venture too close to her domain, dwelling in the rivers and lakes of the Amazon rainforest, with her enchanting presence.

Some stories portray her as a benevolent guardian of the waters, while others depict her as a vengeful temptress, leading wanderers to their watery fate. Lara's tales embody the mystique and allure of the Amazon, blurring the line between reality and myth in the shimmering waters of the rainforest's hidden depth.

Bobinsana grows along the river banks and its roots can be seven to ten times the height of the tree in order to access the water. Among its many properties, they say that it enhances the dream state.

Marco asked his friend Montserrat to design the cover for his book. He requested a Noya Rao tree and primary colors; she could use her imagination for the rest.

Aum also made a brilliant cover depicting a mermaid that Marco will use for his eBook.

When Marco looked at Montserrat's cover, he shed tears of elation.

Her pencils captured the events of the last three years with perfection. Well, that's a figure of speech – she designed it on Canva.

The mermaid is connected to the roots of the Noya Rao, and she gazes upon a creek opening up to the sky like the womb of creation.

I couldn't help drawing parallels between the mermaid and Bhairavi, the Divine Feminine in all its grace and glory.

The three of them had dieted Bobinsana and Noya Rao. They had a symbiotic connection to each other and to those sacred plants. Everything was jelling.

CHAPTER
EIGHTY-THREE

"Become who you are."

— FRIEDRICH NIETZSCHE.

The weather had been miserable for weeks at the Zen retreat in Tamil Nadu where Marco had been staying for over a month. The wind was blowing hard across the valley, with intermittent periods of rain.

I was sitting outside on the balcony of my room, enjoying the timid appearance of the sun.

As I was adding the last few touches to editing this book before sending the manuscript to my publisher, a cicada landed on my chest.

Finally — the mindless Marco and the wise Taj, together with their wordsmith, had merged into ONE.

You may be wondering about the spiritual meaning of a cicada landing on you?

Let me oblige you with these parting words:

It's a powerful sign of transformation and rebirth. The cicada wishes to share its energy of renewal. This insect emerged from its underground chrysalis renewed. By landing on you, it sends you an invitation.

As a messenger, the cicada reminds you to shed old ways. Release what burdens or restricts you. With a fresh mindset, embrace change and start anew. Its presence shows you're entering a positive life transition.

When the cicada graces you, have patience through this metamorphosis. Blossoming into its new form resulted from the insect persevering years underground. Lasting transformation takes time, but rebirth awaits if you persevere. Let the cicada song fill you with hopeful joy.

This spiritual guide appears when you most need healing renewal. Embrace the powerful symbolism of the cicada while you grow into your true self.

I wish you the best on your journey of self-discovery.

Godspeed...

EPILOGUE

A **PRECIOUS HUMAN LIFE**

"Every day, think as you wake up

Today I am fortunate to have woken up.

I am alive, I have a precious human life.

I am not going to waste it.

I am going to use all my energies to develop myself, to expand my heart to others, and to achieve enlightenment for the benefit of all beings.

I am going to have kind thoughts towards others. I am not going to get angry or think badly about others. I am going to benefit others as much as I can."

It would be hard to find a wiser and more compassionate human being than Tenzin Gyatso, the 14th Dalai Lama.

For the reader's benefit, allow me to share some inserts of his talks or writings, regarding universal themes.

In the transcription of these words, Marco felt humbled.

There he was, trying hard to craft a story and put his original thoughts on paper, when countless brilliant minds and spirits had already graced the annals of literature.

Throughout the writing of his book, he was constantly reminded of Oscar Wilde's quote:

"Imitation is the sincerest form of flattery that mediocrity can pay to greatness."

THE TRUE MEANING OF LIFE

"We are visitors on this planet.

We are here for ninety or one hundred years at the very most.

During that period, we must try to do something good, something useful, with our lives.

If you contribute to other people's happiness, you will find the true goal, the true meaning of life."

FRIENDSHIP

"We have genuine friendship when it is based on true human feeling, a feeling of closeness in which there is a sense of sharing and connectedness. I would call this type of friendship genuine because it is not affected by the increase or decrease of the individual's wealth, status, or power.

The factor that sustains that friendship is whether or not the two people will have mutual feelings of love and affection, genuine human friendship is on the basis of human affection, irrespective of your position.

Therefore, the more you show concern about the welfare and rights of others, the more you are a genuine friend. The more you remain open and sincere, the ultimately more benefits will come to you. If you forget or do not bother about others, then eventually you will lose your own benefit."

SELFISHNESS

"We can also approach the importance of compassion through intelligent reasoning. If I help another person and show concern for him or her, then I, myself, will benefit from that. However, if I harm others, eventually I will be in trouble.

I often joke, half sincerely and half seriously, saying that if we wish to be truly selfish, then we should be wisely selfish, rather foolishly selfish.

Our intelligence can help to adjust our attitude in this respect. If we use it well, we can gain insights as to how we can fulfill our own self-interest by leading a compassionate way of life."

LOOKING WITHIN

"The very purpose of religion is to control yourself, not to criticize others. Rather, we must criticize ourselves. How much am I doing about my anger? About my attachment, about my hatred, about my pride, my jealousy? These are the things which we must check in daily life.

Taking your own body and mind as the laboratory, engage in some thoroughgoing research on your own mental functioning, and examine the possibility of making some positive changes within yourself."

THE PARADOX OF OUR AGE

"We have bigger houses but smaller families; more convenience, but less time. We have more degrees, but less sense; more knowledge, but less judgment; more experts, but more problems; more medicines, but less healthiness.

We've been all the way to the moon and back, but have trouble crossing the street to meet the new neighbor. We built more computers to hold more information to produce more copies than ever, but have less communication. We have become long on quantity, but short on quality.

These are times of fast foods but slow digestion; tall men but short character; steep profits but shallow relationships. It's a time when there is much in the window, but nothing in the room."

COMPASSION

"Usually, our concept of compassion or love refers to the feeling of closeness we have with our friends and loved ones. Sometimes compassion also carries a sense of pity.

This is wrong, any love or compassion which entails looking down on the other is not genuine compassion. To be genuine, compassion must be based on respect for the other, and on the realization that others have the right to be happy and overcome suffering, just as much as you. On this basis, since you can see that others are suffering, you develop a genuine sense of concern for them."

FORGIVENESS

"It would be much more constructive if people tried to understand their supposed enemies. Learning to forgive is much more useful than merely picking up a stone and throwing it at the object of one's anger, the more so when the provocation is extreme.

For it is under the greatest adversity that there exists the greatest potential for doing good, both for oneself and others."

HAPPINESS

"I believe that the very purpose of life is to be happy. From the very core of our being, we desire contentment. In my own limited experience I have found that the more we care for the happiness of others, the greater our own sense of well-being. Cultivating a close, warmhearted feeling for others automatically puts the mind at ease.

It helps remove whatever fears or insecurities we may have and gives us the strength to cope with any obstacles we encounter. It is the principal source of success in life. Since we are not solely material creatures, it is a mistake to place all our hopes for happiness on external development alone. The key is to develop inner peace."

NAMASTE.

Tajsimrit.com

BIBLIOGRAPHY

- 'Zero Limits' by Dr. Joe Vitale & Dr. Hew Len
- 'A Return to Love' by Marianne Williamson
- 'Thus Spoke Zarathustra' by Fiedrich Nietzsche
- 'Quantum Love' by Laura Berman
- 'The Map of Consciousness Explained' by David R. Hawkins
- 'The Four Agreements' by Don Miguel Ruiz
- 'The Blue Zones' by Dan Buettner
- 'The Spirit Molecule' by Dr. R. Strassman
- 'The Alchemist' by Paulo Coelho
- "Writing books is not a good idea' by Elle Griffin
- 'Men are from Mars, Women are from Venus' by John Grey
- 'Ayahyasca as a Divine Liquidity' by André Van de Braak
- 'The Celestine Prophecy' by James Redfield
- 'The Yoga Sūtras of Patañjali' by Patañjali
- 'A course in Miracles' by Helen Shucman
- 'Psychology and Alchemy' by Carl Jung
- 'The Untethered Soul' by Michael Singer
- 'Reflections on the Art of Living' by Joseph Campbell
- 'The Adventures of Huckleberry Finn' by Mark Twain
- 'Karma' by Sadhguru
- 'The Finders' by Dr. Jeffery Martin
- 'A View from Above' by Wilt Chamberlain.
- "Autobiography of a Yogi' by Paramahamsa Yogananda
- 'Thrive' by Arianna Huffington
- 'Le Petit Prince' by Antoine de Saint- Exupéry
- 'Relativity: The Special and The General Theory' by Albert Einstein
- "Discourse in the Method' by René Descartes
- 'Transforming Trauma : The Path to Hope and Healing' by Dr. James Gordon
- 'The Supernatural' by Dr Joe Dispenza
- 'Breathing is overrated' by Herbert Nitsch
- 'The Odyssey' by Homer

BIBLIOGRAPHY

- 'The Essential Rumi' by Rumi
- 'The Dark Side of the Light Chasers: Reclaiming Your Power, Creativity, Brilliance, and Dreams' by Debbie Ford
- 'The Attractor Factor' by Dr. Joe Vitale
- 'Journey to Ixtlan' by Carlos Castaneda

www.ingramcontent.com/pod-product-compliance
Lightning Source LLC
Chambersburg PA
CBHW020139170726
47995CB00003BA/593